浙江省普通本科高校"十四五"重点教材

高校国际生成才导论

张宏 主编

An Introduction to
Development of International Students
in Universities

ZHEJIANG UNIVERSITY PRESS
浙江大学出版社
·杭州·

图书在版编目(CIP)数据

高校国际生成才导论 / 张宏主编. —杭州:浙江
大学出版社,2023.12
ISBN 978-7-308-24562-3

Ⅰ.①高… Ⅱ.①张… Ⅲ.①高等学校—留学生教育
—德育—研究—中国 Ⅳ.①G648.9

中国国家版本馆 CIP 数据核字(2023)第 240989 号

高校国际生成才导论

An Introduction to Development of International Students in Universities

张　宏　主编

责任编辑	范洪法　樊晓燕
责任校对	王　波
封面设计	雷建军
出版发行	浙江大学出版社
	（杭州市天目山路 148 号　邮政编码 310007）
	（网址:http://www.zjupress.com）
排　　版	浙江大千时代文化传媒有限公司
印　　刷	杭州钱江彩色印务有限公司
开　　本	710mm×1000mm　1/16
印　　张	18
字　　数	295 千
版 印 次	2023 年 12 月第 1 版　2023 年 12 月第 1 次印刷
书　　号	ISBN 978-7-308-24562-3
定　　价	69.00 元

前　言

当今世界处于百年未有之大变局中。世界多极化、经济全球化势不可挡，人类的命运紧密相连，各国利益深度融合，国家之间的人才竞争日趋激烈，而高等教育则是这种竞争的根本支撑点。能在多大程度上吸引来华留学的国际生，聚天下英才而用之，不仅是衡量一所高校教育水平的标准，更是衡量一个国家高等教育现代化水平的标识。随着中国国际影响力的不断提升，中国教育的国际化程度不断提高，吸引了越来越多的国际生来华留学。教育部的统计数据显示，2018 年共有来自 196 个国家和地区的 492185 名各类外国留学人员在全国 31 个省（区、市）的 1004 所高等院校学习，比 2017 年增加了 3013 人，增长比例为 0.62%。其中，接受学历教育的外国留学生总计 258122 人，占来华留学生总数的 52.44%，比 2017 年增加了 16579 人。然而，由于多种原因，来华留学的国际生教育基本上被视为一种"特殊教育"，其主要集中在专业知识技能的培养上，形成特有的"象牙塔模式"，却忽略了对国际生的世界观、人生观、价值观的形塑。这不仅不利于国际生了解中国、亲近中华文化，而且会直接影响到他们成人成才，进而影响到中国高等教育在世界上的形象。因此，加强来华留学的国际生的德育教育势在必行。

在多元文化背景下对来华留学的国际生开展系统有效的德育工作并非一件易事。其中的关键性问题是对国际生德育的内在规律缺乏深入系统的研究，特别是在以何种价值观来指导和引领国际生方面缺乏共识，也就是说，国际生德育理论一定程度上存在着缺失。这使得国际生的德育课程内容安排过于宽泛，主题不够聚焦，过多关注知华教育、人身安全教育和适应性培养，缺少友华教育、中国情结培养，尤其是缺少关于中国理念、心理健康、法律法规、职业道德等方面的教育。国际生的德育肯定不能照搬中国学生的德育内容，必须根据国际生的心理认知特点，以中国国家领导人习近平提出的和平、发展、公平、正义、民主、自由的全人类共同价值为理论基础进行内容构建。全人类共同价值是联合国的崇高目标,强调人类普遍的伦理道德与价值认同,反映了人类未来发展的价值理想,超越国界、种族、文化差异,有利于各国最大限度地凝聚发展共识。全人类共同价值作为超越时代和文化的理论价值和实践价值,无论是在形成的时代背景、出发点,还是主体性、话语权等方面,与西方的"普世价值"存在着本质性的差异。可见,基于全人类共同价值的国际生德育是新时代国际生的最优选择,是提升国际生道德素养、传播中国文化、中国发展理念的重要途径。

高校国际生德育课程的内容构建应以全人类共同价值理念为基础,以多元文化背景下国际生的心理认知规律为依据,通过多种教学方式和手段,加强高校国际生的世界观、人生观、价值观、道德观、公德观、法治观、心理健康观、职业生涯观等教育。在此,我们提出了由全人类共同价值理念、德育普遍规律、具身认识理论组成的高校国际生德育教育三维理论。《高校国际生成才导论》这本教材正是基于这一理论谋篇布局的。全书由导论和六章构成,以什么是大学、为什么读大学、高校国际生应有的核心素养为引导,以树立正确的人生观、弘扬全人类共同价值、遵守中国的社会公德、崇尚法治精神、合理规划职业生涯、保持心理健康为内容。其中,全人类共同价值是理论基础,人生观、公德观、法治精神、心理健康和职业生涯规划等是具体内容。我们希望对高校国际生开展较为系统的成才成长教育,使其快速适应中国高校学习生活环境,不断提高思想道德水平和综合素养,成为合格的国际化人才。

Preface

The world today is undergoing profound changes unseen in a century. The trend towards multipolarity and economic globalization is unstoppable, and the fate of humanity is closely interconnected. The interests of various countries are deeply intertwined, and the competition for talents between nations is becoming increasingly fierce. Higher education is the fundamental support for this competition. The ability to attract international students to come to China and gather talents from around the world is not only a measure of the educational level of a university but also a symbol of a country's level of modernization in higher education.

As China's international influence continues to grow, the internationalization of Chinese education is also increasing, attracting more and more international students to study in China. According to statistics from the Ministry of Education, in 2018, a total of 492,185 foreign students from 196 countries and regions studied in 1,004 higher education institutions in 31 provincial-level regions across the country. This represented an increase of 3,013 people compared to 2017, with a growth rate of 0.62%. Among them, 258,122 foreign students were enrolled in degree programs, accounting for 52.44% of the total number of international students in China, an increase of 16,579 people from 2017.

However, for various reasons, education for international students studying in China is often considered a form of "special education," primarily focusing on the cultivation of professional knowledge and skills. This has led to a unique "ivory tower model" that neglects the shaping of their worldviews, outlooks on life, and values. This not only hinders international students from understanding China and embracing Chinese culture but also directly affects their personal development, which, in turn, impacts the image of Chinese higher education on the world stage. Therefore, it is imperative to strengthen the moral and character education of international students studying in China.

In a multicultural context, it is not an easy task to conduct systematic and effective moral education for international students studying in China. One of the key issues is the lack of in-depth and systematic research into the inherent laws of moral education for international students. Specifically, there is lack of consensus on which values should guide and lead international students, indicating a certain degree of deficiency in the theory of moral education for international students. This has led to a broad and unfocused arrangement of moral education curriculum content, with an excessive focus on knowledge about China, personal safety education, and adaptability training. It lacks education on becoming friendly to China and fostering emotional connections with China, and particularly, it lacks education on Chinese ideas, mental health, laws and regulations, and professional ethics.

Moral education for international students cannot simply replicate the moral education content designed for Chinese students. It must be reconstructed based on the psychological and cognitive characteristics of international students, with the theoretical foundation rooted in the common values of humanity proposed by Chinese President Xi Jinping: "peace, development, fairness, equality, democracy, and freedom." The common values of humanity are the lofty goals of the United Nations, emphasizing universal ethics and value identity among humanity. They reflect the value ideals for human future development, transcending borders, races, and cultural differences, and are conducive to pooling as much strength as possible for reaching consensus for development among nations.

The common values of humanity, as theoretical and practical values that transcend eras and cultures, have essential differences from Western universal values in terms of their historical background, starting points, subjectivity, and voices. Therefore, moral education for international students based on common values of humanity is the optimal choice for international students in the new era. It is also an important way to enhance the moral literacy of international students, promote the dissemination of Chinese culture, and convey China's development ideas.

The content construction of moral education courses for international students in universities should be based on the concept of common values of humanity, grounded in the psychological and cognitive patterns of international students within a diverse cultural context. Through various teaching methods and approaches, it aims to strengthen the education of international students in universities in areas such as their worldview, outlook on life, values, ethics, public morality, legal awareness, mental health awareness, and career planning perspectives. In this regard, we propose a three-dimensional theory for moral education of international students in universities, consisting of common values of humanity, general moral education principles, and embodied cognition theory. The textbook *An Introduction to the Development of International Students in Universities* is structured based on this three-dimensional theory.

The book consists of an introduction and six chapters. The introduction offers a guidance on what a university is, why one should attend university and the core qualities international students should possess. The rest covers topics such as developing a proper outlook on life, promoting common values of humanity, adhering to social ethics in China, advocating the spirit of the rule of law, planning one's career reasonably, and maintaining mental health. In particular, the common values of humanity serve as the theoretical foundation, while specific contents include the outlook on life, public morality, the spirit of the rule of law, mental health, and career planning.

By providing international students in universities with more systematic education on growth and talent development, it enables them to adapt quickly to the university environment in China, continuously improve their ethical and intellectual levels, and become qualified international talents.

目　录

Contents

导　论

　　同学们,当你们怀着激动好奇的心情走进中国大学的美丽校园,脑海里一定有无数个为什么。大学是什么？为什么要读大学？读大学能得到哪些能力的提升？也许对于这些问题的答案仁者见仁、智者见智,每个人都会有自己不同的见解。在中国读大学的四年学习生活中,你们需要不断地去体会和寻找这些问题的答案。

【思维导图】

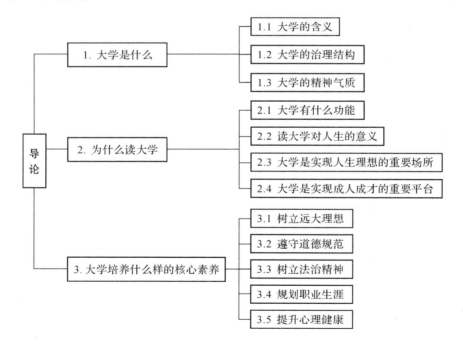

第一节　大学是什么

一、大学的含义

大学是实施高等教育的教育共同体,是提供教学和研究条件、授权颁发学位的综合性的高等教育组织。广义的大学指的是在中等教育基础上设立的、实施高等教育的学校。在中国其包括大学、学院、高等专科学校和高等职业学校,合称普通高等学校。狭义的大学指的是在普通高等学校中办学规模较大的一种。大学是社会发展的产物,是应社会对经过专门培训的人才需要而产生的。

中国的高等教育被公认为是从春秋时期儒家学说创始人孔子办私学开始,到汉代开办的太学,到科举制度下各朝代的国子监,以及民间力量开办的各类学堂、书院。

现代大学起源于西方。在非洲,摩洛哥的卡鲁因大学创办于859年,埃及的艾孜哈尔大学创办于988年。欧洲公认的办学最早的大学——博洛尼亚大学创建于1088年。英文词university在中国最早被翻译成"书院",后又称为"大学堂""大学校",1912年以后"大学"成为正式的称呼。

【知识拓展】

孔子介绍

孔子(公元前551年—前479年),子姓,孔氏,名丘,字仲尼,春秋时期鲁国陬邑(今山东省曲阜市)人,中国古代伟大的思想家、政治家、教育家,儒家学派创始人,"大成至圣先师"。孔子开创私人讲学之风,倡导仁义礼智信,有弟子三千,其中贤人七十二。他曾带领部分弟子周游列国十四年,晚年修订六经(《诗》《书》《礼》《乐》《易》《春秋》)。孔子去世后,其弟子及再传弟子把他及其弟子的言行语录和思想记录下来,整理编成《论语》。该书被奉为儒家经典。孔子是当时社会上最博学者之一,其思想对中国和世界都有深远的影响,其人被列为"世界十大文化名人"之首。

二、大学的治理结构

在现代社会中,组织与治理密不可分,有组织的地方就有治理。治理一般是指运用权力去指导、控制以及用法律来规范和协调影响人们利益的行为。大学的治理结构就是在大学治理主体多元化以及所有权与管理权分离的情况下,协调大学治理主客体之间的相互关系,降低办学成本,提高大学功能效益的一系列制度安排。大学的治理结构是现代大学制度的基石,是大学为实现其目标和理念而进行的制度安排,其本质是建构激励与约束相容、能应对利益冲突的权力结构,让学校的决策机构、执行机构和监督机构分工协作,形成权力制衡。

治理结构包括外部治理结构和内部治理结构。内部治理结构是指组织内部的各种治理主体之间的相互关系和治理主体与治理客体之间的相互关系。外部治理结构是指组织外部各种治理主体的相互关系和外部治理主体与组织之间的相互关系。组织内外治理结构之间相互影响,外部治理结构必然对内部治理结构产生多方面的影响。大学内部治理结构是指对大学内部及外部各利益主体的正式和非正式关系的一种制度安排。使得各利益主体在责任、权力和利益上相互制衡,有利于实现大学内部效率和公平的合理统一。

从世界范围来看,国外高校实行的治理结构,大多数是董事会、理事会、教授会、校务委员会等委员会领导下的校长负责制。《中华人民共和国高等教育法》(1998 年通过,2015 年修订)第三十九条规定:"国家举办的高等学校实行中国共产党高等学校基层委员会领导下的校长负责制。"这明确了中国现阶段大学内部治理结构为党委领导下的校长负责制。

【知识拓展】

哈佛大学内部治理结构

哈佛大学现行的治理体制是双会制,分别是董事会和监理会。后者由校外人士组成,负责对大学的监督。哈佛宪章规定,董事会由哈佛大学的校长和 6 名董事组成,即校长、司库(会计)和其他 5 名教师。哈佛领导层权力维护这种非民主程序,以保持多年一贯的高度统一与和谐。由此可见,董事会是哈佛大学治理团队的最高机构,它拥有最终的决定权。哈佛大学的监

21 世纪大学的根本任务。为此,大学要鼓励学生的探究精神、创新精神,努力培养全面发展的高素质人才,使他们不仅掌握科学文化知识,同时兼备科学精神与人文精神,拥有健康的体魄、完善的人格。

(二)科学研究的功能

大学是科学研究的神圣殿堂,负有探索真理和追求知识的重大责任。因此,大学除了具有教育和培养人才的功能,还有科学研究的功能。曾任北京大学校长的著名教育家蔡元培先生说:"大学者,研究高深学问者也。"英国教育家纽曼在《大学的理念》中指出:"大学是一切知识和科学、事实和原理、探索和发现、实验和思索的高级保护力量。"大学的使命是探究人类从物质世界到精神世界发展的历史,21 世纪的大学的核心理念是重建科学与人文精神的统一性。

(三)服务社会的功能

大学是直接服务于国家和社会发展的科学技术资源基地。大学是社会服务的阵地。大学服务功能的出现,使大学的内涵更加丰富,推动大学从社会边缘走向社会生活的中心。《中华人民共和国高等教育法》规定:高等教育必须贯彻国家的教育方针,为社会主义现代化建设服务,为人民服务,与生产劳动和社会实践相结合。今天的大学,不仅体现了所在国的综合国力和经济社会发展的先进程度,而且对这个国家的政治、经济、科学、技术、文化、教育、生态、国防等方方面面的发展都起到巨大的推动作用,同时也不断为人类的文明和进步做出重要贡献。优质高效的社会服务是 21 世纪大学的一项重要任务。大学的社会服务功能是多方面的,不仅仅满足当前的社会需求,还要有前瞻性,要能有科学预见并满足社会发展的长远要求,在促进科技发展的同时,为社会提供精神支持和道德指引。

(四)传承文明的功能

所谓传承文明,就是大学对于人类文明成果的保存传递,并且通过创造新的文明来充实人类文明的宝库。大学的传承文明主要表现在保存传递人类文明、创新发展人类文明、吸收融合不同文明等三个方面。

大学教育历来是国际学术文化交流的最主要领域,在历史上大学在沟通东西方文明方面发挥了极为重要的作用。特别是在当代,随着高等教育的国际化,国际高等教育的交流日益频繁,许多国家互派教师、互派留学生合作开展科学研究,联合培养学生以及进行学术文献和信息的交流等,为世界不同文化的相互理解、相互吸收、相互融合提供了条件。

大学也是社会批评的中心。大学承载着追求真理,探索未知、创新提升的任务。从这个角度说,大学是最富创造力、最富批判力的场所。

【观点交流】

大学社会功能的发展演变。

【知识拓展】

大学社会功能的发展演变

二、读大学对人生的意义

大学阶段是人生成长的黄金阶段。大学是思想最活跃、最富有创造力的学术殿堂,是新知识、新思想的摇篮。作为人类神圣的精神家园,大学有着崇高的教育理念和价值追求,有着超凡脱俗的治学品质,担负起引导整个社会前进的重大使命,是青年人塑造自我、实现人生意义与目标追求的最佳场所。在大学校园里,相对宽松、多元文化氛围为各种创新思想、质疑精神的碰撞与新文化的萌芽提供了良好的成长沃土和交汇平台。

对于大学的主体——大学生来说,大学阶段是由求学期向创造期转变的过渡时期,正处在个人生理、心理、思想和求知的成长期。大学生在这样一种良好的文化氛围和人文环境中将自然而然地受到熏陶和激励。这使得大学生逐渐培养起强烈的民族责任感、赤诚的爱国心、积极进取的精神境界、团结奋斗的合作精神、宽广扎实的专业知识、良好的人文关怀意识,勇于承担民族的重担和希望,努力将自身塑造成国家的栋梁之材。因此,大学学习阶段能够为青年学子在知识、生理、心理、人格、品质诸方面进一步完善自我、成人成才,为今后的成功奠定坚实的基础。

进入大学学习这一阶段主要是为人生发展、为实现人生价值打基础的阶段。这个阶段的基础越扎实,人性就越完善,将来也就能够更好地服务他人、服务社会、服务国家。与读大学之前的学习阶段相比,大学阶段在人生发展过程中的不同之处在于大学教育内容的特殊性,这是人们在人生发展中的一个转折时期,是一个为人们踏入社会作最后准备的时期。大学阶段既是人才成长、择业定向、走向社会承担社会责任的准备时期,也是个体人生发展在身心、知识各方面承前启后、积蓄发展潜能的转折时期。大学是人生起飞的加油站,它将为理想的实现奠定基础,为人生的腾飞插上翅膀,是直接影响一个人一生的关键阶段。

大学阶段对就读的青年学子的人生重要意义,简要来说表现在以下五个方面:第一,大学是身心发展的成熟期;第二,大学是"成人成才"的关键期;第三,大学是价值观、世界观、人生观的塑造期;第四,大学是社会角色的准备期;第五,大学是主动学习的养成期。总之,大学的学习阶段是青年人为自己成人成才,进而实现自身人生价值做准备的关键阶段,是成功人生和梦想实现的重要过渡阶段。

三、大学是实现人生理想的重要场所

人生指人的生存和生活的总体。人生的主体是人,人生的主题是活动,人生过程也就是人能动的活动过程。人的需要、动机、目的和追求是人生活动的发动者和动力源。人生理想就是人生的奋斗目标,追求美好的理想,对人民和社会多做贡献,才是有价值的人生,才是人生的本质。

大学生的人生理想是指大学生对未来的憧憬和向往。从人生观的角度来说,大学生的人生理想是指人们在组织、管理和计划自己人生活动的过程中,是基于对现实发展的某种可能性的认识而形成的对人生终极目的的向往和追求,是大学生的政治立场和世界观在奋斗目标上的集中体现。大学生的人生理想,应是依据自身所具备的现实条件,为国家奉献自己的才智。青年时期是学生形成价值观、人生观、世界观的重要阶段,也是孕育人生理想的关键时期。在大学阶段,明确"成为什么样的人""为什么读大学""今后走怎样的路",是大学生面临的人生课题。因此,大学生只有树立崇高的社会理想,明确职业理想,有清晰的生活理想和道德理想,才会有人生的奋斗目标,才能提高人的精神境界,才能有不断前进的动力,最终最大化实现人生价值,到达人生成功的彼岸。

四、大学是实现成人成才的重要平台

作为一个特殊而重要的群体,高校国际生求学的主要目标就是成人和成才。在成人和成才的关系上,二者缺一不可,成人重于成才,成人是成才

的前提和基础。高校国际生应加强自身的思想品德修养,努力使自己成人。同时还要加强自身的专业理论和专业技能的学习与研究,只有这样才能把自己逐步培养成为国家和人民所需要的人才。

成人,不单指人生理上的成熟,更强调的是成为具备正确的世界观、人生观和价值观,对社会有用的品德高尚的人。成才通常是指成为一定社会中具备从事物质文明和精神文明建设的素质,并以创造性劳动为社会发展和人类进步做出贡献的人。在大学中所进行的"成人"教育,就是使高校国际生学会为人处世,懂得做人的道理,真正树立正确的世界观、人生观、价值观。大学中所进行的"成才"教育,则是用人类社会创造的优秀成果武装高校国际生,使他们有知识、有技能、有独特的才华。

【知识拓展】

"四有"青年

"四有"青年是指"有理想、有道德、有文化、有纪律"的青年。"四有"是国家对公民的基本要求,也是提高整个中华民族的思想道德素质和科学文化素质的基本内容。任何一个民族、任何一个国家的人民都有自己的素质。这种素质的好坏,决定着一个民族、一个国家的成就和进步。因此,要实现社会主义现代化,就要培养一代有理想、有道德、有文化、有纪律的人才,推进现代化建设。"四有"是一个整体,缺一不可,其中的理想和纪律特别重要。我们这个地大物博、人口众多的国家,靠理想,靠纪律,组织起来才有力量。否则,就会像一盘散沙,不仅革命和建设不会成功,还会遭人宰割。

第三节　大学培养什么样的核心素养

一、树立远大理想

理想信念是人的心灵世界的核心,有无远大的理想信念决定了人生是高尚充实还是庸俗空虚。一方面,远大的理想不仅使人更加充实,而且能以一种科学信念的力量,帮助人们选择正确的人生发展道路。另一方面,远大的理想是人们生活中一股强大的动力,它提升我们的人格,促使我们奋发前进，它拓宽我们的视野，开发我们的能力，激发我们的潜能。

追求远大理想，坚定崇高信念，是高校国际生健康成长、成就事业、开创未来的精神支柱和前进动力。加强思想道德修养，提高精神境界，应牢牢把握理想信念这个核心。高校国际生应当正确认识自身肩负的历史使命，确立科学的信仰，树立远大的理想和奋斗目标。

二、遵守道德规范

大学时期是人生道德意识形成和发展的一个重要阶段，在这个时期形成的思想道德观念对高校国际生一生影响很大。加强社会公德修养，做一个知荣辱、讲道德的人，是国家和社会提出的高要求，也是高校国际生自身全面发展健康成长的重要条件。

高校国际生应当具备的道德品质包括：孝敬父母，尊重师长；谦虚礼让，团结和睦；诚实守信，律己宽人；勤奋学习，学会学习；公正无私，见义勇为等。高校国际生通过深刻领会并践行社会基本道德规范，加强诚信道德建设，增强道德修养的自觉性，是提高自身道德素质、锤炼道德品质的重要途径。

三、树立法治精神

现代法治精神包含了正义、公平、公正、自由、民主、人权、秩序等多位一体的精神内核，是法律意识、法制观念、法律素质、法律信仰的复合体。高校国际生法治精神是指高校国际生在先天生理基础上，历经后天社会法治环境影响和高校法治教育作用，通过法律学习内化和行为实践而逐渐形成的相对稳定的基本品质和活力面貌。

高校国际生是法律知识的拥有者、法律意识的先行者、法律文明的传播者，是法治精神、理念的践行者。高校国际生的法律意识直接反映一个国家的法治水平，直接关系到一个国家法治建设的成败。因此，高校国际生既要具备良好的思想道德素质，也应具备良好的法律素质。当今世界，法治已经成为各国政府治国理政的基本方式，在国家治理和社会管理中发挥着重大作用。高校国际生不仅要学习法律知识，增强法律意识，还要树立法治精神，培养法治思维，维护法律权威，成为具有良好法律素质的国家建设者和接班人。

自由、平等、公正、法治，是对美好社会的生动表述，是对全人类共同价值基本理念的凝练,反映了全人类共同价值的基本属性。其中,自由是指人的意志自由、存在和发展的自由,是人类社会的美好向往,也是人类社会的价值目标;平等指的是公民在法律面前一律平等,其价值取向是不断实现实质平等,它要求尊重和保障人权,人人依法享有平等参与、平等发展的权利;公正即社会公平和正义,它以人的解放、人的自由平等权利的获得为前提,是国家、社会应然的根本价值理念;法治是治国理政的基本方式,依法治国是社会主义民主政治的基本要求,它通过法制建设来维护和保障公民的根本利益,是实现自由平等、公平正义的制度保证。

四、规划职业生涯

职业生涯规划就是根据自己的实际情况,结合决定个人职业生涯的制约因素和眼前的机遇,为自己确定职业目标,选择职业道路,确定教育培训内容和发展计划等,并为自己实现职业目标对行动的时间、行动的顺序、行动的方向等做出合理的安排。职业生涯规划的目的不仅是帮助个人按照自己的条件找到一份合适的工作,达到与实现个人目标,更重要的是帮助个人真正了解自己,更好地筹划未来,并根据主客观条件设计合理可行的职业生涯发展方向,尽快实现自己的社会价值和个人价值,最大限度地实现职业发展的成功。具体来说,第一,科学的职业生涯规划能帮助高校国际生了解自己的实力,准确进行自我评估和职业定位;第二,科学的职业生涯规划能激发高校国际生自我实现价值的需要,培养积极的人生观;第三,科学的职业生涯规划能促进高校国际生树立明确的职业目标和职业理想;第四,科学的职业生涯规划能有助于高校国际生提高学习的自觉性、主动性、目的性,增强就业竞争力;第五,科学的职业生涯规划能有助于高校国际生树立正确的就业、择业观念,有助于未来职业生涯的持续科学发展。

高校国际生正处在职业生涯的探索阶段和职业准备阶段。对于高校国际生来说,在这一阶段科学地规划职业生涯、准确定位、树立职业目标并采取措施以全面提高自身职业素质,对其就业和职业生涯的成功具有非常重大的意义。随着经济社会和高等教育大众化的快速发展,当前的就业市场竞争日趋激烈,高校国际生面临的就业形势越来越严峻,就业压力越来越大。为实现精彩人生,高校国际生们的职业生涯规划应尽早进行,让职业规划从读大学的第一天开始,与大学学习生活同步。

五、提升心理健康

健康是人生幸福的标志之一。随着人类社会生活的发展,人们对健康的认识不断深化并发生着变化。人们日益认识到心理健康对保证人的生存和生活质量具有重要意义,因为发生心理障碍并不比生理疾病对自身生存的威胁小。心理健康是指个体应该具有的基本的认知能力、和谐的人际关系、良好的社会适应能力、有效的调控情绪的能力和良好的人格品质等。

正确认识心理健康概念及其作用十分重要,它能够帮助高校国际生提高自身的健康意识,重视心理健康。保持良好适应的心理状态,创造性地进行学习和工作。身心健康是高校国际生的成才之本、事业成功之源,良好的心理素质在促进高校国际生身体素质,塑造优良品德和人格,奠定未来就业的心理基础和顺利完成学业等方面都具有重要意义。

高校国际生心理健康的标准可以概括为以下七条:

(1)保持对学习较浓厚的兴趣和求知欲望。

(2)能保持正确的自我意识,接纳自我。

(3)能协调与控制情绪,保持良好的心境。

(4)能保持和谐的人际关系,乐于交往。

(5)能保持完整统一的人格品质。

(6)能保持良好的环境适应能力。

(7)心理行为符合年龄特征。

高校国际生常见的心理问题有四类:第一类是一般性的心理问题,如适应问题、学习问题、人际关系问题、恋爱与性心理问题、性格与情绪问题等;第二类是常见的神经症,包括焦虑症、强迫症、恐惧症、疑病症和神经衰弱;第三类是常见人格障碍,主要有偏执型人格障碍、分裂样人格障碍、反社会型人格障碍、冲动型人格障碍、表演型人格障碍、强迫型人格障碍、焦虑型人格障碍、依赖型人格障碍等;第四类是心境障碍,包括躁狂发作、抑郁发作、双相发作、持续性心境障碍等。高校国际生要学会心理自我调节,积极地保持自己的心理健康,促进和实现身心和谐。应当了解一些心理健康知识,掌握必要的心理调适方法,学会做自己的“心理医生”。必要时也可以求助于大学校园内的心理咨询机构与心理辅导机构的支持援助。

【知识拓展】

社会主义核心价值观

中国共产党提出,倡导富强、民主、文明、和谐,倡导自由、平等、公正、法治,倡导爱国、敬业、诚信、友善,积极培育和践行社会主义核心价值观。富强、民主、文明、和谐是国家层面的价值目标,自由、平等、公正、法治是社会层面的价值取向,爱国、敬业、诚信、友善是公民个人层面的价值准则,这24个字是社会主义核心价值观的基本内容。

富强、民主、文明、和谐是中国特色社会主义现代化国家的建设目标,也是从价值目标层面对社会主义核心价值观基本理念的凝练,在社会主义核心价值观中居于最高层次,对其他层次的价值理念具有统领作用。富强即国富民强,是社会主义现代化国家经济建设的应然状态,是中华民族梦寐以求的美好夙愿,也是国家繁荣昌盛、人民幸福安康的物质基础。民主是人类社会的美好诉求。我们追求的民主是人民民主,其实质和核心是人民当家作主。它是社会主义的生命,也是创造人民美好幸福生活的政治保障。文明是社会进步的重要标志,也是社会主义现代化国家的重要特征。它是社会主义现代化国家文化建设的应有状态,是对面向现代化、面向世界、面向未来的,民族的、科学的、大众的社会主义文化的概括,是实现中华民族伟大复兴的重要支撑。和谐是中国传统文化的基本理念,集中体现了学有所教、劳有所得、病有所医、老有所养、住有所居的生动局面。它是社会主义现代化国家在社会建设领域的价值诉求,是经济社会和谐稳定、持续健康发展的重要保证。

【思考题】

1. 结合本章学习内容,谈谈你选择读大学的目的是什么。

2. 你认为大学在一个国家经济社会发展中发挥着什么样的作用和功能?

3. 谈谈你对大学实现"成人"和"成才"作用的理解。你有哪些人生抱负和理想,你希望成为一个什么样的人?

4. 高校国际生应具有什么样的核心素养?

Introduction

As you step onto the beautiful campus of a Chinese university, you may find yourself filled with excitement and curiosity. You might wonder: What exactly is a university? Why should I attend one? What kind of skills and knowledge can I gain from my studies here? The answers to these questions will likely vary from person to person, and each individual will have their own unique perspective. Throughout your four years of study and life on a Chinese campus, it will be up to you to explore and discover the answers to these questions for yourself.

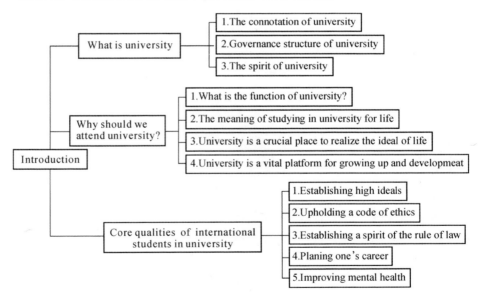

Section One   What Is University?

1. The Connotation of University

A university is an educational community that implements higher education, and it is an authorized comprehensive higher education organization that provides teaching and research conditions and grants degrees. In a broad sense, a university refers to a "school" that provides higher education based on secondary education. In China, it includes universities, colleges, higher technical institutes, and higher vocational schools, collectively known as ordinary institutions of higher education. While in a narrow sense, university refers to those institutions with a larger scale than the ordinary institutions of higher education. Universities are the results of social development and arise from the need to train specialized talents.

Ancient China had the earliest higher education organization similar to modern universities that can be traced back to 770 BC—476 BC. Higher education in China is recognized to have started with Confucius, the founder of Confucianism, who established a private school in the Spring and Autumn Period. This was followed by the establishment of the Imperial Academy during the Han Dynasty, the imperial college during various dynasties under the imperial examination system, as well as various private schools and academies established by civil power.

Modern universities originated in the West. The University of Al-Karaouine in Morocco was founded in 859, and the University of Azhar in Egypt was founded in 988. The earliest recognized university in Europe was the University of Bologna, founded in 1088. The English word "university" was first translated into Chinese as "shuyuan" (书院), later referred to as "daxuetang" (大学堂) and "daxuexiao" (大学校), and 1912, "daxue" (大学)became the formal term.

【**Knowledge Expansion**】

Introduction to Confucius

Confucius (551 BC—479 BC), with the family name Kong and given name Qiu, courtesy name Zhongni, was a great thinker, statesman and educator in the ancient state of Lu (nowadays Qufu, Shandong Province) during the Spring and Autumn Period. He was the founder of the school of Confucianism and was honored as the "Supreme Sage and First Teacher in China". Confucius pioneered the trend of private teaching and advocated the virtues of benevolence, righteousness, propriety, wisdom, and faith. He had three thousand disciples, among whom seventy-two were outstanding. He once led a group of his disciples on a fourteen-year tour to various states. In his later years, Confucius revised and edited the six classics (*Book of Songs*, *Book of History*, *Book of Rites*, *Book of Music*, *Book of Changes*, and *Spring and Autumn Annals*). After his death, his disciples and their followers recorded his teachings and compiled them into the book *Analects of Confucius*, which is regarded as a Confucianist classic. Confucius was one of the most knowledgeable scholars of his time, and his ideas have had a profound influence on both China and the world in general. He was listed as one of the "Top Ten Cultural Celebrities in the World".

2. Governance Structure of University

In contemporary society, organization and governance are closely linked. Where there is organization, there is a need for governance. Governance generally refers to the use of power to guide, control, and regulate behavior that affects people's interests through laws and regulations. The governance structure of a university is a series of institutional arrangements that coordinate the relationship between the multiple subjects of university governance with the separation of ownership and management, to reduce the cost of education and improve the efficiency of university operation. The governance structure of a university is the cornerstone of the modern university system and is the set of institutional arrangements that a university implements in order to achieve its goals and philosophy. Its essence is to construct a power structure that is compatible with incentives and constraints and can address conflicts of interest, so that the decision-making, execution, and supervision of the university can be collaborative and form a balance.

The governance structure includes internal structure and external structure. The internal governance structure refers to the relationships among various governance entities within the organization, as well as the relationships between governance entities and governance subjects. The external governance structure refers to the relationships between various governance entities external to the organization, as well as the relationships between those external governance entities and the organization. These two structures interact with each other, and the external governance structure would definitely exert multiple impacts on the internal governance structure. The internal governance structure of a university refers to a systematic arrangement of the formal and informal relationships between the internal and external stakeholders of the university. This ensures that the various stakeholders are balanced in terms of responsibility, power, and interests, which is conducive to achieving a reasonable unity of efficiency and fairness within the university.

From a global perspective, the governance structures implemented by foreign universities mostly involve a system of Principal Accountability System under the leadership of committees such as the board of directors, board of trustees, professor committee, and school administration committee. Article 39 of the *Higher Education Law of the People's Republic of China* (passed in 1998 and revised in 2015) stipulates that "Higher education institutions established by the state shall implement the Principal Accountability System under the Leadership of the University's Party Committee of the Communist Party of China." This clearly defines the current internal governance structure of Chinese universities.

【Knowledge Expansion】

Internal Governance Structure of Harvard University

Harvard University's current governance system is a dual-board system consisting of a board of directors and a board of supervisors. The latter is composed of individuals outside the university who are responsible for overseeing the university. According to the Charter of Harvard, the board of directors is composed of the university president and six fellows, including the treasurer (accountant) and five other faculty members. The Harvard leadership strongly upholds this non-democratic process to maintain a consistent and harmonious high level of unity over the years. Thus, it is evident that the board of directors is the highest institution of Harvard University's governance and has the power to make the final decision. The board of fellows at Harvard University is currently composed of 32 members, mainly social elites from the fields of education, business, and law.

3. The Spirit of University

Each university possesses a unique spirit, just like the first impression a person leaves on others when interacting with them, reflecting in his spiritual state and behavioral style with a distinct personality. When studying at a university, after four years of immersion and experience, one will be influenced and nourished by the university's unique spirit, and will also be equipped with such a unique spiritual temperament which will be an important quality to help individuals achieve success in their growth process.

The university spirit is an achievement of unique temperament formed during the development of the university itself. As the soul of a university, the university spirit is a symbol and the concrete embodiment of the scientific spirit and a high-level human social civilization. Different universities have different university spirits, which also provide international students with different temperaments. The university spirit is usually reflected in a university's motto. A motto often embodies a university's history, reflects its cultural background or founding process, or reveals a university's mission and its spiritual pursuit. The mottoes of many world-renowned universities can fully reflect the unique management style and humanistic spirit that this university reveres and adheres to. For example, the University of Cambridge's motto is "From here, light and sacred draughts", the University of Oxford's is "The lord is my illumination", Harvard University's is "Let Plato be your friend, and Aristotle, but more let your friend be truth", and Yale University's is "Truth and Light". The motto of Tsinghua University, a prestige Chinese university, is derived from the ancient book *The Book of Changes* and the original sentence reads "Heaven trip key, the gentleman to self-improvement. Earth trip key, the gentleman to Virtuous". The university spirit can be seen from the mottoes such as "Self-discipline and Social Commitment" of Tsinghua University, "Seeking Truth, Pursuing Innovation" of Zhejiang University, "Rich in Knowledge and Tenacious of Purpose, Inquiring with Earnestness and Reflecting with Self-practice" of Fudan University, "Improve Yourself, Carry Forward Stamina, Seek Truth and Develop Innovations" of Wuhan University. Meanwhile, the motto of Shaoxing University is "Cultivate Virtue and Pursue Truth".

【Knowledge Expansion】

The Mottoes of Some World-famous Universities

(1) Harvard University: Let Plato be your friend, and Aristotle, but more let your friend be truth.

(2) Massachusetts Institute of Technology: Mind and Hand.

(3) Stanford University: The Wind of Freedom Blows.

(4) Yale University: Light and Truth.

(5) Cambridge University: From Here, Light and Sacred Draughts.

(6) Princeton University: Under God's power she flourishes.

（7）Cornell University： I would find an institution where any person can find instruction in any study.

（8）University of California Berkeley： Let There Be Light.

（9）University of Chicago： Let knowledge grow from more to more, and so be human life enriched.

（10）California Institute of Technology： The truth shall make you free.

Section Two   Why Should We Attend University?

In order to understand the question of why one should attend university, it is necessary to consider what value universities can provide to the country and society. This is the purpose of universities. Based on this, we can then discuss what kind of abilities, values and significance students can gain from attending university as individuals.

1. What is the Function of University?

The function of a university refers to the effects and roles that a university can provide. The value and importance of a university lie in the functions it serves. These functions of a university mainly include cultivating talents, conducting scientific research, serving society, and inheriting civilization.

（1）The Function of Cultivating Talents

Universities are the cradle of talent development and they bear the dual mission of education and academic research. Since its establishment in the Middle Ages, education and talent cultivation have always been the eternal themes in universities. According to the *Higher Education Law of the People's Republic of China*, the mission of higher education is to cultivate socialist country builders and successors with comprehensive development in moral, intellectual, and physical as well as in arts and labor aspects. The competition for national strength today and in the future ultimately depends on talent competition. Therefore, cultivating high-level specialized talents with a sense of social responsibility, innovative spirit, and practical ability is the fundamental task of universities in the 21st century. Universities should encourage students to explore and innovate, achieve all-around development and become high-quality talents so that they can not only master scientific and cultural knowledge, but also have a scientific and humanistic spirit as well as a healthy body and perfect personality.

(2)The Function of Scientific Research

Universities are sacred places of scientific research, bearing great responsibility for seeking truth and pursuing knowledge. Therefore, in addition to its role in education and cultivating talent, universities also have a function in scientific research. Cai Yuanpei, the former president of Peking University and a famous educator, once said, "A university is a place profound knowledge is studied". British educator Newman pointed out in *The Idea of a University* that "the university is a high-level protective force for all knowledge and science, facts and principles, exploration and discovery, experiment and contemplation". The mission of the university is to explore the history of human development from the material world to the spiritual world. The core philosophy of 21st century universities is to reconstruct the unity of scientific spirit and humanity.

(3) The Function of Serving Society

Universities are the resource bases of science and technology that directly serves the development of the country and society. Therefore, it is also the frontier of social services. The emergence of the university's service function has enriched its connotation and pushed the university from the margin of society to the center of social life. According to the *Higher Education Law of the People's Republic of China*, higher education must implement the state's education policy, serve socialist modernization construction and the people, and integrate with social production and social practice. Today's universities not only reflect the comprehensive national strength and the advanced level of economic and social development of its country, but also play a huge role in promoting the development of the country's politics, economy, science, technology, culture, education, ecology, national defense, and more, and constantly makes important contributions to human civilization and progress. Providing high-quality and efficient social services is an important task of the university in the 21st century. The function of the university in servicing society is multifaceted. It satisfies current social needs while having foresight and can scientifically anticipate and meet the long-term requirements of social development. While promoting the development of science and technology, universities also provide spiritual support and moral guidance to society.

(4) The Function of Inheriting Civilization

Inheriting Civilization means that universities preserve and pass on the achievements of human civilization and enrich its treasure by creating new forms of civilization. This inheritance of civilization by universities is mainly manifested in three aspects: preserving and transmitting human civilization, innovating and developing human civilization, and integrating different civilizations.

University education has always been the main field of international academic and cultural exchange. Throughout history, universities played an extremely important role in facilitating communication between Eastern and Western civilizations. In contemporary times, with the internationalization of higher education, international exchanges in higher education are increasingly frequent. Many countries send teachers and exchange students to cooperate in scientific research, joint student training, academic literature and information exchange, etc. , providing conditions for mutual understanding, learning and integration of different cultures in the world.

Furthermore, universities are the centers of social criticism. Universities bear the task of pursuing truth, exploring the unknown, and innovating for development. From this perspective, universities are places with the most creative strength and critical power.

【Opinion Exchange】

The evolution of university's social function.

【Knowledge Expansion】

The Evolution of the Social Function of University

2. The Meaning of Studying in University for Life

Time spent in universities can be regarded as the golden stage in personal growth, during which time one is most intellectually active and academically creative. University is the cradle of new knowledge and new ideas. As a sacred spiritual home for humanity, the university has lofty educational ideals and values, extraordinary academic qualities, and bears the important mission of guiding the progress of society. It is the best place for young people to shape themselves, realize the meaning of life, and pursue their goals. On the university campus, a relatively relaxed and diverse cultural atmosphere provides a fertile soil as well as an exchange platform for the collision of various innovative ideas and questioning spirit, also the germination of new culture.

For college students, the stage of the university is a transitional period from "learning" to "creating", during which they are in a process of physical, psychological, ideological, and intellectual growth. College students receive guidance and inspiration in such a good cultural atmosphere and a humanistic environment. As a result, university students can gradually develop a strong sense of national responsibility, sincere patriotism, an enterprising spirit, a spirit of unity and striving, broad and solid professional knowledge, a good sense of humanistic care, the courage to bear the burden and hope of the nation and to become the pillars of the country. Therefore, the learning stage in university can further improve young students' knowledge, physical, psychological, personality, and quality aspects, laying a solid foundation for their future success.

Studying in university is mainly a stage to lay the foundation for the development of life and the realization of life value. The more solid the foundation laid during this stage, the better the development of one's character and personality will be, enabling one to better serve others, society, and the country in the future. Compared to the stages of learning before university, the unique feature of the university stage in the process of personal development is the special content of university education. It is a turning point in people's life development and a period for preparing them for society. The university stage is both a preparatory period for students' personal growth, career orientation, and growing awareness of social responsibility, and a turning point for individual life development in terms of improving physical and mental health, expanding knowledge, and accumulating potential. University is the launching pad for life, laying the foundation for realizing one's ideals and providing wings for one to take off, making it a critical stage that directly influences a person's entire life.

The importance of the university stage for young students lies primarily in the following aspects: first, it is a period of physical and mental maturity; second, it is a critical period for them to grow into adults and become talents; third, it is a period for them to shape their values, world view, and life philosophy; fourth, it is a preparatory period for their social roles; fifth, it is a period for developing active learning habits. In short, the period of the university is a critical stage for young people to prepare themselves for becoming adults and achieving success, realizing their own values in life and a crucial transitional stage for achieving a successful life and realizing their dreams.

3. University is a Crucial Place to Realize the Ideal of Life

Life refers to the overall existence and living of a person. The subject of life is human beings, and the theme of life is activity. The process of life is the process of human activities. Human needs, motives, purposes, and pursuits are the initiators and sources of the driving force of life activities. The life ideal is the goal a person strives for and pursuing a beautiful ideal and making more contributions to the people and society is the value and the essence of life.

For college students, the life ideal refers to their aspirations and longing for the future. From the perspective of life philosophy, it is the pursuit of the ultimate goal of life that is formed based on their understanding of the possibility of real-world development in the process of organizing, managing, and planning their own life activities. It is also a concentrated reflection of the political stance and worldview of college students in their goals. College students' life ideals should be the contribution to their country based on their own realistic conditions. The period of youth is an important period for students to form their values, life philosophy, and worldview, as well as to conceive their life ideals. In the university stage, students are faced with life issues such as "what kind of person to become," "why attend university," and "what kind of path to take in the future". Therefore, college students must establish lofty social ideals, clarify their career ideals, life ideals and moral ideals, and finally build up a life goal to strive for. Only then can they improve their spiritual realm, have the motivation to continuously move forward, and ultimately maximize their life value, achieving success in their lives.

4. University is a Vital Platform for Growing Up and Development

As a special and important group of people, the primary goal of international students in colleges and universities is to grow up and develop personally, which are both indispensable. Growing up is more important than personal development, as it is the premise and foundation of personal development. International students should strengthen their ideological and moral cultivation, and try to grow up with a sound personality. At the same time, they should strengthen the study of theories and the practice of skills. Only in this way, can they gradually cultivate themselves to become the talents for their country and people.

Growing up does not only refer to physical maturity but also emphasizes becoming an individual with correct views of the world, life and values, who possesses noble moral character and are useful to society. Personal development of an individual usually refers to his possession of the qualities to engage in the construction of material civilization and spiritual civilization in a society and make contributions to the development of society and human progress through creative work. The "growing up" education in universities is to help international students learn how to conduct themselves in society and understand the principles of being a good person, helping them truly establish correct views of world life and values. The "personal development" education conducted in universities is to equip international students with excellent achievements created by human beings, enabling them to possess knowledge, skills, and unique talents.

【Knowledge Expansion】

Young People with "Four Characteristics"

Young people with "four characteristics" refer to the youth who possess ideals, morals, culture, and discipline. Young people with "four characteristics" is the basic requirement of the state for its citizens, and it is also the basic content of education to improve the ideological and moral quality as well as the scientific and cultural quality of the entire Chinese nation. Every nation or country has its own unique qualities that determine its level of achievements and progress. Therefore, to achieve socialist modernization, it is imperative to cultivate a generation of talented people with ideals, morals, culture, and discipline. "Four characteristics" is an integrated unity, and all of them are indispensable, among which ideals and discipline are particularly important. In our cast, resource-rich and densely populated country, we can only be powerful by relying on ideals and discipline to organize ourselves. Otherwise, we will be like a pile of sand, unable to succeed in our socialist revolution and construction, and vulnerable to attacks from others.

Section Three   Core Qualities of International Students in University

1. Establishing High Ideals

Ideals and beliefs lie at the heart of a person's spiritual world. They determine whether one's life is noble and fulfilling or vulgar and empty. On the one hand, lofty ideals not only make people feel more fulfilled but also, as the power of scientific faith, enable them to choose the correct path for their personal development. On the other hand, lofty ideals are the great force in our lives that enhance our character and drive us to move forward, broaden our horizons, improve our abilities, and stimulate our potential.

Pursuing lofty ideals and maintaining a strong and noble belief are spiritual pillars and driving forces for the growth and success of international students in universities, as well as for helping them to create a bright future. To strengthen their moral and ideological cultivation and promote their spiritual realm, international students should firmly grasp ideals and beliefs as the core of their development. They should have a correct understanding of their historical mission, establish a scientific faith, and set high ideals and goals for their struggle.

2. Establishing High Ideals

University years are crucial for the formation and development of moral consciousness in one's life. The moral concepts and beliefs formed during this period have a great influence on the rest of the lives of international students in universities. Only by strengthening social morality cultivation and becoming a person who understands what is right and wrong and who upholds moral principles, would one meet the high expectations put forward by the country and society. This is also an important condition for the comprehensive development and healthy growth of international students in universities.

International students in universities should possess moral qualities such as filial piety, respect for elders, humility, honesty, self-discipline, diligence, the ability to learn, impartiality, selflessness, courage to uphold solidarity and justice etc. By deeply understanding and practicing basic social ethics, strengthening the building of integrity and honesty, and enhancing the consciousness of moral development, international students can improve their morality and cultivate their personal character.

3. Establishing a Spirit of the Rule of Law

The modern spirit of the rule of law includes the integrated core values of justice, fairness, impartiality, freedom, democracy, human rights, and order. It is a composite of legal consciousness, legal concepts, legal literacy, and legal faith. The spirit of the rule of law of international students refers to the relatively stable basic quality and vitality gradually formed through the internalization of legal learning and practice on the basis of innate physiology, with the influence of the social environment of the rule of law as well as the legal education in universities.

International students in universities are the hope for national development and social progress, the future of a country, as well as the possessors of legal knowledge, pioneers of legal consciousness, and disseminators of legal civilization. They are practitioners of the rule of law spirit and concept. The legal consciousness of international students directly reflects the level of a country's rule of law and is directly related to the success or failure of a country's rule of law construction. Therefore, international students in universities should not only have good ideological and moral qualities but also good legal awareness. In today's world, the rule of law has become a fundamental way of governing worldwide. It plays a significant role in national governance and social management. International students should not only learn legal knowledge and enhance legal consciousness but also establish the rule of law spirit, cultivate legal thinking, and maintain the authority of law. They should become constructors and successors of the country with their good legal qualities.

Freedom, equality, justice, and the rule of law are vivid description of a desirable society, and they are also a condensed expression of the basic principles of the socialist core values. They reflect the fundamental attributes of socialism with Chinese characteristics and is the core value that the common values of all humanity. Freedom refers to the freedom of will, existence, and development of human beings. It is the beautiful aspiration of people in society and also the goal of social value. Equality refers to the equal treatment of citizens under the law, and its value orients towards the achievement of substantive equality gradually. This requires respect for and protection of human rights, and each individual has the right to equal participation and equal development under the law. Justice refers to social fairness and justice. It takes the liberation of people and the acquisition of freedom and equal rights as a prerequisite, and it is the fundamental concept of value that the state or society should provide. The rule of law is the fundamental method of governing the country, which according to law is the basic requirement of socialist democratic politics. It maintains and safeguards the fundamental interests of citizens through legal construction and is the institutional guarantee for realizing freedom, equality, fairness, and justice.

4. Planning One's Career

Career planning is a process of determining one's career goals, selecting a career path, and creating a plan for education, training, and development based on one's current situation, constraints, and opportunities. It involves making reasonable arrangements for the timing, sequence, and direction of actions towards achieving career goals. The purpose of career planning is not only to help individuals find suitable jobs according to their qualifications and preferences, but also to assist them in understanding themselves better, planning for the future, and designing a feasible career development direction based on the objective and subjective conditions, in order to maximize their social and personal values and achieve career success as soon as possible. Specifically, scientific career planning can help international students in universities to understand their strengths, accurately assess themselves, and position themselves for a career; inspire them to pursue self-realization and cultivate a positive outlook on life; encourage them to establish clear career goals and ideals; enhance their self-awareness, initiative, and purposefulness in learning, and improve their employability; and foster the right attitudes towards employment and career, helping them to achieve the continuous and scientific development in their future.

International students in universities are at the stage of career exploration and preparation. If they can scientifically plan their career, accurately set career goals, and take measures to improve their professional skills comprehensively during this stage, it will have a significant impact on their successful employment and career development. With the rapid development of the society and the popularization of higher education, the current competition in job market is becoming increasingly fierce. International students are facing more severe employment situations and greater employment pressure. To achieve a wonderful life, international students should start their career planning as early as possible, and synchronize their career planning with their university life from the first day of university.

5. Improving Mental Health

Health is a key indicator of happiness in life. With the development of human society, people's understanding of health has deepened and changed over time. People increasingly recognize that mental health is equally important for ensuring the survival and quality of life of individuals. This is because psychological disorders are just as threatening to one's survival as physical illnesses. Mental health encompasses basic cognitive ability, harmonious interpersonal relationships, good social adaptation ability, effective adjustment of emotions, and positive personality traits.

Having a correct understanding of mental health and its role in life is very important, as it can help international students in universities to improve their awareness of health and psychological well-being. By maintaining a good psychological state of adaptation, they can study and work creatively. Mental and physical health is the basis of success for international students, and good psychological qualities are important in promoting their physical health, shaping their moral character and personality, and laying the psychological foundation for their university study and future employment.

The standards of mental health for international students can be summarized as follows:

(1) Maintain a strong interest in learning and a desire for knowledge.

(2) Maintain correct self-consciousness and accept yourself.

(3) Coordinate and control emotions, and maintain a good mood.

(4) Maintain harmonious interpersonal relationships and be willing to communicate.

(5) Maintain an integrated and unified personality.

(6) Maintain an ability to adapt to the environment.

(7) Conduct psychological behavior that is consistent with one's age.

International students in universities commonly face four types of psychological problems: first, general psychological problems, such as problems of adaptation, learning, interpersonal relationship, love and sexual psychology, personality and emotions; second, common neurosis, including anxiety, obsessive-compulsive disorder, phobia, hypochondria and neurasthenia; third, common personality disorders, mainly including paranoid personality disorder, schizoid personality disorder, antisocial personality disorder, impulsive personality disorder, histrionic personality disorder, obsessive-compulsive personality disorder, anxious personality disorder, dependent personality disorder, etc.; fourth, mood disorders, including manic episodes, depressive episodes, bipolar episodes, persistent mood disorders, etc. International students in universities should learn to regulate their own psychology, actively maintain their mental health, and achieve physical and mental harmony. They should acquire some knowledge of mental health, master necessary psychological adjustment methods, and learn to be their own "psychologist". When necessary, they can also seek support and assistance from psychological counselling organizations on campus.

【Knowledge Expansion】

Core Socialist Values

The Communist Party of China proposed to advocate prosperity, democracy, civility, and harmony, to advocate freedom, equality, justice, and the rule of law, to advocate patriotism, dedication, integrity, and friendship, actively cultivating the socialist core values and put them into practice. Prosperity, democracy, civility, and harmony are the national-level value goals, while freedom, equality, justice, and the rule of law are the social-level value orientations. Patriotism, dedication, integrity, and friendship are the individual-level value criteria of citizens. These 24 Chinese characters contain the basic content of the socialist core values.

Prosperity, democracy, civility and harmony are the goals for building a modern socialist country in China, and also the condensation of the socialist core values in terms of value targets. They are the highest level of values and play a leading role among all the values. Prosperity means a prosperous country and wealthy people, which is the result of the economic development of a socialist modernization country. It is the long-cherished dream of the Chinese and also the material foundation for the prosperity of the country and the well-being of the people. Democracy is an aspiration of humans in society. The democracy we pursue in China is called people's democracy, and its essence and core are the people's position as masters of the country. It is the essence of the socialist system and the political guarantee for creating a better and happier life for the people. Civility is an important sign of social progress and a key feature of a socialist modernization country. It results from the cultural construction of socialist modernization and the summary of the national, scientific, and popular socialist culture which orient towards modernization, the future and the world. It is also an essential support for realizing the great rejuvenation of the Chinese nation. Harmony is a basic concept of traditional Chinese culture which describes a vivid situation of education for all, work for all, medical care for all, elderly care for all, and housing for all. It is the value pursued in the social construction of a socialist modernization country and the important guarantee for the harmonious, stable, sustained, and healthy development of the economy and society.

【Questions for Discussion】

1. Based on the content of this chapter, what is your purpose for attending university?

2. What role do you think universities play in the economic and social development of a country?

3. Discuss your understanding of the role universities play in helping individuals' growth and personal development. What are your aspirations and ideals in life, and what kind of person do you hope to become?

4. What is the core educational content that international students should receive while studying at a university?

第一章　领悟人生真谛　启航幸福人生

如何领悟人生真谛？如何在变化的世界中成就出彩人生？这是每个人都必须认真思考的问题。对于高校国际生而言，领悟人生真谛，应该在各民族文化的对话与沟通中，通过树立科学的人生观，刻苦学习，增强本领，成就出彩人生。

【思维导图】

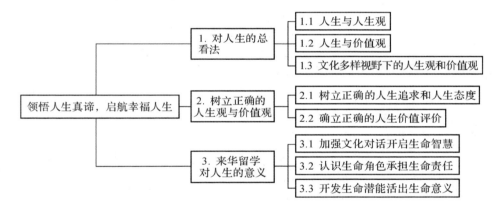

第一节　对人生的总看法

一、人生与人生观

在思考和规划自己的人生之路时，高校国际生要掌握人生观的基本理论，学会科学看待人生的根本问题。

人生是指人从出生至死亡所经历的过程。人不同于动物，不仅要经历生存繁衍、生老病死等自然过程,还要进行生产创造等一系列活动,做出思考、判断和决定。人的一生从出生开始,身边就充满各种社会关系,如家庭、地域、法律关系等。因此,任何人的人生都具有社会性,都是处于一定社会关系中的。在面对不同境遇时,人要不断地去实践人生,在现实生活中感悟人生,树立科学的人生观,才能使自己的人生变得有意义。

人生观是人们对人生的总看法和根本观点。人生观在一定的社会历史条件下形成,决定着人们实践活动的目标、人生道路的方向,也决定着人们如何对待生活。人生观的主要内容为人生目标、人生态度和人生价值,三者相互影响、紧密关联。

（一）人生目标

人生目标是指人们在社会实践中关于自身行为的根本指向和人生追求①。人生目标回答"人为什么活着"这一人生根本问题。人生目标在人生活动中起到的作用主要表现为以下三个方面。

第一,人生目标决定人生道路。人生目标决定了人们人生活动的大方向,从而对具体活动起着定向作用。许多仁人志士,在青年时期就确立了正确的人生目标,因此当站在面对人生重大抉择的十字路口时,能够做出正确的选择,沿着正确的道路前行。

第二,人生目标决定人生态度。不同的人生目标会使人采取不同的人生态度,正确的人生目标会使人积极进取、顽强拼搏、乐观向上;错误的人生目标会使人悲观消极、虚度光阴,甚至违法犯罪。一个人的人生目标越高尚、越明确,其内心所能激发出的驱动力就越强,在困难面前越不容易放弃,反之相反。

第三,人生目标决定人生价值的选择。正确的人生目标会使人懂得人生的价值首先在于奉献,从而在工作、生活、学习中尽职尽责;错误的人生目标则会使人把人生价值理解为向社会或他人索取,漠视对国家、社会、集体和他人的义务与责任。

高校国际生在大学期间,应当尽快树立人生目标,积极思考"人为什么活着"这一问题。如果一时无法设立人生目标,可以设置阶段性目标,比如大学整个阶段的目标,或者一年、一个学期,甚至一个月、一周的目标,从小

---

① 本书编写组.思想道德与法治[M].北京:高等教育出版社,2023:17.

目标入手完成大目标。同时,保持开放包容的心态,努力学习,广泛阅读,积极参加各种活动,在学习实践中拓宽自身视野,也有助于高校国际生尽快树立人生目标。

(二)人生态度

人生态度是指人们通过生活实践形成的对人生问题的一种相对稳定的心理倾向和精神状态[1]。作为人生观的主要内容,人生态度探讨人以怎样的情感状态进行人生实践,回答"人应当如何活着"这一问题。

人生目标如一面旗帜,指引着人们逐步地实现自我价值,而人生态度决定能否形成主观能动性顺利地实现人生价值。如果一个人始终保持乐观向上的人生态度,他往往会充满希望和激情,珍惜生命,在有限的人生中实现更大的价值。一个人如果长期对人生持有消极悲观态度,很可能碌碌无为、厌世轻生,体会不到生命的意义。

对任何人来说,上大学无可避免会遇到各种各样的问题,对于高校国际生更是如此。身处异国他乡,面对一张张陌生的面孔,体验着截然不同的语言文化,高校国际生往往会比其他大学生遇到更多困难。有些同学因此可能会出现消极悲观的态度。短暂的消极悲观是正常的,但如果一直沉浸其中,则有百害而无一利。凡事都有坏的一面,也有好的一面。换个角度看人生中遇到的困难,对人生保持积极乐观的态度,或许你就能发现人生的美妙之处。与其担心在异国他乡求学会遇到困难,不如将其看作是一场在异国有趣的冒险之旅。与其害怕听不懂语言理解不了文化,不妨以此为机会交一些朋友,学一门新的语言、一种新的文化和思维方式。乐观向上的人生态度会让你在高校的国际生活中收获满满。

(三)人生价值

人生价值是指人的人生目标及其实践活动对于社会和个人所具有的作用和意义[2]。当人在选择人生目标,或处理重大人生问题时,会依据一定的标准进行,人生价值便回答了"怎么样的人生才有价值"这一问题。

人生价值包括了人生的自我价值和人生的社会价值,两者强调人生价值的不同方面。人生的自我价值指个体的生活活动对自我生存和发展所具

[1] 本书编写组.思想道德与法治[M].北京:高等教育出版社,2023:18.
[2] 本书编写组.思想道德与法治[M].北京:高等教育出版社,2023:18.

有的意义,主要表现为个体对物质和精神需要的满足程度。人生的社会价值指个体的实践活动对社会、他人所具有的价值。二者构成了人生价值的矛盾统一体,既相互区别,又密切联系、相互依存。一方面,社会是由众多个体构成的,个人自我价值的实现,是个体为社会创造更大价值的前提。另一方面,人是社会的人,没有社会价值,人生的自我价值就无法存在,人生的社会价值是社会存在和发展的重要条件。

怎么样的人生才有价值? 高校国际生们要主动创造实现自我价值和社会价值的机会。在学习、活动、社会实践中,可以培养自我价值;与此同时,要尽可能将实现自我价值和实现社会价值结合在一起。

人生目标、人生态度、人生价值三者相互联系、相辅相成。人生目标决定了人们对实际生活的基本态度和对人生的价值评判,人生态度影响着人们对人生目标的持守和人生价值观的实现,人生价值制约着人们对人生目标和人生态度的选择。认识三者的内涵及其相互之间的辩证关系,才能准确把握人生方向盘,树立正确的人生观。

【案例分析】

高校国际生志愿者 A 积极响应公益课堂号召,来到当地小学,通过图文、视频、现场演示、互动问答等形式,向孩子们介绍了她的祖国马达加斯加的风土文化,在新冠疫情防控期间为孩子们带来了一次意义特殊的线上旅行。

【观点交流】

通过参加该活动,高校国际生志愿者 A 实现了自我价值和社会价值的结合了吗? 如果是,她是通过什么途径实现的?

除了利用语言优势参加语言类志愿活动,你是否能列举其他事情使高校国际生志愿者既可以实现自我价值,又能实现社会价值?

二、人生与价值观

人生是一个人生存在世界的岁月,每个人的人生都是千差万别的。在这段岁月里,有渴望追寻,有成功收获,有失败落寞,这些社会实践伴随着你的人生,体现着人生的价值。价值观是人们关于价值及其相关内容的基本观点和看法,是人们认定事物、判定是非的一种思维或取向,为人们判断善恶美丑提供基本准则。

价值观反映着特定的时代精神。人的社会存在和生活是属于一定时代的,因此,作为反映社会存在和生活的价值观也表现出鲜明的时代性。不同的时代存在不同的价值观,不存在超历史的或一成不变的价值观。

价值观体现着鲜明的民族特色。民族通过长期的共同生活形成了具有民族特色的价值观,其经过历史的沉淀,构成了该民族文化的内核。

价值观蕴含着特定的阶级立场。阶级社会中,不同阶级由于阶级地位和经济利益不同,有着不同的价值观。

价值观是一定社会形态、社会性质的集中体现。它体现着社会制度的阶级属性、社会运行的基本原则和社会发展的基本方向。价值观对社会生活的各个方面和社会中的每个成员都有着深刻的影响。

价值观与人生观、世界观紧密联系、相辅相成,对于人生的具体行为有重要的引导作用。树立什么样的价值观,会直接影响人们对人生目标、人生意义等问题的思考,左右他们对人生道路的选择,影响他们的人生态度。

来华学习后,高校国际生会接触各种各样的人,也会面对形形色色的价值观。在大多数情况下,人们有着人类共同的价值观,对于是非对错、善恶美丑有着类似的分辨标准。由于价值观体现着鲜明的民族性、时代性、阶级性,因此每个人的价值观多多少少有些不同。在一个陌生的国家,接触到不同的价值观很正常,在明辨是非善恶的基础上,不妨以一颗包容的心来看待这个事实,以免陷入一种无法与自我、与环境和解的矛盾中荒废宝贵光阴。

【观点交流】

不同时代存在不同的价值观,你能和我们分享那些以前存在的但现在已改变的价值观吗?

三、文化多样视野下的人生观和价值观

全球化的浪潮推动着世界各国的文化交融,高校国际生身处其中,感受着丰富多样的思想文化,面对着多种多样的人生观和价值观。高校国际生要深刻认识人生观和价值观的内涵与意义,准确把握人生方向,以文化多样性的视野,树立正确的人生观,服务大众,奉献世界。

【知识拓展】

世界是丰富多彩的,多样性是人类文明的魅力所在,更是世界发展的活力和动力之源。"非尽百家之美,不能成一人之奇。"文明没有高下、优劣之分,只有特色、地域之别,只有在交流中才能融合,在融合中才能进步。

——习近平在中华人民共和国恢复联合国合法席位50周年纪念会议上的讲话①

当今世界是文化多样性的世界,世界上的每个民族、国家都有自己独特的文化。全球化的浪潮一方面推动着文化的交融,一方面也使得文化多样性面临严重威胁。我们既要认同本民族文化,又要尊重其他民族文化,相互借鉴,求同存异,尊重世界文化多样性,共同促进人类文明繁荣进步。

来自不同国家、民族与文化的高校国际生,在文化多样性的今天,应该如何树立科学的人生观和价值观? 首先,要了解和尊重自己民族的文化,坚持本民族中正确的人生观和价值观。其次,承认世界文化的多样性,尊重不同民族文化,学习他们的优秀之处。最后,在多元文化交流过程中,要尊重差异,和睦共处,锻炼国际视野,树立正确的人生观,服务大众,奉献世界。

第二节　树立正确的人生观与价值观

一、树立正确的人生追求和人生态度

大学期间是一个人思想最为活跃的时期之一,是人生观形成的关键阶段。在这个阶段,高校国际生要树立正确的人生观,明确人生目标,端正人生态度,领悟人生价值,为今后的人生道路奠定良好的基础。

(一)树立高尚的人生追求

关于人生目标的探索,思想家们给出了数不清的答案,形成了众多思想。马克思认为,高尚的人生目标总是与奋斗和奉献联系在一起。它以历

---

① https://www.fohb.gov.cn/info/2023-01/20230110160300.4768.html.

史唯物主义关于人民群众是历史的创造者的基本观点为理论基础,指明了人在成长和发展过程中确立的人生目标和方向。当一个人确立了服务人民、奉献社会的人生追求,才能深刻理解为什么而活、应当如何活着、怎么样的人生才有价值等人生问题。他能够不为私心所困,不为名利所累,不为物欲所惑,将自己融入社会中,成就大我,推动社会进步,创造不朽业绩。

(二)树立积极进取的人生态度

在树立高尚的人生追求的同时,高校国际生们也要采取积极进取的人生态度,以认真务实、乐观向上、积极进取的姿态,面对学习、生活、工作中的各种挑战,处理各种各样的难题。

人生须认真。高校国际生要学会认真做人、认真做事,以认真的态度对待人生,严肃思考生命的意义,清醒地看待生活,对自己负责,对家人朋友负责,对周围的人和更多的人负责,进而担起对社会和国家的责任,成为一个有担当的人。当面对人生中出现的问题时,高校国际生们要做好规划、认真处理,而不是得过且过、半途而废。

人生当务实。做人做事要脚踏实地,将远大理想付诸实际行动中,以科学的态度看待人生,从小事做起,从身边事做起,一步一个脚印实现人生目标。高校国际生切忌脱离实际、急功近利、华而不实,要以务实的态度过好每一天,解决每一个问题。

人生应乐观。高校国际生在面对学习、生活、工作中遇到的问题时,应当有正确的认识,以乐观豁达的心态对待挫折。人在一生中,难免遇到一些磕磕碰碰,许多事情不会一帆风顺。如果一味为"失"叹息,就无法看到事情的另一面,容易产生消极悲观情绪,严重者甚至颓废堕落、自暴自弃。高校国际生不妨调整心态,选择积极的生活方式,乐观地面对生活。

人生要进取。人生要不断进取,不断超越。以进取的姿态面对人生道路上的各种问题,才能增强自身能力,挖掘自我价值,收获成果,取得快乐。不思进取、故步自封、贪图安逸只会让生活失去应有的光彩。高校国际生要采取主动进取的人生态度,拒绝"躺平",保持年轻人的蓬勃朝气,自强不息。

【案例分析】

来自肯尼亚的 B 同学是浙江某大学的一名国际生,她和中国同学一起参加了浙江省"互联网+"大学生创新创业大赛。以下是她的描述:

"我负责比赛的陈述和答辩。为了尽可能完美地展示项目成果,每天的排练必不可少,有时会排练到深夜,甚至让我与凌晨的月亮有了好多次邂逅。如果说,有什么比月亮的温柔陪伴更温暖,那一定是和队友们同甘共苦的经历。老师、队友们给了我很多暖心的鼓励和帮助。他们不厌其烦地听我的每一遍陈述,帮助我反复纠正发音和语调。越来越熟练的表达让我鼓起了直面比赛的勇气,坚定了我的信心。

来到中国学习、参加创新创业大赛的经历也在为我的人生'充电'。这份生命中独一无二的财富,将激励我回国后为家乡、为肯尼亚、为非洲贡献出属于自己的一份力量。感谢老师、同学及家人们一路上对我的帮助和支持,更要感谢那个在奋斗路上永远不服输、不放弃的自己!"

【知识拓展】

来华留学生讲中国故事

【观点交流】

1.当 B 同学面临准备比赛中的挑战时,她的态度是怎么样的?

2.她放弃了吗?她在这次经历中收获了什么?

二、确立正确的人生价值评价

对人生价值的正确评价,是人们迈向目标前进,实现人生价值的先决因素。

(一)正确评价人生价值

评价人生价值的根本尺度是看一个人的实践活动是否符合社会发展的客观规律,是否促进了历史的进步。在今天,衡量人生价值的标准,最重要的就是看一个人是否用自己的劳动和聪明才智为国家和社会真诚奉献,为人民群众尽心尽力服务。

既要看贡献的大小,也要看尽力的程度。对一个人的人生是否有价值或价值大小的评价,要看他对社会是否做出了贡献和贡献的大小。不同人由于不同的身体状况、家庭情况、努力程度,所从事的职业、做出的贡献量也不同。但如果仅仅从贡献量的维度去衡量一个人的价值，是不准确的。人无论从事什么职业，只要对于自己的岗位兢兢业业，尽职尽责，积极地为社会发展做出贡献，他的人生价值就应该得到肯定。

既要尊重物质贡献，也要尊重精神贡献。生产劳动是物质生产劳动和精神生产劳动的统一，人的社会劳动分工有的侧重物质财富的创造，有的侧重精神财富的创造，有的侧重体力劳动，有的侧重脑力劳动，都值得尊重。

既要注重社会贡献，也要注重自身完善。评价一个人的人生价值主要看他对社会做的贡献，但这并不代表要否认个人的自我价值。实现人的全面发展是社会发展的根本目标，因此，人的自身完善，既要实现个人自我价值，又要为社会创造价值。

（二）把握人生价值的实现条件

人们在实践中努力实现自己的人生价值。但是人们的实践活动从来都不是随心所欲的，任何人都只能在一定的主客观条件下去实现自己的人生价值。作为高校国际生，要想实现人生价值，需要把握人生价值的实现条件。

从社会客观条件出发实现人生价值。人生价值的实现，需要依赖于一定的社会客观条件。历史上有些仁人志士，因为客观的社会条件，未能实现人生价值。随着社会的进步，尤其是改革开放以来，我国社会实现了巨大的发展，为人们实现人生价值提供了良好条件。高校国际生们要珍惜难得的社会客观条件，抓住机遇，勇于探索，努力拼搏，把自己的人生价值实现建立在正确把握当今中国和世界发展的基础上。

从个体自身条件出发实现人生价值。个人的自身条件有所差异，在实现自身价值时，难易程度各不相同。高校国际生们正处于人生中最美好的时期之一，但是也会受到社会经历不足等方面的限制，过于主观地看待自身条件，导致在做出种种决定时产生判断偏差。这就需要高校国际生客观认识自我，理性把握自身条件，实现人生价值。

不断增强实现人生价值的能力和本领。人生价值的实现，很大程度上由个人的主观努力决定。高校国际生要努力学习，勇于实践，通过各种途径增强实现人生价值的能力和本领，为实现人生价值做好准备。

第三节　来华留学对人生的意义

一、加强文化对话开启生命智慧

生命智慧是生命本身所具有的智慧，这种智慧来源于生命本身，又保护生命。从整个生命的大视野出发，生命智慧可分为本能智慧与生活智慧。本能智慧存在于一切生命中，而生活智慧在此专指人所有的。生命的本能智慧存在于大自然的动物和植物中。鸟兽虫鱼为了生存下来，无不在自然界中展现出强大的生命本能智慧。章鱼在受到威胁或攻击时，会将身体缩小挤压，得以穿过小于自己的小小缝隙。壁虎在遇到对手时，能够断尾求生。鹰为了训练雏鹰飞翔会把雏鹰叼向天空，再摔向悬崖峭壁。植物的种子被随意地撒在土地上，根总是向下扎，芽向上冒，寻求更多大自然的养分。人既有本能智慧，又有生活智慧。生活智慧基于本能智慧，由生活中后天的经历体验形成，它是人通过观察或面对生或死、有限与无限等形成对生命的感悟。

从所涉及的领域看，生命智慧分为大生命智慧、类生命智慧和个体生命智慧。大生命智慧是整个生命世界的智慧，包括人类和动植物之间的智慧，理解生命之间的共性与相互依存的关系。类生命智慧指关乎人类命运的智慧，从人类生命视角出发，理解人类生命中不同国家、地区、民族之间的命运与关系。个体生命智慧指个体生死攸关的智慧，从个体生命出发，理解生老病死的意义。高校国际生要特别理解类生命智慧，理解不同国家、地区、民族之间的生命智慧，明白他山之石可以攻玉，在各民族文化对话与会通中思考人生矛盾，开启生命智慧。

生命智慧无形却不可或缺，在人的一生中，它的价值无可寻迹却又无处不在，它体现在以下三个方面：

生命智慧具有抚慰心灵的价值。浮躁的人生大多是缺乏生命智慧，无法感觉到满足，不能以一颗平和的心看待人生。生命智慧是喜悦之源，能帮助人们抚慰心灵，找到心灵之家。

生命智慧由于含有本能智慧这一属性，具有保卫生命这一价值。当遇到危险时，人会感到害怕，能发出求救，采取自我防卫或回击。生命智慧具有找到希望的价值。当人们身处逆境时，如果懂得生命智慧，明白生命生生不息,就会找到希望,不气馁,不灰心,充满希望地活着。

生命智慧具有冲破限制的价值。人的生命中存在许多限制,如生理上的或心理上的,有形的或无形的等,生命存在于限制中,又无时不在冲破限制,逐渐成长。

二、认识生命角色承担生命责任

责任是做好分内的事,并且承担做不好分内应做的事的后果。生命责任不仅指对于自我生命需求的主动反应,如生理、安全、社交、尊重、认知、审美、自我实现等,也指对于社会角色、法律条文、承诺契约等承担责任,以及对他人、团体、国家等的责任。

一个负责的生命,除了对自我生命负责,也对社会角色、他人、家庭、国家民族负责,对于人类共同责任负责,如保护环境、节约资源、和平发展等。作为一名高校国际生,应当理解生命责任的含义,学会对自我生命、社会他人、国家民族、人类共同责任负责,构建服务大众、奉献世界的价值认同,成长为负责任的生命。

要理解生命责任的内涵,个人首先要承担对自我生命的责任,学会保护自己的生命。一个人如果连自己的生命都无法保护,何谈对家人、国家、人类负责?在学会保护自己生命的同时,人也要学会保护他人生命,保护动植物的生命。如果没有对其他生命的尊重,那么人就倾向于认为生命是无价值的,从而做出危险的行为。

【案例分析】

某大学 50 多名来自不同国家的高校国际生组成了环保小分队,在校园内开展校园垃圾清理志愿服务活动。他们戴着口罩和手套,手持垃圾袋,从公寓楼到操场,从校园主干道到沿河小道,搜寻垃圾、装袋收集、分类投放。他们的行为体现了一个负责的生命不仅对自我生命负责,也对于人类共同责任如"保护环境"的负责,用实际行动践行了服务大众、奉献世界的理念。

角色表示人在社会关系中的地位和作用,是人生命中的一部分,每个人在社会中都扮演着多种多样的角色,比如父母、儿女、学生、工人、教师、医生等。

角色责任就是扮演这些角色所需要承担的责任。一个人不仅要承担生命责任,也要承担角色责任。

高校国际生的角色由大学生、来华国际生等要素组成,因此需要承担大学生和来华国际生几个角色所要求的责任。这几个角色要求高校国际生在人类共同价值的指引下,努力学习、刻苦钻研、开拓创新、勇于奉献,兼具国际视野、中国情怀,拥有良好的思想道德与专业素养。

【案例分析】

来自贝宁共和国的大明同学是中国武汉某高校的在读博士研究生。新冠疫情防控期间,他毅然选择留下来与武汉人民共同面对,用自己的方式加入中国的抗"疫"斗争。他和来自多个国家的几十名高校国际生自发成立了志愿服务队,帮助学校开展物资搬运分发、订餐送饭等工作。此外,他还多次在国内外社交平台和媒体上积极正面发声,传递正能量,为中国呐喊、为武汉加油,从亲历者角度讲述真实的中国抗"疫"故事。

【观点交流】

1. 从大明同学的案例中,你获得了什么启发?

2. 新冠疫情防控期间,公民的角色责任是什么? 高校国际生的角色责任又是什么?

三、开发生命潜能活出生命意义

生命潜能是人的生命所具有的一种能量,一般在特殊环境中才会爆发。每个人、每个生命都有生命潜能。一方面,生命潜能源于生命遗传,无法超越基因而存在。另一方面,生命潜能虽然无法超越基因,但其多样性往往远远超出人类想象,且每个人的潜能的发达程度不同。比如音乐家、舞蹈家的音乐潜能较强,运动员的运动潜能较强,数学家、律师等逻辑潜能更为发达,等等。因为生命潜能的存在,每个生命都有可能成为优质自我。比如你种下了一棵小树苗,只要有阳光雨露、适宜的温度和土壤等,加上辛勤耕作,小树苗就很有可能成长为参天大树。人也一样,只要努力为自己创设将生命潜能可能性转为现实的主客观条件,就可以开发潜能,成长为优质自我。

开发生命潜能,要充分利用自己的优势,掌握可控资源,将自我优势最大化。来自不同国家和地区的高校国际生有着不同的优势,有些同学擅长音乐体育,有些同学交际表达能力强,有些同学动手操作能力强等。在中国学习期间,他们可以在课堂、学校课外活动、社会实践等形式中,充分挖掘自身优势,从而挖掘出更强的生命潜能。

开发生命潜能,要破除意识中设立的障碍,勇于尝试,不断努力挑战自我,超越自我。高校国际生在中国学习期间,受语言、文化、思维差异等因素影响,不可避免地会遇到各种各样的困难。一部分同学受挫后,会无形中设立思维障碍,不愿意突破自我。这就需要高校国际生突破思维限制,敞开心扉,勇敢地去尝试,不断在新环境中努力学习新的知识,超越自我。

开发生命潜能,要努力过好当下生活,一步一个脚印,脚踏实地地耕耘。许多高校国际生,尤其是刚来中国学习时,或许由于学习生活环境发生骤然变化,会感到迷茫空虚,仿佛一下子失去了生活方向。大部分同学在老师和同学们的关心下,可以在较短时间内找到目标,开始脚踏实地地在中国学习和生活,逐渐挖掘、开发自我潜能。但仍有一部分同学长期处于这种状态中无法走出,严重者甚至萎靡不振,无法过好当下生活。这就需要高校国际生树立活在当下的心态,认真对待自己的生活,走好每一步,刻苦学习,增强本领,开发自我生命的潜能,成就出彩人生。

【案例分析】

高校国际生 John(化名)初来中国学习时,由于语言、文化差异等原因,受挫感较强,不愿与他人沟通。在大一时他成绩较差,甚至出现了挂科现象。课后大部分时间他将自己封闭在寝室内,对学校组织的活动也较为冷淡,基本上不参加。在老师和同学们的关心下,他逐渐意识到自己的问题,主动寻求办法改变自己的大学生活。课堂上,他积极与任课老师互动,认真完成每一次作业,脚踏实地完成学习内容,让老师们刮目相看。课后,他积极参加各类活动,如汉语朗诵大赛、高校国际生乒乓球比赛等,不断突破自己,打破思维障碍。大三时,John 的成绩已达到了全班第一,并在各类活动中锻炼了自己的各项才能,获得浙江省政府来华奖学金。

【观点交流】

1. 从 John 的案例中,你获得了什么启发?

2. 高校国际生可以通过哪些途径开发生命潜能?

【思考题】

搜索并阅读高校国际生大明和他的"钢铁侠"志愿者团队相关新闻,结合该章节所学内容:

1.描述他们的人生观和价值观。

2.分享他们的人生故事带给你的启发。

Chapter One　Understanding the True Meaning of Life, Setting Sail for a Happy Future

What is the true meaning of life? How can we lead a remarkable life in a world that is constantly evolving? These are questions that demand our serious contemplation. For international students in universities, understanding the true meaning of life should be achieved through intercultural communication, and by establishing a scientific outlook on life, they should study hard, enhance their abilities, and finally achieve a fulfilling life.

【Mind Map】

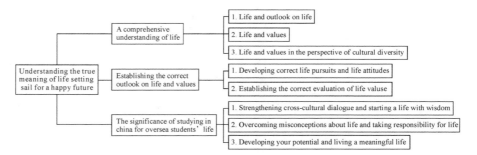

Section One　A Comprehensive Understanding of Life

1. Life and Outlook on Life

To reflect on and plan their own life path, international students in universities should know the basic theories concerning outlook on life and learn to scientifically approach the fundamental issues of life.

Life refers to the process that people go through from birth to death. Unlike animals, humans not only experience natural processes such as survival, reproduction, aging, and death, but also engage in a series of activities such as communication, production, and creation which demand making thoughts, judgments, and decisions. Since birth, people are embedded in various social relationships derived from family, locality, and legal systems. Therefore, everyone's life is of sociality and is situated in certain social relationships. In facing different circumstances, people need to constantly practice in life, perceive life, establish a scientific outlook on life, and make their lives meaningful.

Outlook on life is people's general view and fundamental standpoint on life. It is formed under certain social and historical conditions, and it determines the goals of people's practical activities, the direction of their life paths, and their attitude towards life. The main contents of outlook on life are life purpose, life attitude, and life value, all of which are interrelated, closely linked and unified as an organic whole.

(1) Life Purpose

Life purpose refers to the fundamental direction and utmost pursuit of one's life in their social practice. It answers the fundamental question of "why people live" and reveals the fundamental desire and goal of life. As the core of worldview, life purpose plays a crucial role in life practice, which can be seen in the following three aspects.

Firstly, life purpose determines one's life path. Life purpose determines the general direction of one's life activities and serves as a guide for specific actions. Many noble-minded individuals establish a correct life purpose during their youth, which enables them to make the right choices when facing major life decisions and continue on the right path.

Secondly, life purpose determines one's attitude towards life. Different life purposes will lead to different attitudes towards life. A correct life purpose will inspire one to be proactive, tenacious, optimistic, and positive. On the contrary, an incorrect life purpose will lead to pessimism, negativity, waste of time, or even criminal behavior. The higher and clearer one's life purpose is, the stronger the driving force within oneself will be, and the less likely one will give up in the face of difficulties.

Thirdly, life purpose determines the choice of one's life values. A correct life purpose will make one understand that the value of life lies in dedication, and thus fulfill one's duty in study, work, and life. An incorrect life purpose, on the other hand, will make one understand the value of life as a demand for social or personal gains, neglecting one's obligations and responsibilities to the country, society, groups, and other individuals.

International students in universities should establish their life purpose as soon as possible and actively think over the fundamental question "why do we live". If they cannot set a life purpose immediately, they can set a phased goal, such as the goal for the entire university period, or a goal for a year, a semester, or even a month or a week, and start with small goals before achieving larger ones. At the same time, maintaining an open and inclusive attitude, studying diligently, reading widely, and participating actively in various activities to broaden their horizons will also help them to establish their life purpose as soon as possible.

(2) Life Attitude

Life attitude refers to a relatively stable psychological tendency towards and mental state on life issues formed by people through their life practice. As the main content of the outlook on life, life attitude explores how people carry out life practice with their emotional state, and answers the question of "how should people live".

The purpose of life is like a banner, guiding people to realize their own value gradually, while life attitude determines whether one's subjective initiative can be formed to achieve life value smoothly. If a person always maintains a positive and upward life attitude, he/she will often be full of hope and passion, cherish life, and realize greater value in his/her limited life. Conversely, if a person holds a negative and pessimistic attitude towards life for a long time, he/she may be idle and suicidal, unable to understand the meaning of life.

Going to university inevitably involves various problems, especially for international students. International students in universities often encounter more difficulties than their domestic counterparts as they are in a foreign country, facing unfamiliar faces and experiencing different languages and cultures. As a result, some students may develop a negative and pessimistic attitude. Short-term negative and pessimistic attitudes are normal, but if one remains immersed in them, there will be no benefit. Everything has a positive and negative side. Looking at the difficulties encountered in life from a different perspective and maintaining a positive and optimistic attitude towards life, you may discover the beauty of life. Rather than worrying about encountering difficulties while studying abroad, why not see it as an interesting adventure in a foreign country? Instead of being afraid of not understanding the language and culture, why not take this as an opportunity to make friends, and learn a new language, a new culture and a new way of thinking? A positive and upward life attitude will enable you to harvest a lot in your life as an international student.

(3) Life value

The term "life value" in Chinese refers to the function and significance of one's life practice to the society and the individual. When people are choosing life goals or dealing with major life issues, they will follow certain standards, and the concept of "life value" answers the question of "what kind of life is valuable".

Life value includes both the personal value and social value of one's life, emphasizing different aspects of the value. The personal value of life refers to the significance of individual activities for one's own survival and development, mainly manifested in the degree of satisfaction with material and spiritual needs. The social value of life refers to the significance of individual activities for society and others. These two aspects constitute the "contradictory unity" of the value of life, both distinct from each other and closely related, and even mutually dependent. On the one hand, society is composed of numerous individuals, and the realization of personal value is a prerequisite for individuals to create greater value for society. On the other hand, people are social beings, and without social value, their personal value of life cannot exist. The social value of life is an important condition for the existence and development of a society.

What kind of life is valuable? International students in universities should actively create opportunities to realize their personal value and social value. Through learning and social practice, one can cultivate their personal value. At the same time, they should try to combine the realization of their personal value with the realization of social value.

Life purpose, life attitude and life value are interrelated and complementary. Life purpose determines people's basic attitude towards practical life and their evaluation of life value. Life attitude affects people's adherence to life goals and the realization of their values, while life value constrains people's choices of life goals and life attitudes. Understanding the connotations of these three aspects and their dialectical relationship is essential to accurately set the direction of life and establish a correct view of life.

【Case Analysis】

International student A from the university participated actively in the public welfare classroom, went to a local primary school, and introduced the culture and customs of her home country, Madagascar, to the children through pictures, videos, on-site demonstrations, interactive Q & A, etc. She brought a special online journey for the children during the epidemic.

【Opinion Exchange】

Did international student A achieve a combination of personal value and social value through participating in the voluntary class? If so, how did she achieve it?

Besides participating in language-related volunteering activities that utilize their language advantage, can you list other ways for international students to achieve both personal and social value?

2. Life and Values

Life is a period of time in which a person exists in the world, and each person's experience of life is different. During this period, people have desires to pursue, successes to achieve, and failures and loneliness to experience. These social practices accompany your life and reflect the value of life. Values reflect people's basic opinions and views of the world. They are a kind of thinking or orientation that people use to identify things, judge right from wrong and provide basic criteria for people to judge good and evil, beauty and ugliness.

Values reflect a specific spirit of the times. People can only live in a certain time, and therefore, as a reflection of social existence and life, values also show a distinct characteristic of the time. Different times have different values, and there are no values that are beyond history or unchanged.

Values reflect distinct national characteristics. A nation forms values with its own characteristics since its people live together for a long time, which, after historical sedimentation, constitute the core of its culture.

Values embody specific positions of different classes. In a society with different classes, each class has different values due to its different social status and economic interests.

Values epitomize the form and nature of a certain society. They reflect the classes of the social system, the basic principles of social operation, and the basic direction of social development. They have a profound influence on every aspect of social life and each individual.

Values are closely related to one's view of life and the world, playing an important guiding role in one's specific behavior. The values one holds directly influence their thoughts on the purpose and meaning of life and can affect their attitude toward life and their choices in life.

After coming to China to study, international students in universities will encounter a variety of people and face different values. In most cases, people share common values in distinguishing right from wrong, good from evil, and beauty from ugliness. However, as values embody distinct temporal, national and class characteristics, everyone's values differ to some extent. It is normal to encounter different values in a foreign country. In case one can distinguish right from wrong, it is advisable for him to take a tolerant attitude towards diversified values to avoid wasting precious time in a conflict that cannot be reconciled with the new environment.

【Opinion Exchange】

Different times have different values. Can you share with us some values that existed in the past but have now changed?

3. Life and Values in the Perspective of Cultural Diversity

The tide of globalization is driving cultural integration among countries around the world, and international students in universities are immersed in this environment, experiencing diverse and rich cultural and ideological perspectives, and facing a variety of life views and value systems. International students in universities should have a profound understanding of the connotations and significance of life and values, accurately maintain the direction of life, and with a culturally diverse perspective, establish a correct outlook on life to serve the public and contribute to the world.

【Knowledge Expansion】

The world we live in is diverse and colorful. Diversity makes human civilization what it is, and provides a constant source of vitality and driving force for world development. As a Chinese saying goes, "Without achieving the good of one hundred various schools, the uniqueness of one individual cannot be achieved". No civilization in the world is superior to others; every civilization is special and unique to its own region. Civilizations can achieve harmony only through communication, and can make progress only through harmonization.

——Speech by Xi Jinping at the 50th anniversary of the restoration of the People's Republic of China's lawful seat in the United Nations①

Today's world is a world of cultural diversity. Every nation and country in the world has its own unique culture. While globalization promotes cultural integration, it also poses a serious threat to cultural diversity. We should not only recognize our own national culture, but also respect the cultures of other nations. We should learn from each other, seek common ground while reserving differences, respect the world's cultural diversity, and jointly promote the prosperity and progress of human civilization.

How could international students from different countries, nations and cultures establish a scientific outlook on life and values in today's world of cultural diversity? First, they need to understand and respect their own national culture, and adhere to the correct outlook on life and values within their own nation. Second, they need to acknowledge the diversity of world cultures, respect the cultures of different nations, and learn from their strengths. Finally, in the process of multicultural exchange, they should respect differences, live in harmony, cultivate an international perspective, establish a correct outlook on life, serve the public and contribute to the world.

① https://www.fohb.gov.cn/info/2023-01/20230110160300_4768.html.

Section Two   Establishing the Correct Outlook on Life and Values

1. Developing Correct Life Pursuits and Life Attitudes

The period of university is one of the most intellectually active periods for a person and a crucial stage in the formation of their worldview. At this stage, international students in universities should establish a correct outlook on life, identify their life goals, adopt a positive attitude towards life, and recognize the value of life, so as to lay a solid foundation for their future life journey.

(1) Establishing a noble pursuit in life

Exploring the purpose of life, philosophers have offered countless answers and developed numerous thoughts. Marx believes that a noble life purpose is always linked to striving and dedication. The idea of serving the people and contributing to society, which is scientific and noble in nature, represents the most advanced human pursuit in human society to date. The theoretical viewpoint of historical materialism that people are the creators of history has indicated the life goals and directions one should establish in the process of growth and development. When a person establishes the life pursuit of serving the people and contributing to society, he or she can deeply understand questions like "why should one live", "how to live" and "what kind of life is valuable" etc. They can integrate themselves with society without being trapped by selfishness, fame or material desires, through which they can achieve a better self, promote social progress and create great accomplishment.

(2)Develop a positive and proactive attitude towards life

Besides establishing a noble pursuit in life, international students should also adopt a positive and proactive attitude towards life. They should face various challenges in their studies, life and work with a serious, practical, optimistic and proactive attitude, and learn to handle all kinds of problems.

One should take life seriously. International students in universities should learn to be diligent in their work and life. They should treat life seriously, think seriously about the meaning of life and be responsible for themselves, their families, friends and the people around them. They should take on responsibilities for society and for the country. When faced with problems in life, international students should make good plans and carry them out steadily, rather than just getting by or giving up halfway. Otherwise, they will deviate from the right track of life and waste their time.

One should be practical in life. People should be down-to-earth in their work and life, put lofty ideals into practical action, view life with a scientific attitude, start with small things and things around them and take one step at a time before finally achieving their life goals. International students should avoid being unrealistic, out of touch with reality and aiming too high. They should be practical in dealing with everyday problems and solving every problem.

One should be optimistic in life. When facing problems in their studies, life and work, international students should have the correct perception and treat setbacks with an optimistic and open-minded attitude. In one's lifetime, it is inevitable to encounter ups and downs, and many things may not go smoothly. If one constantly laments over losses, they won't be able to see the other side of things and may develop negative and pessimistic emotions. And in serious cases, one may become discouraged, fall into decadence and even give up on themselves. They should adjust their mindset, choose a positive lifestyle and face life with optimism.

One should be proactive in life. Life demands one to forge ahead and surmount difficulties. Only by facing various problems in life with a proactive attitude can people enhance their own abilities, tap their own values, make accomplishments and achieve happiness. Lack of ambition, being stuck in old ways, and seeking comfort will only make life lose its luster and meaning. International students should adopt a proactive attitude towards life, refusing to "lie flat", which reflects a mentality that young people adopt to reject rat race. Since trying hard can't get what you want, you'd better choose to skate by and become a couch potato. They should always maintain the vigor and vitality of young people and strive to improve themselves.

【Case Analysis】

Student B from Kenya is an international student at a university in Zhejiang Province. She participated in the College Students' "Internet ＋" Innovation and Entrepreneurship Competition in Zhejiang Province with her Chinese classmates. The following is her description.

"I was responsible for presenting and defending our project in the competition. In order to show the project's achievements as perfectly as possible, daily rehearsals were essential. Sometimes we rehearsed until late at night, and several times we could even greet the moon in the early morning hours. If there is anything warmer than the gentle companionship of the moon, it must be the experience of sharing joys and sorrows with my teammates. My teachers and teammates gave me a lot of warm encouragement and help. They patiently listened to my presentations and helped me repeatedly correct my pronunciation and tone in Chinese. The increasing proficiency in expressing myself gave me the courage to face the competition and strengthened my confidence.

The experience of studying in China and participating in the innovation and entrepreneurship competition has also given me a boost in my life. This unique wealth in my life will motivate me to contribute my own strength to my hometown, to Kenya, and to Africa after returning home. I am grateful for the help and support from my teachers, classmates and family along the way, and I am even more grateful to myself who never gave up and never surrendered to difficulties"!

【Knowledge Expansion】

Stories Told by International Students

【Opinion Exchange】

1. What was B's attitude when facing challenges in preparing for the competition?

2. Did she give up? What did she gain from this experience?

2. Establishing the Correct Evaluation of Life Values

The correct evaluation of one's own life values is an important prerequisite for people to strive towards their goals and achieve their life values.

(1) Establishing a Correct Evaluation of Life Values

The fundamental criterion for evaluating the value of life is to see whether a person's practical activities conform to the objective laws of social development and contribute to historical progress. Today, the most important standard for measuring the value of life is to see whether a person has dedicated themselves to the country and society sincerely with their labor and intelligence and has served the people wholeheartedly.

We should consider both the result of the contribution and the effort of the contributor. The evaluation of whether a person's life is valuable or how important their values are depends on whether they have contributed to society and the result of that contribution. Different people have different occupations and contributions due to different physical conditions, family situations, and degrees of effort. However, it is inaccurate to measure a person's value solely based on the result of their contribution. As long as people are diligent in their work, fulfill their duties and actively contribute to social development, their value in life should be affirmed, regardless of their occupation.

We should respect both material contributions and spiritual contributions. Social production consists of both material production and spiritual production. With the division of labor in society, some people focus on creating material wealth while others fucus on creating spiritual wealth, and they are undertaking physical labor or mental labor respectively. Both of these types of labor deserve respect.

We should pay attention to both individuals' social contributions and their personal improvement. Evaluating a person's value of life mainly depends on their contribution to society, but this does not mean that personal value should be denied. Achieving comprehensive development of individuals is the fundamental goal of social development. Therefore, personal improvement not only helps realize individual value but also creates value for society.

(2) Understanding the Conditions for Achieving Personal Values in Life

People strive to realize their own values in practice. However, people's practical activities are never arbitrary, and they can only realize their own values under certain objective and subjective conditions. As international students in universities, in order to realize our own values, we need to identify the conditions for realizing our own values.

To realize life values in objective social conditions. The realization of life values relies on certain objective social conditions. Throughout history, some benevolent people were unable to achieve their life values due to the objective social conditions they lived in. With the progress of society, especially since the reform and opening up, China has achieved tremendous development and provided favorable conditions for people to realize their life values. International students in universities should cherish the favorable objective social conditions, seize opportunities, explore bravely and work hard to establish their own life values based on a correct understanding of the current development of China and the world.

To realize life values in personal conditions. Personal conditions vary, and the difficulty of realizing personal values is different from person to person. Though international students in universities are in one of the best periods of their lives, they may also face limitations such as the lack of social experience. A merely subjective view of their own conditions may lead to misjudgment when making decisions. This requires international students to objectively understand themselves, rationally grasp their own conditions and realize their life values.

To continuously improve the ability and skills to realize life values. The realization of life values is largely determined by personal subjective efforts. International students in universities should strive to enhance their ability and skills through learning and practice by all possible means so as to realize their life values.

Section Three   The Significance of Studying in China for Oversea Students' Life

1. Strengthening Cross-cultural Dialogue and Starting a Life with Wisdom

Life wisdom is the wisdom that life itself possesses. It comes from life itself and also protects life. From the broad perspective of life, life wisdom can be divided into instinctual wisdom and experiential wisdom. Instinctual wisdom can be found in all living things, while experiential wisdom is specific to human beings. The instinctual wisdom of life exists in animals and plants in nature. Birds, beasts, insects, and fish all exhibit strong instinctual wisdom so as to survive in nature. Octopuses can shrink and squeeze their bodies to pass through tiny gaps when threatened or attacked. Geckos can detach their tails to survive when encountering enemies. Eagles can carry their chicks to the sky and drop them from cliffs to train them to fly. If plant seeds are randomly scattered on the ground, their roots always grow downwards while their shoots grow upwards, seeking more nutrients from nature. Humans have both instinctual and experiential wisdom. Experiential wisdom is based on instinctual wisdom and is formed through life experiences. It is the understanding of life gained through observation or when facing life and death, finiteness and infiniteness.

From the perspective of the fields involved, life wisdom is divided into three categories: great life wisdom, cyborg and bionic wisdom, and individual life wisdom. Macro-level life wisdom refers to the wisdom of the entire world of life, including the wisdom between human beings and animals and plants, and the understanding of the commonality and interdependence between lives. Human destiny-related life wisdom refers to the wisdom related to human fate. It focuses on the understanding of fate and the relationship between different countries, regions, and ethnic groups from the perspective of human life. Individual life wisdom refers to the wisdom related to individual life and death. It focuses on the understanding of the meaning of life, aging, illness and death from the perspective of individual life. International students in universities should understand human destiny-related life wisdom, understand the life wisdom between different countries, regions and ethnic groups, think about the contradictions of life through communication among different cultures and build up their own life wisdom.

Life wisdom is intangible but indispensable and in one's life, its value is untraceable yet ubiquitous. It can be manifested in the following three aspects:

Life wisdom has the value of soothing the mind. A restless life is mostly due to the lack of life wisdom, one being unable to feel satisfied and unable to view life with a peaceful mind. Life wisdom is the source of joy and can help people soothe their mind and find their spiritual home.

Life wisdom has the value of protecting life because of its attribute of instinctual wisdom. When faced with danger, people feel afraid, ask for help and take self-defense or counter-attack measures. Life wisdom has the value of finding hope. When people are in adversity, they can go on with their lives if they understand life wisdom because they will find hope and not be discouraged or disheartened.

Life wisdom has the value of breaking through limitations. There are many limitations in human life, whether physical or psychological, tangible or intangible. Life exists within limitations, yet it breaks through limitations and grows gradually.

2. Overcoming Misconceptions about Life and Taking Responsibility for Life

Responsibility means doing what is expected of you and accepting the consequences of not fulfilling those expectations. Life responsibility not only refers to actively responding to your own life needs, such as physiological soundness, safety, sociality, respect, cognition, aesthetic, and self-realization, but also refers to taking responsibility for one's social roles, promises and lawful contracts. It can also refer to the responsibility for others, groups, nations and so on.

A responsible life entails being accountable not only for one's own life, but also for others, family, nation, and humanity as a whole, such as protecting the environment, conserving resources, and promoting peaceful development. As an international student in a university, one should understand the meaning of life responsibility, and learn to be responsible for oneself, others, one's nation and humanity as a whole. He/she should build a sense of value for serving the public and contributing to the world and become a responsible individual.

To understand the connotation of life responsibility, individuals must first take responsibility for their own lives and learn to protect themselves. If a person cannot even protect their own life, how can they be responsible for their family, nation, or humanity? While learning to protect their own life, people should also learn to protect the lives of others, including the lives of animals and plants. Without respect for other forms of life, people tend to believe that life is worthless and may engage in dangerous behavior.

【Case Analysis】

A group of over 50 international students from different countries at a university formed an environmental protection team and carried out volunteer services to clean up the campus. Wearing masks and gloves, they carried trash bags and searched for garbage from the dormitories to the playground, and from the main road of the campus to the riverbank path. They collected the garbage and sorted it properly. Their actions reflect that a responsible life is not only responsible for one's own life but also for the common good of humanity as demonstrated in the action of environmental protection. They have practiced the concept of serving the public and contributing to the world through their own actions.

Role refers to the position and function of a person in social relations, which is part of a person's life. Each person plays various roles in society, such as parents, children, students, workers, teachers, doctors and so on.

Role responsibility is the responsibility that one needs to undertake in order to fulfill these roles. A person should not only bear the responsibility of life but also the responsibility of roles.

The role of international students in universities consists of elements such as college students and international students in China. Therefore, they need to bear the responsibilities required by these roles. These roles require international students to strive to learn, explore, innovate and be willing to contribute. Under the guidance of common human values and with an international vision and Chinese sentiments, they should possess excellent moral and professional qualities.

【Case Analysis】

Daming, a student from the Republic of Benin, is a doctoral student at a university in Wuhan, China. During the epidemic, he resolutely chose to stay and face it together with Wuhan. He joined China's anti-epidemic fight in his own way. He and dozens of international students from other countries formed a volunteer service team to help the university with tasks such as transporting and distributing supplies, ordering and delivering meals, etc. In addition, he also actively voiced his support for China in media and on social media platforms both domestically and internationally, telling the real story of China's anti-epidemic efforts from the perspective of someone who was there, cheering for Wuhan and spreading positive energy for China.

【Opinion Exchange】

1. What inspirations did you draw from the case of student Daming?

2. What is the role responsibility of citizens during the epidemic? What is the role and responsibility of international students in universities?

3. Developing Your Potential and Living a Meaningful Life

Life potential is a kind of energy that exists in human life and it only "erupts" under special conditions. Every person has life potential. On the one hand, life potential comes from genetic inheritance and cannot surpass what the genes could provide. On the other hand, although life potential cannot go beyond genes, its diversity often far exceeds human imagination. The degree to which each person's potential develops is different. For example, musicians and dancers have strong musical potential, athletes have strong athletic potential, mathematicians and lawyers have stronger logical potential, and so on. Because of the existence of life potential, every life has a chance to become a high-quality self. For example, when you plant a sapling, as long as there are sunshine, rain, suitable temperature, and soil, plus your utmost care, the sapling is likely to grow into a towering tree. It is true with people. As long as they work hard to create the subjective and objective conditions that help turn their potential into reality, they can make full use of their potential and grow into high-quality selves.

To develop life potential, a person should master the resources available and maximize their own advantages. International students from different countries and regions have different advantages. Some are good at music and sports, some are good at communication and expression, some have strong hands-on skills, etc. During their study in China, they can fully make use of their advantages in classes, school extracurricular activities and social practice, and thus develop stronger life potential.

To develop life potential, one must break down mental barriers, dare to try and constantly challenge and surpass themselves. During the process of studying in China, international students will inevitably encounter various difficulties due to differences in language, culture and thinking pattern. Some students will unconsciously set up mental barriers after setbacks and be unwilling to break them down by themselves. This requires international students to break through their thinking limitations, open their hearts to try bravely and continuously learn new knowledge in a new environment in order to surpass themselves.

To develop life potential, one must strive to live in the present and work hard to make progress step by step. Many international students, especially those who are new in China, may feel lost and empty due to dramatic changes in their study and living environment as if they have lost their direction in life. Most students, under the care of their teachers and classmates, can refund their goals in a short period and start to work hard and develop their potential in China. However, some students remain "lost" for quite a long time and are unable to get out of it. The most serious ones even will be unable to keep going. This requires international students to establish a mentality of living in the present, taking their lives seriously. They should take each step well, study hard, enhance their abilities and develop their life potential so that they can achieve a brilliant life.

【Case Analysis】

When John, an international student in the university, felt discouraged due to language and cultural differences and was unwilling to communicate with others when he first came to China to study. His grades in the first year were poor, and he even failed some courses. Most of the time after class, he isolated himself in his dorm room and was uninterested in school-organized activities. With concern and care from teachers and classmates, he gradually realized his problem and actively sought ways to change himself. In class, he actively interacted with the teachers, completed each homework seriously and learned his courses well. After class, he actively participated in various activities such as Chinese recitation contests and international students' table tennis competitions, broke through his mental barriers, and challenged himself to higher goals. By the third year, his grades ranked first in the class. He honed his talents and skills through various activities and eventually won a scholarship from the provincial government.

【Opinion Exchange】

    1. What inspiration did you gain from John's case?

    2. How can international students develop their potential in life?

【Questions for Discussion】

Search and read news related to the international student Daming and his "Iron Man" volunteer team at universities. Based on the content learned in this chapter, try to:

    1. Describe their outlook on life and values;

    2. Share the inspirations you gained from their life stories.

第二章 弘扬全人类共同价值
构建人类命运共同体

当今时代,人类是一个相互依存的整体,各国命运与共,人类比以往任何时候都更需要弘扬和坚守全人类共同价值,为构建人类命运共同体凝聚价值共识、奠定价值之基。

【思维导图】

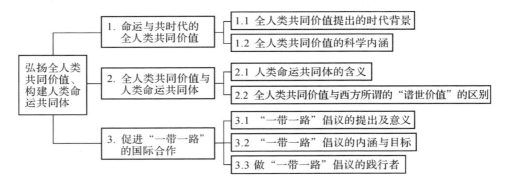

第一节 命运与共时代的全人类共同价值

一、全人类共同价值提出的时代背景

中国共产党第二十次全国代表大会上的报告指出:"当前,世界之变、时代之变、历史之变正以前所未有的方式展开。"①在新的历史时期,国际力量

---

① 习近平.高举中国特色社会主义伟大旗帜 为全面建设社会主义现代化国家而团结奋斗——在中国共产党第二十次全国代表大会上的报告[M].北京:人民出版社,2022:60.

对比深刻调整,影响国际形势发展变化的短期因素与长期因素相互交织,世界面临新的动荡变革。日益增长的全球性挑战让人类命运共同体理念更加深入人心,和平、发展、合作、共赢的历史潮流不可阻挡。全人类共同价值是基于人类命运共同体理念提出的经济全球化时代各国命运与共的价值纽带,它的提出具有深刻的时代背景。

（一）世界经济发展的不平衡性

在经济全球化和互联网时代,世界已变成了互联互通的"地球村"。然而世界共通在带来全球经济蓬勃发展的同时,各地区和国家之间经济发展的不平衡也日渐凸显。其中,发达国家和发展中国家之间发展不平衡的矛盾尤为突出,对世界经济和社会发展的影响十分深刻。目前,世界经济已形成了物质产品由发达国家流向发展中国家,资金、财富则又以各种方式从发展中国家流向发达国家的新局面,由此导致南北差距的继续扩大。同时,发达国家内部收入差距也在扩大,全世界的社会财富进一步集中于少数人手里。世界经济发展的不平衡会引发各种社会矛盾,这种不平衡状况若不采取有力措施而任其发展下去,将直接影响全球经济的健康发展。

【知识拓展】

"地球村"（global village）这一词是加拿大传播学家 M. 麦克卢汉 1964 年在他的《理解媒介：人的延伸》一书中首次提出的。麦克卢汉对现代传播媒介的分析深刻地改变了人们——特别是当代青年人对 20 世纪以及 21 世纪生活的观念,他所预言的地球村在今天的社会已经变成了现实。麦克卢汉认为,"地球村"的主要含义不是指发达的传媒使地球变小了,而是指人们的交往方式以及人的社会和文化形态发生了重大变化。交通工具的发达曾经使地球上的原有"村落"都市化,人与人之间的直接交往被迫中断,由直接的、口语化的交往变成了非直接的、文字化的交往,而电子媒介又实施着反都市化,即"重新村落化",消解城市的集权,使人的交往方式重新回到个人对个人的交往。

不断扩大的贫富差距成为全球最大的挑战

（二）安全与风险的不确定性

当今世界，国际战略格局深刻演变，国际力量加快分化组合，新兴市场国家和发展中国家力量持续上升，战略力量对比此消彼长、更趋均衡，促和平、求稳定、谋发展已成为国际社会的普遍诉求，和平力量的上升远远超过战争因素的增长。但是，霸权主义、强权政治、单边主义时有抬头，地区冲突和局部战争持续不断，国际安全体系和秩序受到冲击。随着社会发展的不稳定性、不确定性因素日益增加，诸如全球疫情、气候灾害、经济危机、恐怖主义、国家间冲突甚至战争等新兴风险与阶层不平等、区域不均衡等传统问题的融合，将使得人类越来越陷入全球风险社会的深度不确定性中。

【知识拓展】

当前全球经济三大不确定性与最大确定性

（三）全球治理体系的不合理性

全球治理是国际社会中的多元行为体为应对全球性挑战而进行协调与合作的过程。当前全球治理体系是第二次世界大战后在美国等西方国家主导下建立起来的，其基本架构仍在发挥有效作用，但不少机制、规则和运作方式已不能适应国际力量对比的变化。在现行的全球治理体系中，少数大国拥有更多的话语权，如在国际货币基金组织、世界银行等机构中，欧美发达国家拥有更多的投票权。进入 21 世纪后，新兴市场国家和发展中国家崛起，国际经济力量对比发生了深刻变化，而全球经济治理体系未能反映这一新格局。目前，新兴市场国家和发展中国家对全球经济增长的贡献率已经达到 80％，成为全球经济增长的主力军。然而，在全球经济治理体系中，新兴市场国家与发展中国家的代表性与发言权与它们对世界经济增长所做出的贡献率明显不相匹配。全球治理体系的包容性与代表性不够，导致现有全球治理体系无法适应经济全球化深入发展的要求，无法有效应对当前人类面临的全球性问题的挑战。

（四）文明与文化的多样性

世界上没有两片完全相同的树叶。在漫长的人类文明的历程中,文明图谱五光十色,每一种文明都是人类劳动和智慧的结晶,都是值得尊重和珍惜的。从人类发展的价值层面看,每个国家、每个民族、每种文化都各有各的价值观,这些价值观之间没有高低、优劣、好坏之别。然而,文化表现形态的差异性并不能遮蔽人类生存共识与共同价值追求的形成;相反,世界范围内的冲突越是剧烈,恐怖主义、霸权主义、资本扩张、贫富差距、生态危机等问题越是严重,人类的共同价值追求便越是迫切与普遍。建设更加美丽的世界、更加美好的生活,绝不是以一种文明代替另一种文明,而是要在尊重各国各民族文明、维护世界文明多样性的基础上,推动不同社会制度、不同意识形态、不同历史文化、不同发展水平的国家在国际事务中利益共生、权利共享、责任共担。

【概念解析】

文化多样性指的是世界上每个民族、每个国家都有自己独特的文化,民族文化是民族身份的重要标志。文化多样性不仅体现在人类文化遗产通过丰富多彩的文化表现形式来表达、弘扬和传承的多种方式,也体现在借助各种方式和技术进行的艺术创造、生产、传播、销售和消费的多种方式。文化多样性是人类社会的基本特征,也是人类文明进步的重要动力。因此,我们应该做到:

（1）既要认同本民族文化,又要尊重其他民族文化,相互借鉴,求同存异,尊重世界文化多样性,共同促进人类文明繁荣进步。

（2）尊重文化多样性,首先要尊重自己民族的文化,培育好、发展好本民族文化。

（3）承认世界文化的多样性,尊重不同民族的文化,必须遵循各民族文化一律平等的原则。

（4）在文化交流中,要尊重差异,理解个性,和睦相处,共同促进世界文化的繁荣。

【观点交流】

如何看待文化的多样性? 你们国家的文化有什么特点?

【案例分析】

　　首次出版于 1996 年的《文明的冲突与世界秩序的重建》是美国政治学家塞缪尔·亨廷顿的代表作。作者认为,冷战后,世界格局的决定因素表现为七大或八大文明,即中华文明、日本文明、印度文明、伊斯兰文明、西方文明、东正教文明、拉美文明,还有可能存在的非洲文明。冷战后的世界,冲突的基本根源不再是意识形态,而是文化方面的差异,主宰全球的将是"文明的冲突"。塞缪尔·亨廷顿认为,不同文明之间的矛盾无法调和,未来的世界冲突将会是文明与文明之间的冲突。

二、全人类共同价值的科学内涵

　　2015 年 9 月 28 日,习近平在第七十届联合国大会一般性辩论时指出:"和平、发展、公平、正义、民主、自由,是全人类的共同价值,也是联合国的崇高目标。"[①]中共二十大报告呼吁世界各国弘扬和平、发展、公平、正义、民主、自由的全人类共同价值,促进各国人民相知相亲,尊重世界文明多样性。全人类共同价值的提出宛如打开了一扇窗户,给处于复杂而深刻变革之中的世界带来全新的发展思路与视野,引发许多国家的热切关注与深入思考,显示出强大的思想感召力和实际影响力。

　　和平、发展、公平、正义、民主、自由是全人类共同价值。这六大价值要素涵盖政治文明、物质文明、精神文明、社会文明、生态文明建设等五大领域,各有侧重、相互补充,有机统一为一整套全新的价值认知体系,实现了人类文明发展史上一场伟大的价值观革命。

　　和平与发展既是人类的共同事业,也是当今时代的主题,关乎所有人的生存权和发展权。其中,和平是全人类共同价值中的底线价值。人类要生存和发展就必须反对战争。只有在和平稳定的环境中,人类才能更好地生存与发展。没有和平,一切都无从谈起。而发展是进步的条件,支撑着生存和希望,唯有发展才能消除冲突的根源,保障人民的基本权利,从而满足人民对美好生活的热切向往。发展与和平相辅相成,和平孕育发展生机,发展保障持久和平。

　　公平、正义是全人类共同价值中的条件和保障。公平是人类和谐相处

---

　　① 习近平.习近平谈治国理政[M].第 2 卷.北京:外文出版社,2017:522.

的基本条件,正义是人类坚定而恒久的价值追求。没有公平、正义的国际秩序,和平、发展就得不到保障,民主和自由也不可能真正实现。公平、正义主要涉及的是全球社会问题,尤其是秩序问题。其中,公平更侧重于国际关系中无差别的主体平等,正义则更侧重于国际秩序中各主体的"得其应得"。坚持公平正义,首要的是坚守主权平等原则。国家不分大小、强弱、贫富,一律平等,主权和尊严必须得到尊重,内政不容干涉,反对以强凌弱,反对把自己的意志强加于人。

民主、自由是全人类共同价值中的理想与方法。民主意味着各国平等参与国际事务,共同掌握世界命运,遵循共商共建共享原则参与国际治理等;自由意味着捍卫主权国家独立自主的权利和自主选择社会制度和发展道路的自由,捍卫国家合理表达利益诉求和合理分享发展成果的自由。在全球社会中,作为方法的民主、自由,就是要让各国正确看待相互差异,理性处理彼此分歧,自觉、平等地以公共性为原则进行讨论、辩驳,以实现真正的公共理性。

【观点交流】

谈谈你对全球人类共同价值的理解。

第二节　全人类共同价值与人类命运共同体

一、人类命运共同体的含义

在世界百年未有之大变局的时代背景下,构建人类命运共同体必然要摒弃西方中心论的价值理念,超越西方的"普世价值",通过弘扬和践行全人类共同价值,有效地推动人类命运共同体的构建。

(一)人类命运共同体的概念

人类命运共同体是 21 世纪初由中国共产党首先提出、倡导并推动的一种价值理念和具体实践。人类命运共同体强调在多样化社会制度总体和平并存,各国之间仍然存在利益竞争和观念冲突的现代国际体系条件下,每一个国家在追求本国利益时兼顾他国合理关切,在谋求本国发展中促进各国共同发展。它的核心理念是和平、发展、合作、共赢,其理论原则是新型义利观,建构方式是结伴而不结盟,最终目的是增进世界人民的共同利益、整体利益和长远利益。

从政治、安全、经济、文明、生态等维度出发,构建人类命运共同体主要包括五个层面的基本内涵:一是坚持对话协商,建设一个持久和平的世界;二是坚持共建共享,建设一个普遍安全的世界;三是坚持合作共赢,建设一个共同繁荣的世界;四是坚持交流互鉴,建设一个开放包容的世界;五是坚持绿色低碳,建设一个清洁美丽的世界。

【概念解析】

这个世界,各国相互联系、相互依存的程度空前加深,人类生活在同一个地球村里,生活在历史和现实交汇的同一个时空里,越来越成为你中有我、我中有你的命运共同体。

——《习近平谈治国理政》第一卷,北京:外文出版社,2018 年,第272 页。

人类命运共同体,顾名思义,就是每个民族、每个国家的前途命运都紧紧联系在一起,应该风雨同舟,荣辱与共,努力把我们生于斯、长于斯的这个星球建成一个和睦的大家庭,把世界各国人民对美好生活的向往变成现实。

——《习近平谈治国理政》第三卷,北京:外文出版社,2020 年,第433 页。

(二)全人类共同价值与人类命运共同体的关系

人类命运共同体从"持久和平、普遍安全、共同繁荣、开放包容、清洁美丽"五个方面构建了基本框架。全人类共同价值明确了"和平、发展、公平、正义、民主、自由"六大价值标准,两者前后呼应,相互贯通,辩证统一。如果说,人类命运共同体描绘了世界的美好生活图景,那么,全人类共同价值则是对于人类命运共同体到底"共在哪里、同在何处"的思想概括。构建人类命运共同体是在应对日益增多且复杂严峻的全球性挑战中提出的,而和平、发展、公平、正义、民主、自由正体现出全人类在解决共同面临的重大问题上的价值诉求。全人类共同价值鲜明体现着主权平等、沟通协商、公平正义、开放包容、人道主义等理念,为构建人类命运共同体提供价值认同基础,确证了人类命运共同体的道义性。全人类共同价值从价值层面最大限度地凝聚共识,在实践中汇聚各国力量向着构建人类命运共同体的方向努力。人类命运共同体是全人类共同价值的实践场域。全人类共同价值对构建人类命运共同体的意义,没有仅仅停留在观念层面,在今天的国际关系中,它正在具体地转化为一些国家的外交政策,体现在越来越多的国际公共政策领域。

【知识拓展】

构建人类命运共同体思想的丰富内涵,可以从政治、安全、经济、文化、生态五个方面来理解:一是政治上,要相互尊重、平等协商,坚决摒弃冷战思维和强权政治,走对话而不对抗、结伴而不结盟的国与国交往新路。二是安全上,要坚持以对话解决争端、以协商化解分歧,统筹应对传统和非传统安全威胁,反对一切形式的恐怖主义。三是经济上,要同舟共济,促进贸易和投资自由化、便利化,推动经济全球化朝着更加开放、包容、普惠、平衡、共赢的方向发展。

二、全人类共同价值与西方所谓的"普世价值"的区别

(一)西方所谓的"普世价值"的实质

西方所谓的"普世价值"伴随着资本主义的发展而发展,是资产阶级价值观和意识形态的集中体现。其主要内容包括以下三个方面:一是在西方自文艺复兴到启蒙运动时期形成的一些政治理念,例如自由、平等、博爱、民主、人权、法治等在资产阶级革命时期形成的核心价值观;二是资本主义社会的政治经济制度模式,例如三权分立、多党制、普选制,私有化、市场经济等;三是与前两者相适应的一些道德准则和行为规范等。

西方所谓的"普世价值"的本质是西方价值,是仅仅根据西方国家发展起来之后的生活提炼而成的,并不是全世界所有国家和民族接受的理念。尽管西方所谓的"普世价值"高举自由、民主、人权大旗,但背后的资本强权逻辑使其世界秩序呈现出实质上的高度不自由、不民主、非人权。因此,西方所谓的"普世价值"本来就不是普世的,它包含了许多资产阶级和资本主义社会具有的特殊政治理念和特定政治经济模式的内涵,体现的是少数强权国家的话语霸权,把它说成是普世的或普适的,具有欺骗性和虚伪性。

【案例分析】

请阅读下面的案例，分析讨论案例中基辛格的观点。

西方宣扬"普世价值"的实质是推销西方的所谓"民主国家体系"和"自由体制"。美国原国务卿亨利·基辛格的《论中国》一书，对西方推行"普世价值"有深刻的论述。该书认为，西方国家包括美国声称自己的价值观和体制普世适用，但中国从古至今都有不同于西方的价值观。"中国社会占统治地位的价值观源自一位古代哲学家的教诲，后人称其为孔夫子。"基辛格进一步指出："中国主张独立自主，不干涉他国内政，不向外国传播意识形态，而美国坚持通过施压和激励来实现价值观的普适性，也就是要干涉别国的内政。"

（二）全人类共同价值对西方所谓的"普世价值"的超越

全人类共同价值是世界各国在价值上的最大公约数，是世界各国人民最基本、最美好的价值追求。全人类共同价值打破了西方中心主义和西方话语霸权，超越了基于地域主义的西方所谓的"普世价值"。

西方所谓的"普世价值"忽视了各个国家、民族、地区的文化背景、历史条件、地理环境、人口状况等具体条件的不同。实现民主、自由的方式必然有其国家、民族的具体特色和选择，而西方所谓的"普世价值"把不具备普遍性的，而具有特殊性、具体性的东西当作"普世性"的价值来追求。人类追求美好幸福的生活，而美好生活的内涵非常丰富，在不同国家、民族、地理位置，以及不同发展程度的社会呈现出不同的样态，从而诞生出璀璨多样的文明形态。多样性与共同性是辩证统一的，璀璨多样的人类文明形态必然具有某些共同性，这些共同性中就蕴含着人类的共同、普遍需要。因此，真正适用于全人类的共同价值，应当根据全人类共同、普遍的生活中蕴含的共同、普遍的需要提炼而成。任何民族或者国家无论在地球哪个位置、处于何种发展程度、信奉何种宗教，都必然追求和平、发展、公平、正义、民主、自由等共同价值。全人类共同价值是根据全人类共同、普遍生活提炼而成的，它以开放的视野、宽广的格局、博大的胸怀观照世界各民族的共同发展，旨在寻求国际间的真诚合作与平等交流，以共同应对全球挑战，回应亟须解决的时代难题，形成共建美好世界的最大公约数。

第三节 促进"一带一路"的国际合作

一、"一带一路"倡议的提出及意义

历史上的古丝绸之路在东西方之间架起了一座政治、经济、文化交往最具象征性的合作桥梁,如今,"一带一路"不仅是和平之路、商贸之路,更是文化和人才的互通通道。在新的历史条件下,中国提出"一带一路"倡议就是要继承和发扬丝绸之路精神,把中国的发展同沿线国家和世界其他国家的发展结合起来,把中国梦同沿线国家和世界其他国家人民的梦想结合起来,赋予古代丝绸之路以全新的时代内涵。共建"一带一路"倡议源于中国,更属于世界。而来华学习的高校国际生运用自身资源和才智服务"一带一路"建设乃题中之义、大势所趋,也是责无旁贷的时代选择。

【概念解析】

"一带一路"(The Belt and Road,缩写 B&R)是"丝绸之路经济带"和"21世纪海上丝绸之路"的简称。2013 年 9 月和 10 月,中国国家主席习近平分别提出建设"新丝绸之路经济带"和"21世纪海上丝绸之路"的合作倡议。依靠中国与有关国家既有的双多边机制,借助既有的、行之有效的区域合作平台,"一带一路"旨在借用古代丝绸之路的历史符号,高举和平发展的旗帜,积极发展与沿线国家的经济合作伙伴关系,共同打造政治互信、经济融合、文化包容的利益共同体、命运共同体和责任共同体。

作为践行人类命运共同体理念和推进构建人类命运共同体的重要实践平台,"一带一路"倡议为实现各国共同发展提供了新思路、新方案和新动力,为完善全球经济治理提供了理念支撑和实践模式。其意义主要有以下两个方面。

一方面,为世界经济复苏和发展注入了强劲动力。"一带一路"倡议坚定地支持多边主义和多边贸易体制,推行自由贸易和投资。得益于共建"一带一路"倡议,世界最大的内陆国哈萨克斯坦拥有了出海通道,白俄罗斯第一次有了自己的轿车制造业,马尔代夫实现了拥有桥梁的梦想,巴基斯坦多个能源项目开工以后,电力短缺问题得到了根本性改善,中老铁路将使老挝从"陆锁国"变为"陆联国"。事实证明,共建"一带一路"倡议为沿线国家的经济发展、民生改善做出了突出贡献。

另一方面,为完善全球治理体系做出了新的贡献。"一带一路"倡议坚持对话协商,坚持共建共享,坚持合作共赢,坚持交流互鉴,推动各国加强政治互信、经济互融、人文互通,推动构建人类命运共同体。"一带一路"建设实现了沿线各国之间政策的相互沟通,增进了对彼此外交政策的了解和理解,通过签订一系列友好协议,为各国之间更加深入的交往提供了政治保障。实践充分证明,共建"一带一路"倡议顺应了全球治理体系变革的内在要求,彰显了同舟共济、共建命运共同体的理念,为完善全球治理体系提供了中国思路、中国方案。

【知识拓展】

共建"一带一路"取得实打实、沉甸甸的成就

二、"一带一路"倡议的内涵与目标

作为一种开放性、平等性和包容性的区域合作平台,"一带一路"倡议是中国向世界提供的国际公共产品,是中国同世界共享机遇、共谋发展的阳光大道,其根本宗旨在于通过对接各国发展战略,开拓新的合作空间,发掘新的合作潜力,实现中国发展机遇与世界发展机遇的双向转化和良性互动。

(一)"一带一路"倡议的内涵

"一带一路"是一项以互利共赢、构建利益和命运共同体为目的的合作倡议,是所有国家均可参与、各方共商共建、共享共赢的大平台,其内涵主要包括以下方面。

共同发展是方向。"一带一路"建设不是仅着眼于中国自身发展,而是以中国发展为契机,让更多国家搭上中国发展的"快车",帮助他们实现发展目标。"一带一路"倡议的发展能量来自共同发展的合作取向,对各国共同发展的追求正是"一带一路"倡议的旗帜方向。

合作共赢是基础。"一带一路"是中国与世界的互利共赢之路,"互利共赢"是贯穿"一带一路"倡议始终的核心价值观。"一带一路"倡议秉承了和平合作、开放包容、互学互鉴、互利共赢的丝路精神,不搞固定、排外机制,是沿线国家合作共赢之路。

共商共建共享是原则。所谓共商,就是沿线各国无论大小、强弱、贫富,都是"一带一路"的平等参与者。所谓共建,就是沿线国家共同参与,各国地方政府、金融机构、跨国公司、国际组织、非政府组织都可以参与其中,各方优势和潜能都能得到充分发挥,从而形成新的合作优势。所谓共享,就是在寻求各方利益契合点和合作最大公约数的基础上,求大同,存小异,努力让合作成果惠及沿线各国,惠及广大民众。

民心相通是人文基础。"一带一路"倡议以文明交流超越文明隔阂、文明互鉴超越文明冲突、文明共存超越文明优越,推动各国相互理解、相互尊重、相互信任。近年来,中国在共建"一带一路"进程中,通过艺术节、影视桥、研讨会、智库对话等人文合作项目,加强同沿线国家的不同文明交流互鉴,拉近了各国人民心与心的距离。

构建人类命运共同体是目标。"一带一路"倡议描绘了构建人类命运共同体的世界大同目标,共建"一带一路"将不断推动沿线各国沿着人类命运共同体的目标迈进,从而走出一条相互尊重、公平正义、合作共赢的光明大道。世界上越来越多的人相信,通过以共建"一带一路"为平台推动构建人类命运共同体,将会让人类生活更加幸福美好。

（二）"一带一路"倡议的建设目标

"一带一路"倡议秉持和遵循共商共建共享原则,努力实现政策沟通、设施联通、贸易畅通、资金融通、民心相通,是发展的倡议、合作的倡议、开放的倡议。这一倡议通过促进基础设施建设和互联互通,加强经济政策协调和发展战略对接,促进协同联动发展,实现共同繁荣。"一带一路"倡议的建设目标是要构建一个政治互信、经济融合、文化包容的利益共同体、命运共同体和义务共同体,是包含欧亚大陆在内的世界各国构建一个互惠互利的命运和义务共同体,其要实现的最高目标就是在"一带一路"建设国际合作框架内,各方携手应对世界经济面临的挑战,开创发展新机遇,谋求发展新动力,拓展发展新空间,实现优势互补、互利共赢,不断朝着人类命运共同体迈进。

三、做"一带一路"倡议的践行者

"一带一路"的建设离不开各国青年的热情参与和深入实践。来华学习的高校国际生既是"一带一路"建设的直接参与者、建设人才和智力资源,同时也是跨文化交流的实践者,是世界了解中国的纽带,是连接两国文化的"桥梁",也理所应当是"一带一路"建设的传播者和践行者。

来华学习的高校国际生应该是讲好中国故事的主角。高校国际生亲身感受了中国的悠久历史、发展成就和面临的问题,学成回国后应成为中外交流的友好使者,以增进各国对中国的了解和信任。他们应以自身的视角对中国故事进行客观讲述,这对于增强各国人民对共建"一带一路"倡议的理解、认同和支持,使本国人民了解"一带一路"倡议对构建人类命运共同体的积极意义,对营造良好的国际合作氛围,促进民心相通作用巨大。不少高校国际生来自发展中国家,他们亲身感受到中国的发展成就,回国后通过向亲人和朋友分享在中国的各种见闻和感受,来传播今日中国形象。同时,来华学习的高校国际生具有"贯通中外"的优势,能够把中国的语言文化带到世界各地,把适合他们国家同胞口味的"中国故事"传播开来。尤其是"一带一路"沿线各国的来华高校国际生,他们在"一带一路"建设的时代背景下来中国留学并成长起来,是未来"一带一路"的建设者、继承者。因此,来华学习的高校国际生要努力学习,使自己成为具有国际视野、知晓国际规则、善于跨文化理解的高素质国际化人才,做"一带一路"的建设者和践行者,为深化中国和各自祖国之间的合作与友谊贡献自己的力量。

【观点交流】

作为来华学习的高校国际生,你能为"一带一路"建设和本国与中国的文化交流做些什么?

【思考题】

1.在当今时代,为什么要推动构建人类命运共同体?

2.全人类共同价值与西方所谓的"普世价值"有什么区别?

3.你如何看待"一带一路"倡议?

Chapter Two Promoting the Common Values of All Humanity and Building a Community with a Shared Future for Mankind

In today's world, humanity is an interdependent whole, and the destinies of all nations are interlinked. More than ever before, humanity needs to promote and uphold the common values of all humanity, consolidate a shared understanding of values, and establish the foundation of values for building a community with a shared future for mankind.

【Mind Map】

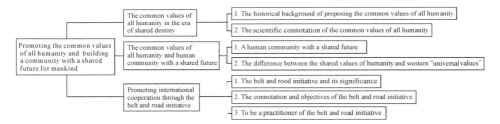

Section One The Common Values of All Humanity in the Era of Shared Destiny

1. The Historical Background of Proposing the Common Values of all Humanity

It is pointed out in the 20th National Congress of the Communist Party of China that "In this time and age, great changes are unfolding in

ways like never before". ① In the new historical era, the balance of
international power has undergone profound adjustments, and short-term
and long-term factors are intertwining, affecting the development and
changes in the international situation. The world is facing new turmoil
and transformation. The increasingly growing global challenges have made
the concept of a community with a shared future for mankind more deeply
ingrained in people's hearts. The historical trend of peace, development,
cooperation and win-win situations is unstoppable. Based on the concept
of a community with a shared future for mankind, the common values of
all humanity are the bond of the interdependence of all nations in the era of
economic globalization. Its proposal has a profound historical background.

(1) The Unbalanced Development of the World Economy

In the era of the internet and economic globalization, the world has
become an interconnected "global village". However, while global
connectivity has led to the flourishing of the global economy, the
unbalanced development between regions or countries has become
increasingly serious. The contradiction in the unbalanced development
between developed countries and developing countries is particularly
prominent, which has a profound impact on the world economy and social
development. Currently, the world economy has formed a new situation
where material products flow from developed countries to developing
countries, while funds and wealth flow from developing countries to
developed countries, widening the gap between the Global North and
South. At the same time, the gap in income within developed countries is
also widening, and the world's wealth is further concentrated in the hands
of a few. The unbalanced development in the world economy will lead to
various social contradictions. If this imbalance is allowed to continue
without effective measures, it will directly affect the healthy development
of the global economy.

---

① https://www.mfa.gov.cn/mfa_eng/zxxx_662805/202211/t20221114_10974580.html.

【Knowledge Expansion】

The term "global village" was first coined by Canadian communication theorist Marshall McLuhan in his book *Understanding Media : The Extensions of Man* in 1964. McLuhan's analysis of modern communication media profoundly changed people's understanding of life in the 20th and 21st centuries, especially among young people. The global village he predicted has become a reality in today's world. McLuhan believed that the main indication of the global village was not that well-developed media made the world smaller, but that people's modes of communication and their social and cultural existence underwent significant changes. The development of transportation has urbanized the original "villages" on earth, breaking the direct communication between people and changing it from direct, oral communication to indirect, written communication. However, electronic media have implemented a process of "reverse urbanization" or "re-villagization", dissolving the centralization of cities and restoring people's modes of communication to personal interactions.

The Ever-expanding Wealth Gap Becoming the World's Biggest Challenge

(2) Uncertainty in Security and Risk

In today's world, the international landscape is undergoing profound changes, and international power is rapidly dividing and gathering. Emerging market countries and developing countries are continuously strengthening their power, and the strategic power is becoming more balanced. Promotion of peace, stability and development has become a consensus of the international community. The rise of peace forces far exceeds the growth of war factors. However, hegemonism, power politics and unilateralism are on the rise, and regional conflicts and local wars continue. The international order and security system are at stake. With the increasing instability and uncertainty in social development, the fusion of new problems and traditional ones such as global pandemis, climate disasters, economic crises, terrorism, national conflicts and even wars, will trap the whole humanity in profound global risks.

【Knowledge Expansion】

The Current Global Economy: Three Major Uncertainties and the One Certainty

(3) The Unbalanced Global Governance System

Global governance is the process of coordination and cooperation among different countries or regions in the international community to address global challenges. The current global governance system was established after World War II, primarily led by Western countries, such as the United States, and its basic framework is still in effect. However, many mechanisms, regulations and operations are no longer able to adapt to the changing dynamics of international power. In the existing global governance system, a few major countries have more influence in institutions like the International Monetary Fund and the World Bank, where developed Western nations have more voting power. Since the beginning of the 21st century, emerging market countries and developing countries have risen in prominence, leading to a profound shift in the balance of international economic power. The global economic governance system has failed to reflect this new reality. Currently, emerging market countries and developing countries contribute around 80% to global economic growth, making them the main driving force behind global economic expansion. However, their representation and voice in the global economic governance system do not match their contributions to world economic growth. The lack of inclusivity and general representation in the global governance system means that it cannot adequately meet the requirements of deepening economic globalization or effectively address the global challenges faced by humanity today.

(4) The diversity of civilization and culture

There are no two leaves in the world that are exactly the same. Throughout the long history of human civilization, the diversity of civilizations makes the world colorful. Each civilization is a crystallization of human activities and wisdom, and each one deserves respect and cherishing. From the perspective of human development, each country, each ethnic group and each culture has its own values, and there is nothing superior or inferior, good or bad between them. However, the differences in cultures cannot forbid the formation of consensus in human survival and the pursuit of common values. On the contrary, the more intense conflicts are in the world, the more serious issues such as terrorism, hegemonism, capital expansion, wealth gap and ecological crisis become, the more urgent and universal is the pursuit of common values by humanity. To build a more beautiful world and a better life, it is not to replace one civilization with another but to promote the development of different countries with different social systems, ideological systems, historical cultures and development levels, so that they can share interests, rights and responsibilities in international affairs on the basis of respecting the diversity of civilizations around the world.

【Conceptual Analysis】

Cultural diversity refers to the fact that every ethnic group and country in the world has its own unique culture which is an important symbol of ethnic identity. Cultural diversity is not only reflected in the various ways in which human cultural heritage is expressed, promoted and inherited through rich and diverse cultural forms, but also in the various ways in which art creation, production, dissemination, sales and consumption are carried out through various methods and technologies. Cultural diversity is a fundamental characteristic of human society and an important impetus of the progress for human civilization. Therefore, we should strive to:

(1)Recognize and respect our own culture as well as other cultures, learn from each other, seek common ground while reserving differences, and respect the world's cultural diversity to promote the prosperity and progress of human civilization together.

(2)First respect one's own national culture and develop it well.

(3)Recognize the diversity of world cultures, respect the cultures of different ethnic groups and follow the principle of equal treatment of all ethnic cultures;

(4)Respect differences in cultural exchange, understand individuality, live in harmony and jointly promote the prosperity of world culture.

【Opinion Exchange】

How do you view the diversity of cultures? What are the characteristics of the culture in your country?

【Case Analysis】

The Clash of Civilizations and the Remaking of World Order, first published in 1996, is a representative work by American political scientist Samuel Huntington. The author believes that after the Cold War, the determining factor of world development is seen in seven or eight civilizations, namely Chinese civilization, Japanese civilization, Indian civilization, Islamic civilization, Western civilization, Orthodox civilization, Latin American civilization and possibly African civilization. In the post-Cold War world, the basic root of the conflict is no longer ideology but cultural differences, and the dominant force of the world will be the "clash of civilizations". Huntington believes that the conflicts between different civilizations cannot be reconciled, and the conflict in future world will be the conflict between civilizations.

2. The Scientific Connotation of the Common Values of all Humanity

On September 28, 2015, during the general debate of the 70th session of the United Nations General Assembly, President Xi Jinping pointed out that "Peace, development, equity, justice, democracy, and freedom are the common values of all humanity and also the lofty goals of the United Nations". [1] The report of the 20th National Congress of the Communist Party of China called for the promotion of the common values of all humanity and the promotion of mutual understanding and respect for the diversity of world civilizations. The proposal of the common values of all humanity is like opening a window, bringing a new development concept and vision to the complex and profound transformation of the world. It has aroused keen attention and in-depth discussion from many countries, demonstrating strong ideological appeal and practical influence.

Peace, development, equity, justice, democracy, and freedom are the common values of all humanity. These six value elements cover the five fields of political civilization, material civilization, spiritual civilization, social civilization, and ecological civilization, each with its own emphasis and complementary to others. They organically unify into a whole new value system, achieving a great value revolution in the development history of human civilization.

Peace and development are both the common cause of humanity and the theme of the present era, which concern the rights of survival and development of all people. Among them, peace is the bottom-line value in the common values of all humanity. If humanity wants to survive and develop, it must oppose war. Only in a peaceful and stable environment can humanity better survive and develop. Without peace, nothing can be achieved. Development is the condition of progress, supporting survival

---

[1] https://search.english.www.gov.cn/en/search.shtml? code = 17dbe3acd9d&data type Id=57&search word=Patriotism, dedication%20to%.

and hope. Only by development, can the root causes of conflicts be eliminated, the basic rights of the people be guaranteed, and the people's strong desire for a better life be satisfied. Development and peace are complementary to each other. Peace breeds the vitality of development, and development guarantees lasting peace.

Equity and justice are the conditions and guarantees of the common values of all humanity. Equity is the basic condition for harmonious coexistence among human beings, and justice is the firm and permanent value pursuit of human beings. Without a fair and just international order, peace and development cannot be guaranteed, and democracy and freedom cannot be truly realized. Equity and justice mainly involve global issues, especially issues of global order. Among them, equity focuses more on the nondiscriminatory equality of subjects in international relations, while justice focuses more on "what each subject deserves" in the international order. To uphold equity and justice, the priority is to uphold the principle of sovereign equality. Regardless of size, strength, wealth or poverty, all countries are equal, and their sovereignty and dignity must be respected. Internal affairs cannot be interfered with, and coercion of the weak by the strong and the imposition of one's own will on others must be opposed.

Democracy and freedom are the ideals of the common values of all humanity as well as the method to implement these values. Democracy means that all countries participate in international affairs on an equal footing, jointly grasp the destiny of the world, and participate in international governance in accordance with the principles of consultation, cooperation, and shared benefits. Freedom means safeguarding the right of sovereign states to independence and autonomy, and the freedom to choose social systems and development paths, as well as the freedom of states to express their demand for their own interests and share development achievements reasonably. In the global society, democracy and freedom as methods are aimed at enabling countries to correctly view their differences, rationally handle their differences and consciously and equally achieve public rationality through public discussions and debates.

【Opinion Exchange】

Can you talk about your understanding of the common values of all humanity?

Section Two   The Common Values of All Humanity and the Community with a Shared Future for Mankind

1. A Community with a Shared Future for Mankind

In the context of the unprecedented transformations in the world in the past century, building a community with a shared future for mankind requires abandoning the values of Western centrism and transcending the so-called "universal values" of the West. By promoting and practicing the common values of all humanity, we can effectively promote the construction of a community with a shared future for mankind.

(1) The concept of a community with a shared future for mankind

The concept of a community with a shared future for mankind is a value system and a concrete practice proposed and advocated by the Communist Party of China in the early 21st century. The concept emphasizes the pursuit of national interests while taking into account the legitimate concerns of other countries in a modern international system characterized by peaceful coexistence of diverse social systems, economic competition and ideological conflicts. Its core values are peace, development, cooperation and mutual benefit, and it uphold the right approach to justice and the pursuit of interests. The way to construct this community is through partnerships rather than alliances, with the ultimate goal of enhancing the common, overall and long-term interests of all peoples in the world.

From political, security, economic, cultural and ecological dimensions, the construction of a community with a shared future for mankind mainly includes five basic contents: (1) upholding dialogue and consultation to build a world of lasting peace; (2) upholding co-construction and sharing to build a world of universal security; (3) upholding cooperation and mutual benefit to build a world of common prosperity; (4) upholding exchanges and mutual learning to build a world of openness and inclusiveness; (5) upholding green and low-carbon development to build a world of clean and beautiful environment.

【Concept Analysis】

Human beings live in the same global village. The degree of interconnection, interdependence, cooperation and mutual promotion among countries is unprecedented deepening. The international community has increasingly become a community of destiny in which you have mine and I have yours.

——Xi Jinping

As the term suggests, "a global community with a shared future" implies that the future of all peoples and all countries in the world are closely linked and that we must stand together through good and bad and work to build a large harmonious global family and to realize humankind's aspiration for a better life.

——Xi Jinping

(https://baijiahao. baidu. com/s? id＝1698354923651381236 & wfr＝spider & for＝pc)

(2) The relationship between the common values of all humanity and the community with a shared future for mankind

The community with a shared future for mankind has constructed a basic framework from five aspects: persistent peace, universal security, common prosperity, openness and inclusiveness, and a clean and beautiful environment. The common values of all humanity have defined six major value standards: peace, development, fairness, justice, democracy, and freedom. The two are interrelated and interdependent. If the community with a shared future for mankind depicts a beautiful picture of the world, then the common values of all humanity summarize "what is in common and what can be shared". The construction of a human community with a shared future was proposed in response to the increasingly complex and severe global challenges, and peace, development, fairness, justice, democracy and freedom embody the value appeals of all humanity in solving major global problems. The common values of all humanity vividly reflect the ideas of sovereignty equality, communication and consultation, fairness and justice, openness and inclusiveness and humanitarianism, providing a basis for value recognition to construct the human community with a shared future and confirming the community's moral legitimacy. The common values of all humanity maximize consensus and converge the strengths of all countries towards constructing the community with a shared future for mankind in practice. The human community with a shared future provides chances for the realization of common values of all humanity. The significance of common values of all humanity in constructing the community with a shared future for mankind is not limited to the conceptual level, but has been applied in the foreign policy of some countries and manifested in more and more international public affairs in today's international relations.

【Knowledge Expansion】

The rich connotations of the idea of building a human community with a shared future can be understood from five aspects: politics, security, economy, culture, and ecology.

First, politically, countries should respect each other, engage in equal communication, firmly reject Cold War mentality and power politics, and pursue a new path of state-to-state interactions that prioritize dialogue over confrontation and partnership over alliance.

Second, in terms of security, countries should settle disputes through dialogue and resolve differences through consultation, coordinate efforts to deal with traditional and non-traditional security threats, and oppose all forms of terrorism.

Third, in terms of the economy, countries should work together to promote trade and investment liberalization and facilitation, and promote economic globalization in a more open, inclusive, beneficial, balanced and win-win direction.

Fourth, culturally, countries should respect the diversity of world civilizations, go beyond cultural barriers through exchanges, and abandon civilization superiority through mutual learning.

Fifth, ecologically, countries should adhere to environmental friendliness, cooperate in addressing climate change, and protect the Earth, our common home, on which humans live.

2. The Difference Between the Shared Values of Humanity and Western "Universal Values"

(1) The nature of Western "universal values"

Western "universal values" evolved along with the development of capitalism and are a concentrated expression of bourgeois values and ideology. Its main content includes: firstly, some political ideas that emerged during the period from the Renaissance to the Enlightenment in the West, such as freedom, equality, philanthropy, democracy, human rights and the rule of law, which were the core values formed during the bourgeois revolution; secondly, the political and economic system of capitalist society, such as separation of powers, multi-party system, universal suffrage, privatization and market economy; thirdly, some moral standards and behavioral norms that are adapted to the first two.

Western "universal values" are "Western" values in nature, which are extracted based solely on the development of Western countries and lifestyles, and are not the ideas accepted by all countries and nations in the world. Although Western "universal values" hold high the banners of freedom, democracy and human rights, the logic of capital hegemony behind them makes the world order essentially non-free, non-democratic and without human rights. Therefore, "universal values" are not really universal because they contain the connotations of specific political and economic models of the bourgeois and capitalist society, and reflect the discourse hegemony of a few powerful countries. Claiming that it is universal or applicable is deceptive and hypocritical.

【Case Analysis】

Please read the following case and analyze Henry Kissinger's viewpoint on "universal values".

The West's promotion of "universal values" is essentially the promotion of its so-called "democratic system" and "free system". Henry Kissinger, former US Secretary of State, had a profound discussion on the West's promotion of "universal values" in his book *On China*. This book argues that Western countries, including the United States, claim that their values and systems are universally applicable, but China has had a different set of values from ancient times to the present. "The dominant values in Chinese society originate from the teachings of an ancient philosopher, later known as Confucius," Kissinger further pointed out. " China advocates independence and non-interference in the internal affairs of other countries and does not seek to spread its ideology to foreign countries. On the other hand, the United States insists on using pressure and incentives to achieve the universality of its values, which means interfering in the internal affairs of other countries".

(2) The transcendence of the common values of all humanity over the Western "universal values"

The common values of all humanity are the greatest common denominator of values among countries in the world, and the most fundamental and noblest value pursuit of people in all countries. The common values of all humanity break Western-centrism and Western discourse hegemony and surpass the so-called "universal values" of the

West based on regionalism.

The so-called "universal values" of the Western ignore the differences in specific conditions such as cultural background, historical conditions, geographic environment and population status among countries, nations and regions. The way to achieve democracy and freedom must be chosen by countries or nations themselves. "Universal values" have mistaken those special and specific things that do not have "universality" as "universal". Humanity pursues a happy and beautiful life. The connotation of a beautiful life is very rich. It presents different forms in different countries, nations, geographic locations and development levels, thus giving birth to brilliant and diverse civilizations. Diversity and commonality are dialectical unity. Diverse forms of human civilization must have certain commonalities which contain the common and universal needs of humanity. Therefore, the common values of all humanity that truly apply to all should be extracted based on the common and universal needs contained in the life of all people. Regardless of which country or nation, regardless of its geographic location, level of development, or religious beliefs, they will pursue common values such as peace, development, fairness, justice, democracy, and freedom. The common values of all humanity are extracted from the common and universal life of all people. It observes the common development of all nations in the world with an open vision, broad pattern, and broad-mindedness. It aims to seek sincere cooperation and equal communication between nations, jointly respond to global challenges, respond to the urgent problems of the times and form the greatest common denominator of building a better world.

Section Three   Promoting International Cooperation through "the Belt and Road" Initiative

1. "The Belt and Road" Initiative and Its Significance

The ancient Silk Road in history has built a symbolic bridge of political, economic, and cultural exchanges between the East and the West. Today, "the Belt and Road" initiative is not only a road of peace and trade, but also a channel for cultural and talent exchanges. Under new historical conditions, China proposed "the Belt and Road" initiative to inherit and carry forward the spirit of the Silk Road, to combine China's development with the development of countries along the route and other countries in the world, to integrate the Chinese dream with the dreams of people from countries, and to give the ancient Silk Road a new connotation of the era. "The Belt and Road" initiative originated from China but belongs to the world. It is of great significance for international students in universities who come to study in China to use their own resources and talents to serve the construction of "the Belt and Road" initiative. It is also an inevitable choice of the times and a responsibility that cannot be shirked.

【Concept Analysis】

"The Belt and Road" is the abbreviation for "the Silk Road Economic Belt" and "the 21st-Century Maritime Silk Road". In September and October 2013, Chinese President Xi Jinping proposed the initiatives to build "the New Silk Road Economic Belt" and "the 21st-Century Maritime Silk Road" cooperation. With the help of existing bilateral and multilateral mechanisms between China and relevant countries, and by leveraging effective regional cooperation platforms, "the Belt and Road" initiative, using the historical symbol of the ancient Silk Road, aims to uphold the banner of peaceful development, actively develop economic partnership with countries along the route, and jointly create a community of shared interests, shared destiny and shared responsibility based on political mutual trust, economic integration and cultural inclusiveness.

As an important practical platform for implementing the concept of the human community with a shared future and promoting the construction of such a community, "the Belt and Road" initiative provides new ideas, new plans and new impetus for achieving common development among countries and improving global economic governance. Its significance can be seen from two aspects.

On the one hand, it injects strong impetus into the world economy for recovery and development. "The Belt and Road" initiative firmly supports multilateralism and a multilateral trading system, promoting free trade and investment. Thanks to "the Belt and Road" initiative, Kazakhstan, the world's largest landlocked country, now has access to sea routes, Belarus has its own car manufacturing industry for the first time, the Maldives has realized its dream of having bridges, and Pakistan's power shortage problem has been radically improved after the building of several energy projects. The China-Laos railway will also transform Laos from a landlocked country to a land-linked country. The facts have proved that "the Belt and Road" initiative has made outstanding contributions to the economic development and the improvement of people's livelihoods in countries along the route.

On the other hand, it has made new contributions to improving the global governance system. "The Belt and Road" initiative adheres to dialogue, co-construction, sharing, cooperation, mutual benefit, and exchanges and mutual learning. It promotes political mutual trust, economic integration, and cultural exchange among countries, and promotes the construction of a human community with a shared future. The building of "the Belt and Road" has enhanced understanding of each other's foreign policies among countries along the route, and provided political basis for more in-depth exchanges among countries through signing a series of agreements. The practice has fully proved that "the Belt and Road" initiative conforms to the inherent requirements of transformation in global governance systems, demonstrates the concept of solidarity and shared destiny, and provides Chinese ideas and solutions for the global governance system.

【Knowledge Expansion】

Substantial Accomplishments Achieved in
Co-building "the Belt and Road"

2. The Connotation and Objectives of "the Belt and Road" Initiative

As an open, inclusive and equitable platform for regional cooperation, "the Belt and Road" initiative is an international public product offered by China to the world, and a sunlit path for China to share opportunities and seek common development with the world. Its fundamental purpose is to connect the development strategies of different countries, create new opportunities and tap into new potential for cooperation, and achieve a two-way conversion and positive interaction between China's development opportunities and those of the world.

(1) The connotation of "the Belt and Road" initiative

"The Belt and Road" initiative is a cooperative proposal aiming at achieving mutual benefit and building a community with shared interests and future. It provides a large platform on which all countries can participate, collaborate and finally win together. It can be further explained in the following aspects.

Common development is the direction. The construction of "the Belt and Road" is not only focused on China's own development but also provides an opportunity for more countries to catch up with China's development and help them achieve their development goals. The energy of "the Belt and Road" initiative comes from a cooperative approach to common development, and the pursuit of common development among countries is the guiding direction of the initiative.

Win-win cooperation is the foundation. "The Belt and Road" is a win-win path for China and the world. Win-win cooperation is the core value of the initiative. "The Belt and Road" initiative upholds the spirit of the Silk Road, which emphasizes peaceful cooperation, openness and inclusiveness, mutual learning, and mutual benefit. It does not promote fixed, exclusionary mechanisms but instead is a path of cooperation and mutual benefit among countries along the route.

Consultation, co-construction, and sharing are the principles. Consultation means that all countries along the route, regardless of size, strength or wealth, are equal participants in "the Belt and Road" initiative. Co-construction means that countries along the route can jointly participate, and local governments, financial institutions, multinational companies, international organizations and non-governmental organizations can also participate in the initiative. With each party's strengths and potential being fully utilized, there will be new cooperation advantages. Sharing means that, on the basis of seeking points of convergence and cooperation, the initiative seeks common ground while shelving differences, making every effort to ensure that the benefits of cooperation reach all countries and their people along the route.

People-to-people bonds are the foundation of culture. "The Belt and Road" initiative transcends civilization barriers through civilization exchange, transcends civilization conflict through mutual learning, and promotes civilization coexistence beyond civilization superiority. It thus promotes mutual understanding, mutual respect and mutual trust among countries. In recent years, China has strengthened cultural cooperation with countries along the route through various cooperation projects, such as art festivals, film and television bridges, seminars and think-tank dialogues, bridging the gap between people's hearts along the route.

Building a human community with a shared future is the goal. "The Belt and Road" initiative depicts the world's common goal of building a human community with a shared future, and the co-building of "the Belt and Road" will continuously promote countries along the route towards this common goal. The initiative aims to build a bright avenue leading to mutual respect, fairness and justice, and win-win cooperation. More and more people around the world believe that by promoting the construction of a human community with a shared future through the platform of "the Belt and Road" initiative, human life will become happier and more prosperous.

(2) The construction goals of "the Belt and Road" initiative

The construction of "the Belt and Road" initiative adheres to the principle of consultation, collaboration and sharing, and strives to achieve policy exchange, facility connectivity, trade flow, capital financing and people-to-people bonds. It is an initiative for development, cooperation, and openness. Through promoting infrastructure construction and connectivity, strengthening economic policy coordination and development strategy alignment, and promoting coordinated and interconnected development, this initiative aims to achieve common prosperity. The construction goals of "the Belt and Road" initiative are to build a community of shared interests, shared destiny, and shared obligations based on political mutual trust, economic integration, and cultural inclusiveness. This community includes countries from around the world to build a mutually beneficial community of interests, destiny, and obligations. The ultimate goal is to join hands with all parties within the international cooperation framework of "the Belt and Road" initiative to address the challenges facing the world economy, create new development opportunities, seek new sources of development, expand new development space, achieve complementary advantages, mutual benefit and win-win results, and continuously move towards a human community with a shared future.

3. To be a Practitioner of "the Belt and Road" Initiative

The construction of "the Belt and Road" cannot be separated from the enthusiastic participation and in-depth practice of young people from various countries. International students who come to study in China are direct participants, talents and intellectual resources for the construction of "the Belt and Road", as well as the practitioners of cross-cultural communication. They are a link for the world to understand China and a "bridge" connecting the cultures of China and their own countries. They are also disseminators and practitioners in the construction of "the Belt and Road".

International students who come to study in China should play a major role in telling China's story. Through their firsthand experience of China's long history, development achievements and challenges, they can become ambassadors of China in foreign exchanges and help promote mutual understanding and trust between China and other countries. By objectively telling the story of China from their own perspectives, they can enhance people's understanding, recognition and support of "the Belt and Road" initiative, help build a positive atmosphere for international cooperation and promote people-to-people connectivity. Many international students come from developing countries and have experienced China's development achievements. They can share their experiences and feelings about China with their families and friends when they return home and spread the image of China today to the world. Moreover, international students who come to study in China have the advantage of "bridging China and foreign countries" and can bring Chinese language and culture to different parts of the world, as well as spread "China's story" that suits the taste of their compatriots. Especially for international students who come from countries along the route of "the Belt and Road", and study in China in the background of the initiative, they can become the inheritors and future builders of the initiative.

Therefore, international students in China should strive to become high-quality international talents with an international perspective, knowledge of international rules and skills for cross-cultural communication. They should become builders and practitioners of "the Belt and Road" and contribute their strength to deepening cooperation and friendship between China and their respective countries.

【Opinion Exchange】

As an international student studying in China, what can you do for "the Belt and Road" initiative as well as for the cultural exchanges between your home country and China?

【Questions for Discussion】

1. Why should we promote the building of a human community with a shared future in today's world?

2. What is the difference between the common values of all humanity and the so-called "universal values" of the West?

3. What is your opinion on "the Belt and Road" initiative?

第三章 遵守社会公德 维护公共秩序

每个人都是生活在一定的社会关系之中。在社会公共生活中,只有自觉遵循社会公共生活秩序,社会才能和谐发展。维持公共生活的正常运行,维护社会公共秩序,就必须约束自身行为,遵守社会公德。高校国际生来华留学时,必须了解和遵守社会公德,尊重社会公序良俗,自觉维护公共秩序。

【思维导图】

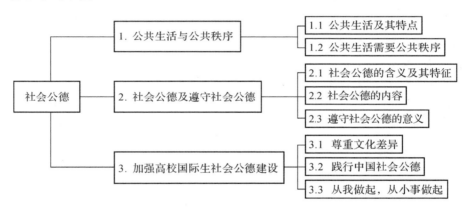

第一节 公共生活与公共秩序

一、公共生活及其特点

公共生活是指人们在公共空间里发生相互联系、相互影响的共同生活。人们在公共活动中必须遵循的一些基本的、起码的行为准则。公共生活的适用范围很广泛,涉及人与人、人与社会、人与自然之间的各种复杂关系。

当代社会公共生活的特征主要表现在以下几个方面。

（一）活动范围的广泛性

经济社会的发展，使公共生活的场所和领域不断扩展，从传统的公交车、影剧院、图书馆、公园、集体宿舍等到新兴的证券交易所、人才市场等，互联网的发展使公共生活领域进一步扩展到虚拟世界。

【概念解析】

今天，任何一个国际航空公司的飞机在 17 小时内都可以到达世界上任何一个角落。现代传媒手段的普及和推广，使人们可以真正做到"秀才不出门，尽知天下事"。20 世纪末以来，信息技术、互联网的迅猛发展正在把地球变成一个"村落"，人类公共生活进入了一个崭新的阶段。互联网使人们的公共生活进一步扩展到虚拟世界。虚拟世界是公共生活的一部分，不是法外之地，因此在虚拟世界中，我们也同样要遵守社会公德，维护公共秩序。

（二）活动内容的公开性

公共生活是社会生活中最普遍、最基本的公众性生活，它是由社会成员共同参与、共同创造的公共空间，能为社会全体成员所共享，不具排他性，因此它涉及的内容是公开的、透明的。

（三）交往对象的复杂性

在很长的历史时期内，人们往往是在"熟人社会"中活动，交往圈子很小。当今社会，科学技术的发展和社会分工的日益细化，社会公共生活领域不断扩大，使人们在公共生活中的交往对象不再局限于熟识的人，而是进入公共场所的任何人。这更像一个"陌生人社会"，增加了人际交往信息的不对称性和行为后果的不可预期性，从而造成了交往对象的复杂性。

（四）活动方式的多样性

当代社会的发展使人们的生活方式发生了新的变化，也极大地丰富了人们公共生活的内容和方式。如商场购物、歌厅娱乐、广场漫步、公园休闲、图书馆学习、体育馆健身、互联网冲浪等，人们可以根据自身的需要及年龄兴趣、职业、经济条件等因素，选择和变换参与公共生活的具体方式。公共场所的增加和公共设施的完善，也为丰富人们公共生活的内容和方式提供了良好的条件。

【案例分析】

中国古代社会公共生活和社会关系

在中国古代社会,人们认为有五种人际关系,即君臣、父子、夫妻、长幼和朋友之间的关系需要规范,这五种关系也称为"五伦"。中国儒家圣人之一的孟子强调"父子有亲,君臣有义,夫妇有别,长幼有序,朋友有信"(见《孟子·滕文公上》)。这几句话的大意是:父子之间有骨肉之亲,君臣之间有礼义之道,夫妻之间有男女之别,老少之间有尊卑之序,朋友之间有诚信之德。孟子的这一思想对几千年来中国人的行为规范有深刻影响,尤其是孟子很早就已经注意到男女之间存在的差别,而不是简单地追求男女平等。

【观点交流】

为什么在中国古代社会,人们的公共生活会比较简单?

【知识拓展】

孟子生平及思想简介

孟子(约公元前 372 年—公元前 289 年),名轲,字子舆,邹国(今山东邹城东南)人。战国时期哲学家、思想家、教育家,是孔子之后、荀子之前的儒家学派的代表人物,与孔子并称"孔孟"。

孟子宣扬"仁政",最早提出"民贵君轻"思想,被韩愈列为先秦儒家继承孔子"道统"的人物,元朝追封其为"亚圣"。

二、公共生活需要公共秩序

公共秩序也称社会秩序,为维护社会公共生活所必需的秩序。在经济全球化加速发展的今天,公共生活领域不断扩大,人们相互之间的交往也随之扩大,公共生活日益成为社会成员生活的重要组成部分,维护公共秩序显得尤为迫切和重要。公共秩序关系到人们的生活质量,也关系到社会的文明程度。

【概念解析】

比如人们每天出行要过马路、乘坐相应的交通工具,购物要去商店,休闲娱乐要去公园或者电影院,学习要去学校的教室,这些公共场所是人们社会交往和公共生活的地方,其中不只有家人、朋友、同事、同学,还有许多陌生人,我们每天都要和这些不同类型的人群产生各种各样的社会关系。如过马路要看红绿灯,如果随意行走,就会和他人产生冲撞;乘坐公交车要排队,乱插队则会和其他乘客发生冲突;在商店购物要公平交易,不能强买强卖;在电影院看电影不可大声喧哗;在教室学习要服从教师的安排。可见,任何公共场所都会产生人际互动的关系,都需要一定的公共秩序。

第二节　社会公德及遵守社会公德的意义

一、社会公德的含义及其特征

社会公德是指存在于社会群体中间的道德,是生活于社会中的人们为了群体的利益而约定俗成的应该做什么和不应该做什么的行为规范。社会公德本质上是一个国家,一个民族或者一个群体,在历史长河中、在社会实践活动中积淀下来的道德准则、文化观念和思想传统。其基本特征主要表现为以下几方面。

(一)继承性

继承性是一切道德的重要特征,公共道德也不例外。千百年来,人类在共同生活、相互交往的过程中,形成了共同遵守的为人处世的道德传统,这些道德传统凝结着人类的道德智慧,构成了社会公德的重要组成部分。

(二)基础性

社会公德是社会道德体系的基础层次,被视为每个社会成员应遵守的最起码的道德准则,是社会为维护公共生活而提出的最基本的道德要求。每一个社会成员都应当具备社会公德素养。

(三)广泛性

社会公德是全体社会成员都必须遵守的道德规范,具有最广泛的群众基础和适用范围。在一个社会中,社会成员无论具有何种身份、职业和地位,都必须在公共生活中遵守社会公德。

（四）简明性

社会公德大多是生活经验的积累和风俗习惯的提炼,往往不需要作更多的说明就能被人们理解,如讲礼貌、讲卫生、讲秩序等就是起码的生活共识,"不随地吐痰""不乱穿马路"等公德规范,更是简单明了。

（五）渗透性

社会公德具有广泛的渗透性,它作为调节公共生活的准则,包含着非常广泛的内容,诸如遵守公共秩序、保持公共卫生、敬老爱幼、尊师爱生、言而有信、互相关心、互相尊重、礼貌待人、互相谦让、济困扶危、拾金不昧、见义勇为等。

【知识拓展】

曼德拉生平简介

纳尔逊·罗利赫拉赫拉·曼德拉（Nelson Rolihlahla Mandela,1918 年 7 月 18 日—2013 年 12 月 5 日）,出生于南非特兰斯凯,先后获南非大学文学士和威特沃特斯兰德大学律师资格。曾任非国大青年联盟全国书记、主席。于 1994 年至 1999 年间任南非总统,是南非的首位黑人总统,被尊称为"南非国父"。

在任职总统前,曼德拉是积极的反种族隔离人士,同时也是非洲国民大会的武装组织"民族之矛"的领袖。当他领导反种族隔离运动时,南非法院以密谋推翻政府等罪名将他定罪。依据判决,曼德拉在牢中服刑了 27 年。1990 年出狱后,曼德拉转而支持调解与协商,并在推动多元族群民主的过渡期挺身领导南非。自种族隔离制度终结以来,曼德拉受到了来自各界的赞许,包括从前的反对者。2013 年 12 月 5 日,曼德拉在其位于约翰内斯堡的住所逝世,享年 95 岁。

曼德拉在 40 年来获得了超过一百项奖项,其中最显著的便是 1993 年的诺贝尔和平奖。2004 年,他被选为最伟大的南非人。

【案例分析】

曼德拉为结束种族隔离制度而斗争

人与人之间、民族与民族之间、种族与种族之间应该是平等的,理应相互尊重。在实际生活中,有色人种诸如亚裔、非裔常常受到歧视,他们不能和白人一起乘坐交通工具,不能一起读书,这显然是有违社会公德的行为。被称为"南非国父"的曼德拉为结束南非存在已久的不人道的种族隔离制度,进行了数十年的斗争,最终赢得胜利。

【观点交流】

在日常生活中,你是否存在不尊重他人,歧视其他民族、种族的情形?或者你有没有被别人不尊重的经历?

二、社会公德的内容

公共活动中有一些必须遵循的简单的、基础的行为准则。它们的适用范围很广泛,涉及个人与个人、个人与社会、人类与自然之间的各种复杂关系。随着现代社会生活领域的不断扩大,生活质量和文明程度的提高,特别是随着现代高科技的日益发展及其成果的广泛运用,人们活动空间及道德视野的更加广阔,社会公德的内容也越来越丰富。比如人与自然环境之间的关系,甚至人在外层空间活动应当遵守什么样的伦理规则等问题,也显得越来越突出了。在这方面,社会公德的新内容主要表现为人与自然的伦理关系。从我国社会的实际出发,结合当前整个世界人类生活发展的要求,现代社会的社会公德规范主要有下述的一些内容。

(一)文明礼貌,提倡人们互相尊重

作为社会公德的一个基本规范,文明礼貌是人际交往中的一种道德信息,它说明了一个人对别人的尊严和人格的尊重。今天,倡导和普及文明礼貌,是继承和弘扬中华民族传统美德、提高人们道德素质的迫切需要;建立尊重人、理解人、关心人、帮助人,形成团结互助、平等友爱、共同前进的新型人际关系的迫切需要。

(二)助人为乐,发扬互帮互助的人道主义精神

在社会公共生活中,每个人都会遇到困难和问题,总有需要他人帮助和

关心的时候。因此,在社会公共生活中倡导助人为乐精神,是社会主义道德核心和原则在公共生活领域的体现,也是社会主义人道主义的基本要求。助人为乐是中国的传统美德,中国自古就有"君子成人之美""为善最乐""博施济众"等广为流传的名言。把帮助别人视为自己应做之事,看作是自己的快乐,是每个社会成员应有的公德,有助于提升社会公共生活领域的道德温度。

(三)爱护公物,增强社会主义主人翁的责任感

爱惜和保护公共财物是社会公德的基本要求,它要求公民要关心、爱护和保护国家财产,同一切破坏和浪费公共财物的行为作斗争。

(四)保护环境,强化生态伦理观念

保护环境是中国的基本国策,也是社会公德的基本内容之一,它涉及每个人的切身利益。保护环境不仅仅是指讲究公共卫生,美化个人生活环境等,主要是指保护自然环境,如水环境、大气环境、土壤环境、绿色环境、矿产资源、动物资源等,也包括保护文物资源、文化资源、社会管理资源等人文环境,还包括减少环境污染,维护生态平衡,合理开发利用自然资源、能源等广泛内容。

(五)遵纪守法,自觉维护公共秩序

遵纪守法是社会公德最基本的要求,是维护公共生活秩序的重要保障。遵纪守法的实践是提高人们社会公德水平的一个重要途径,在社会生活中,每个社会成员既要遵守国家颁布的有关法律、法规,也要遵守特定公共场所和单位的有关纪律规定。高校国际生来自全球各地,尤其应当全面了解中国公共生活领域中的各项法律法规,熟知校纪校规,牢固树立法治观念,"以遵纪守法为荣、以违法乱纪为耻",自觉遵守有关的纪律和法律。

【概念解析】

了解微塑料的危害

关于这个问题,早在100多年前恩格斯就提出过警告:我们不要过分陶醉于我们人类对自然界的胜利。然而,对于每一次这样的胜利,自然界都对人类进行了报复。每一次胜利,起初确实取得了我们预期的结果,但是往后和再往后却发生了完全不同的、出乎预料的影响,常常把最初的结果又消除

了。作为有较高文化素养的一代有为青年，高校国际生要牢固树立环境保护意识，身体力行，从小事做起，从身边做起，从自己做起，带头宣传和践行环境道德要求，做保护环境的模范。

【知识拓展】

看不见的微塑料正在威胁人类健康

【知识拓展】

碳达峰、碳中和

为构建新发展格局，推进产业转型和升级，走上绿色、低碳、循环的发展路径，实现高质量发展，保护地球生态，推进全球应对气候变化，2020年9月，中国提出"二氧化碳排放力争于2030年前达到峰值（碳达峰），努力争取2060年前实现碳中和（通过植树造林、节能减排等形式，抵消自身产生的二氧化碳排放量，实现二氧化碳零排放）"的目标和愿景，这是中共中央经过深思熟虑作出的重大战略决策，事关中华民族永续发展和构建人类命运共同体，意味着中国更加坚定地贯彻新发展理念。

【案例分析】

"中国人民志愿军是坚强而凶狠的斗士，也是更加文明的敌人"

自古以来，战争都是非常残酷的，不仅会造成大量士兵在战场上死亡，也会给无辜平民带来巨大灾难。在伟大的抗美援朝战争中，中国人民志愿军从不伤害平民，即使是在缺衣少食的时候，志愿军也是拿钱向朝鲜人民购买补给，而不是像其他军队那样直接抢劫。志愿军不仅不杀害平民，也优待俘虏，只要对方放下武器，志愿军就会给予他们最好的待遇。如果俘虏受伤了，他们也会及时得到治疗。曾在这场战争中担任"联合国军"总司令的美国将军范弗利特在回忆录中写道："中国人释放俘虏的做法与别人截然不同。有一次,中国人甚至将重伤员用担架放在公路上,而后撤走;在我方医护人员接运伤员时,他们没有向我们射击。……我们后来体会到,中国人是坚强而凶狠的斗士,他们常常不顾伤亡地发起攻击。但是,他们是更加文明的敌人。有很多次,他们同俘虏分享仅有的一点食物,对俘虏采取友善的态度。……我们在夺回汉城时发觉,中国人并未恣意毁坏我们运到汉城准备用以修复这座遭到轰炸的城市的建筑材料。"

【知识拓展】

抗美援朝战争

【观点交流】

为什么中国人民志愿军能够做到优待俘虏,这和中国的文化传统有什么关系?

三、遵守社会公德的意义

社会公德在维护公共秩序方面的作用日益突出,具有无可替代性。社会公德发挥着维护现实的稳定、公道、扬善惩恶的功能,在社会生产和生活中起着强大的舆论监督作用和精神感召作用。社会公德以规范方式来促进社会和个人弃恶扬善,扶正祛邪,从而指导人们的思想和行为,非强制性地调节和规范着社会生活中人们的言论和行动,维护社会公共生活秩序,有效地为满足社会与社会成员的需要服务。自觉遵守社会公德有着重要意义。

(一)遵守社会公德是维护公共利益和公共秩序的必要条件

如果每个社会成员都能自觉遵守社会公德的基本规范,社会维护公共生活秩序的难度和成本就会大大降低,社会成员往往就不会产生大的纠纷,或者能够自行调解纠纷,化解矛盾,避免因琐碎小事而酿成剧烈纷争和严重混乱,使人们能够在稳定而有序的环境中安居乐业。

(二)遵守社会公德是现代社会道德体系的基石

遵守社会公德对职业道德、家庭美德等方面的建设都有着重要的促进作用。社会公德是社会道德的基石和支柱之一,社会公德对社会道德风尚包括职业道德和家庭美德的影响稳定而深刻、广泛而持久。

(三)遵守社会公德是体现社会文明程度的重要尺度

遵守社会公德是一个国家、民族文明的"窗口"。社会公德是社会精神文明的重要组成部分,所以从人们实践社会公德的自觉程度和普及程度,可以看出整个社会精神文明建设的状况。今天,人们不仅要以建筑、道路等物质环境来评价某一国家或地区的文明程度,更要从人们的公德水平来衡量这个国家或地区的文明程度。

第三节　加强高校国际生社会公德建设

中国现阶段的社会公德继承和发扬了中华优秀传统道德,它是根植于社会主义社会经济关系而产生的,也是对以往社会公德观念的扬弃所取得的成果。"礼让""诚信""惜物"以及强调人和自然和谐相处等,都属于中华优秀传统道德范畴。高校在设定教育目标时,不仅要重视专业技能的教学,更要不断地全面提升高校国际生的道德素养。这既是高校国际生在中国遵纪守法、友善交际、顺利学习及生活的重要保证,也是中国教育对世界培育优秀人才自觉承担的责任。高校国际生来自世界各地,其文化背景、生活习惯、宗教信仰和个人爱好各有不同,来到陌生的国度学习和生活,应尤其注意学习和了解中国社会公德和公共秩序的特点和要求,力争早日适应周围环境,融入当地社会。高校国际生应从以下几个方面加强社会公德建设。

一、尊重文化差异

高校国际生入学后,要通过学校的始业教育和亲身体验,认真学习中国的法律法规、校纪校规、道德规范和公序良俗,了解中国社会公德的内容和特点。

高校国际生在学习的过程中,要特别留意中国和自己的国家在法律法规、社会公德、人际交往、公民习惯等方面的差别,避免因误解和误会造成的不便和麻烦。比如中国人习惯用点头表示"是"的意思、用摇头表示"不"的意思,但是在伊朗、保加利亚和希腊的一些地方,点头表示否定,摇头表示肯定。中国人伸出食指表示"1",而欧美人则是伸出大拇指表示"1";中国人伸出食指和中指表示"2",欧美人伸出大拇指和食指表示"2",而中国人伸出大拇指和食指表示的是"8"。手势"OK"在印度表示"正确",在泰国表示"没问题",在日本、缅甸、韩国表示"金钱",在法国表示"微不足道"或"一钱不值",在巴西、希腊和意大利的撒丁岛表示这是一种令人厌恶的污秽手势。高校国际生尊重不同文化间的差异,有助于避免和化解法律风险以及人际交往中的误解和尴尬,形成良好的人际关系和人际互动,并加深对社会公德的理解和维护良好的公共秩序。

二、践行中国社会公德

高校国际生要在实践中增强公德意识,自觉践行公德规范。知易行难,高校国际生掌握中国的社会公德内容和法律法规知识,了解不同文化间的差异并不存在很大困难,困难的是在实践中始终如一地按照社会公德要求规范自己的行为。

中国有句古语叫"入乡随俗",西方也有谚语"在罗马,就要像罗马人那样行事"。但在实际生活中,很多高校国际生因为多年来养成的行为习惯和思想观念,很难在中国读书期间自觉调整自己的行为方式,无法顺利融入周围环境。比如2019年底新冠疫情暴发以来,各高校的中国学生都能积极响应中国政府的号召,自觉遵守学校的疫情防控管理规定,按照要求上报个人行程信息,严格遵守进出校门规定,出现密接或次密接情形的按规定进行隔离,定期做核酸检测,这些对于他们都是习以为常的行为,但部分高校国际生却不理解、不认同、不执行,多次出现违反学校规定私自离校、不愿积极报告个人行程和健康状况的对抗行为,给各个学校的疫情管控造成不小的麻烦,也违反了社会公德要求。有的高校国际生在华学习期间,禁不住外界诱惑,非法就业,违法追求高薪工作。这一行为已经不仅是违法社会公德的问题,还触犯了中国的法律。可见,高校国际生自觉践行社会公德,绝不是一句空话,而是时时处处都需要特别留意、特别警惕的问题。

三、从我做起、从小事做起

社会公德所规范的行为包括社会公共生活中最微小的行为细节,这些细节极容易被人们忽视,而它一旦被社会群体中的大多数人所忽视,往往就可能形成不良的社会风气。因此,较高的公德意识要在点点滴滴的日常小事中培养。古人云"勿以善小而不为,勿以恶小而为之",讲的就是这个道理。

【概念解析】

就高校国际生的实际情况而言,有些学生主要存在以下几个问题。首先是时间观念较差。参加一个活动,很多留学生都不能做到准时登车、准时到达指定地点。和导师见面,迟到、爽约的情形屡见不鲜。其次是诚信有问题。不少高校国际生借钱不还、考试作弊、答应的事情又反悔等。其实,践行公德并不难,比如,上课不迟到、不早退是公德;诚实守信、不撒谎是讲公德;见到老师、长辈主动问候是讲公德;乘坐公交车主动让座是讲公德;在银行、邮局等公共场所排队时站在"一米线"外是讲公德;最后离开教室时随手关灯是讲公德;外出旅游时不在景点设施上随意刻画是讲公德。社会公德的境界,就是在这些不起眼的举手投足间慢慢升华的。

【知识拓展】

程门立雪的故事

北宋时期,杨时和游酢前来拜见程颐,在窗外看到老师在屋里打坐冥想。他俩不忍心惊扰老师,又不愿放弃求教的机会,就静静地站在门外等他醒来。可天上下着鹅毛大雪,并且越下越大,杨时和游酢仍一直站在雪中。等程颐醒来后,门外的积雪已有一尺厚了。这时,杨时和游酢才踏着一尺深的积雪走进去。后来杨时成为天下闻名的大学者,这件事也被作为尊师重道的范例,由此演变成成语"程门立雪"。杨时千里寻师,程门立雪,诚心讨教的行为被传为佳话,流传千古。"程门立雪"这则成语告诉人们,在求学路上,只有虚心才会不断获得进步,只有礼貌才会得到他人的肯定。没有多少人会对粗俗无礼、骄傲自满者积极主动地伸出援助之手。

通过本章的学习,主要是使高校国际生能基本理解和掌握中国社会生活、公共秩序和社会公德的含义和内容;在日常生活和学习中,能自觉遵守中国法律法规、校纪校规和社会公德,顺利完成学业。各位高校国际生一定要把这些期望化为提高自身修养的强大动力,努力培养自己的公德意识,树立遵守公德的良好形象,争做践行社会公德的合格公民,以实际行动推动全社会的公德建设。

【思考题】

1.作为一名高校国际生,在华学习和生活中,是否存在诸如迟到、早退、不信守承诺、借钱不还等不守公德的行为? 应该怎样加强自身的公德修养?

2.高校国际生对中国社会的公共交往习惯和公德规范有怎样的体验和感受? 和你们自己的国家相比,中国在公共交往习惯和公德规范有哪些异同?

Chapter Three   Observing Social Morality and Maintaining Public Order

Everyone is a member of a certain society. In social life, only by consciously following the public order can a society develop harmoniously. To maintain public life and public order, individuals must constrain their own behavior and abide by social public morality. International students who come to Chinese universities must understand and abide by social public morality, maintain public order and respect social customs.

【Mind Map】

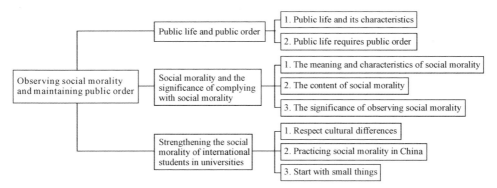

Section One   Public Life and Public Order

1. Public Life and its Characteristics

Public life refers to the collective life of people who are interconnected and influenced by each other in public spaces. There are some simple and basic behavioral norms that must be followed in public activities. The scope of public life is very wide, involving various complex relationships between individuals and individuals, individuals and society as well as humans and nature. The characteristics of contemporary public life are mainly manifested in the following several aspects.

(1) The Extensive Scope of Activities

The development of economy and society has expanded the places and fields of public life, from traditional places such as buses, cinemas, libraries, parks and dormitories to emerging places like stock exchanges and talent markets, etc.

【Conceptual Analysis】

Today, any aircraft of an international airline can reach any corner of the world within 17 hours. The popularity and promotion of modern media means that people can truly "know everything without leaving their house". Since the end of the 20th century, the rapid development of information technology and the internet have been turning the earth into a "village", and human public life has entered a new stage. The internet has further expanded people's public life into the virtual world. The virtual world, as part of public life, is not a lawless place, so we must also abide by social morality and maintain public order in the virtual world.

(2) The Public Nature of the Activities

Public life is the most common and fundamental form of life in a society. It can be enjoyed by all members of society without exclusivity. Its content is open and there are no secrets involved.

(3) Complexity of Communication Objects

For a long period in history, people often lived and interacted in "a society of acquaintances" with a small circle of limited number people. In today's society, the development of science and technology and the increasing specialization of social labor have continuously expanded the field of social public life, allowing people's social interactions to extend beyond familiar acquaintances to anyone in public places. This is more like "a society of strangers" which increases the asymmetry of interpersonal communication information and the unpredictability of behavioral consequences, resulting in the complexity of communication objects.

(4) Diversity of Activity Modes

The development of contemporary society has brought about new changes in people's way of life, and greatly enriched the content and methods of public life. For example, shopping in malls, entertaining in karaoke bars, strolling in squares, relaxing in parks, studying in libraries, exercising in sports centers and surfing on the Internet, people can choose their specific ways of participating in public life based on their own needs, interests, occupations, economic conditions and other factors. The increase of public places and the improvement of public facilities have also provided good conditions for enriching the content and methods of public life.

【Case Analysis】

Public Life and Social Relations in Ancient Chinese Society

In ancient Chinese society, people believed that there were five types of interpersonal relationships that needed to be regulated: ruler and subject, father and child, husband and wife, elder and younger siblings, and friends. These relationships were also known as the "Five Relations" or "Wulun" in Chinese. Mencius, one of the Confucian sages, emphasized the importance of these relationships by stating, "Between father and child there should be affection, between ruler and subject there should be righteousness, between husband and wife there should be attention to their separate functions, between old and young there should be proper order, and between friends there should be faithfulness" (from *Mencius Teng Wengong Shang*). This idea has deeply influenced Chinese behavior norms for thousands of years. Mencius also recognized the differences between men and women, rather than simply advocating gender equality.

【Opinion Exchange】

Why was public life relatively simple in ancient Chinese society?

【Knowledge Expansion】

Introduction to Mencius' Life and Thought

Mencius (approximately 372 BC —289 BC), whose birth name was Ke and courtesy name was Ziyu, was a philosopher, thinker, and educator in the Warring States Period in ancient China. He was a representative figure of the Confucian school of thought between Confucius and Xunzi and is often listed alongside Confucius as "Confucius and Mencius".

Mencius advocated the concept of "benevolent governance" and was the first to propose the idea that "the people are more important than the ruler". He was regarded by Han Yu as one of the inheritors of the Confucian "orthodox tradition" and was posthumously awarded the title of "Sub-Sage" in the Yuan Dynasty.

2. Public Life Requires Public Order

Public order, also known as social order, is necessary to maintain public life. With the accelerated development of economic globalization, the scope of public life is constantly expanding, and people's interactions with each other are also expanding. Public life has become an important part of the lives of social members, and maintaining public order is particularly urgent and important. Public order is related to people's life quality and also to the level of civilization of society.

【Conceptual Analysis】

Every day, people have to cross the road and take different kinds of transportation, go to stores for shopping, visit parks or cinemas for leisure and entertainment and go to classrooms for learning. These public places are where people socialize and participate in public life. In addition to family members, friends, colleagues and classmates, there are also many strangers with whom we interact in various ways on a daily basis. For instance, we need to obey traffic signals when crossing the road, or we may collide with others if we walk randomly. We need to line up for buses, and we may cause conflicts with other passengers if we cut in line. We should trade fairly and not engage in unfair practices when shopping in stores. We must refrain from making loud noises while watching movies in cinemas. We should also follow the instructions of teachers when studying in classrooms. Therefore, it can be seen that any public place will generate interpersonal interactions, and certain public order is needed.

Section Two   Social Morality and the Significance of Complying with Social Morality

1. The Meaning and Characteristics of Social Morality

Social morality refers to the morality that exists within social groups. It is a set of behavioral norms that people living in society have agreed upon for the benefit of the group. Essentially, social morality refers to a set of moral standards, cultural values and traditional ideas that have been accumulated by a country, a nation, or a group throughout its history and social practices. The basic characteristics of social morality are manifested in the following aspects.

(1) Inheritance

Inheritance is an important feature of all morality, and public morality is no exception. For thousands of years, in the process of living together and interacting with each other, humans have formed moral traditions that they abide by in their dealings with others. These moral traditions condense human moral wisdom and form an important component of social morality.

(2) Fundamentality

Social morality is the fundamental level of the social moral system and is regarded as the most basic ethical standard that every member of society should abide by. It is the most fundamental moral requirement proposed by society to maintain public life. Every member of society should possess social morality literacy.

(3) Extensiveness

Social morality is a moral norm that must be followed by all members of society and thus it has the widest mass base and scope of application. In a society, regardless of their identity, profession and status, all members of society must abide by social morality in public life.

(4) Simplicity

Social morality is mainly the accumulation of life experience and the refinement of customs and habits. It often can be understood by people without further explanation. For example, being polite, hygienic and orderly is the basic consensus in life, and the norms of social morals such as "no spitting" and "no jaywalking" are plain and clear.

(5) Permeability

Social morality has extensive permeability. As a criterion for regulating public life, it includes a wide range of content, such as observing public order, maintaining public hygiene, respecting the elderly and caring for the young, respecting teachers and loving students, keeping promises, caring for each other, helping the needy, returning lost property, being brave in standing up for what is right, etc.

【Knowledge Expansion】

Introduction to Mandela's Life

Nelson Rolihlahla Mandela (1918—2013) was born in Transkei, South Africa. He obtained the degree of Bachelor of Arts from the University of South Africa and the qualification of lawyer from the University of

Witwatersrand. Mandela served as the National Secretary and President of the African National Congress Youth League. He was the first elected black President of South Africa from 1994 to 1999, and was widely known as the "Father of the Nation".

Before his presidency, Mandela was an active anti-apartheid campaigner and the leader of the armed wing of the African National Congress, Umkhonto we Sizwe. He was convicted of conspiracy to overthrow the government by the South African courts during his time as an anti-apartheid activist, and served 27 years in prison. After his release in 1990, Mandela advocated reconciliation and negotiation, and became a key figure in the transition period of South Africa into a nation with a multi-racial democracy. Since the end of apartheid, Mandela has been widely praised, even by former opponents. Mandela passed away at the age of 95 at his home in Johannesburg on December 5, 2013.

During his 40 years of activism, Mandela was awarded more than 100 honors, including the Nobel Peace Prize in 1993. In 2004, he was voted as South Africa's greatest person.

【Case Analysis】

Mandela Fought to Abolish the System of Racial Segregation

People, ethnic groups, and races should be equal and respect each other. In real life, people of color, such as Asians and Africans, often face discrimination. They could not ride public transportation or attend school with white people. This behavior is obviously against social ethics. Known as the "father of South Africa," Mandela fought for decades to abolish the long-standing and inhumane system of racial segregation in South Africa, and ultimately achieved victory.

【Opinion Exchange】

Have you ever been disrespectful to others or displayed discrimination against other ethnic groups or races in daily life? Have you ever been disrespected by others?

2. The Content of Social Morality

In public activities, there are some simple and basic codes of conduct that must be followed, involving various complex relationships between individuals and society, individuals and individuals and humans and nature. With the continuous expansion of modern social life, the improvement of living quality and the development of civilization, especially with the increasing development of modern high-tech and its widespread application, people's activity space and moral vision have become broader, and the content of social ethics has become richer. For example, the relationship between humans and the natural environment, or even the ethical rules that should be followed when humans are in outer space, have become increasingly important. In this regard, the new content of social morality mainly manifests in the ethical relationship between humans and nature. Based on the actual situation in China and the development requirements of human life around the world, the main contents of modern society's norms of social morality can be summarized as follows.

(1) Displaying Good Manners and Promoting Mutual Respect Among People

As a basic norm of social morality, good manners promote mutual respect between individuals. It indicates a person's respect for the dignity and personality of others in interpersonal communication. Today, advocating and promoting good manners is an urgent need to inherit and carry forward the traditional virtues of Chinese culture and improve people's moral quality. It is also an urgent need to establish new interpersonal relationships that respect, understand, care for and help each other, and form a united, equal and friendly relationship.

(2) Helping Others and Promoting the Humanitarian Spirit of Mutual Assistance

In public life, everyone may encounter difficulties and problems and there are always times when they need help and care from others. Therefore, advocating the spirit of helping others and promoting mutual assistance is the embodiment of the socialist moral core and principles in public life, as well as the basic requirement of socialist humanism. Helping others is a traditional Chinese virtue, and there are widely spread sayings such as "a noble man helps others to fulfill their dreams", "the greatest joy comes from doing good deeds", "to benefit the masses through generosity", etc. Regarding helping others as something that one should do and finding it a source of personal happiness is a public morality that every member of society should have. And that is an expression of love.

(3) Cherishing Public Property and Enhancing the Sense of Responsibility as Socialist Masters

Protecting public property is a fundamental requirement of social morality, which requires citizens to care for, cherish and safeguard national assets and fight against any acts of destruction and waste of public property.

(4) Protecting the Environment and Strengthening Ecological Ethics

Protecting the environment is a fundamental national policy of China. It is also one of the basic contents of social morality and concerns everyone's vital interests. Environmental protection is not only about public health and beautifying personal living environments but mainly refers to the protection of the natural environment, such as water environment, atmospheric environment, soil environment, mineral resources, animal resources, and other cultural and social resources by reducing environmental pollution, maintaining ecological balance and utilizing natural resources and energy rationally.

(5) Abiding by Laws and Regulations and Consciously Maintaining Public Order

Complying with laws and regulations and consciously maintaining public order is the most basic requirement of social morality, and an important condition for maintaining public life order. Conducting law-abiding behavior is an important way to improve people's social morality. In social life, every member of society should not only abide by relevant laws and regulations issued by the state but also comply with relevant discipline and regulations in specific public places and units. International students from all over the world should have a comprehensive understanding of various laws and regulations in China's public life, be familiar with school rules and regulations, firmly establish a legal concept of "be proud of compliance with laws and regulations and ashamed of violating laws and discipline", and consciously abide by relevant regulations and laws.

【Conceptual Analysis】

Understand the Hazards of Microplastica

Over 100 years ago, Engels warned: Let us not overestimate our human victories over nature. For each such victory, nature takes its revenge on us. Each victory, it is true, in the first place brings about the results we expected, but in the long run, it has quite different, unforeseen effects, which only too often cancel out the earlier results. As a capable and cultured generation of youth, international students in universities should firmly establish environmental protection awareness, take action with small steps, start from themselves, take the lead in promoting and practicing environmental ethics, and become role models in protecting the environment.

【Knowledge Expansion】

Microplastics Being a Threat to Human Health

【**Knowledge Expansion**】

Carbon Emission Peak and Carbon Neutrality

In order to build a new development pattern, promote industrial transformation and upgrading, embark on a green, low-carbon, and circular development path, achieve high-quality development, protect the earth's ecology, and advance global response to climate change, China proposed the goal of "striving to carbon dioxide emission peak before 2030 (carbon peaking), and achieving carbon neutrality before 2060 (offsetting its own carbon dioxide emissions through tree planting, energy conservation and emission reduction, achieving zero carbon dioxide emissions)" in September 2020. It is a major strategic decision made after careful consideration by the Central Committee of the Communist Party of China, and is related to the sustainable development of China and the construction of a human community with a shared future, signifying that China is more firmly implementing the new development concept.

【**Case Analysis**】

"The Chinese People's Volunteers were strong and fierce fighters but also more civilized enemies."

Throughout history, wars have always been very cruel, causing not only a large number of soldiers to die on the battlefield, but also bringing huge disasters to innocent civilians. In the War to Resist US Aggression and Aid Korea (1950—1953), the Chinese People's Volunteers (CPV) never harmed civilians. Even when they lacked clothing and food, they bought supplies from the Korean people with money, rather than plundering them like other armies. The CPV not only did not kill civilians but also treated prisoners of war well. As long as the enemies laid down their weapons, the CPV would give them the best treatment. If they were injured, they would be promptly treated. General Van Fleet, who served as the commander-in-chief of the

"United Nations Forces" in the war, wrote in his memoirs: "The Chinese practice of releasing prisoners of war was different from that of others. Once, they even put heavily wounded soldiers on stretchers and left them on the road, and did not shoot at our medical personnel when we transported the wounded... Later, we realized that the Chinese were strong and fierce fighters who often attacked regardless of casualties. However, they were more civilized enemies. There were many times when they shared their only food with prisoners and treated them kindly. We discovered that when we recaptured Seoul the Chinese did not recklessly destroy the building materials we had transported to the city to repair the bombed-out city."

【Knowledge Expansion】

The War to Resist US Aggression and Aid Korea

【Opinion Exchange】

Why were the Chinese People's Volunteers able to treat prisoners of war well? Is it related to China's cultural traditions?

3. The Significance of Observing Social Morality

The role of social morality in maintaining public order is increasingly important and irreplaceable. Social morality plays a crucial role in maintaining stability and justice, and punishing evil while promoting good. It has a powerful influence on social production and life through public opinion monitoring and spiritual inspiration. Social morality promotes individuals and society in general to abandon evil and promote good in a standardized way, guiding people's thoughts and behaviors without coercion, regulating and standardizing people's speech and actions in social life, maintaining public order, and effectively serving the needs of society and its members. It is of great significance to voluntarily comply with social morality.

(1) Observing Social Morality Is a Necessary Condition for Maintaining Public Interests and Public Order

If every member of society can consciously abide by the basic norms of social morality, the difficulty and cost of maintaining public order in society will be greatly reduced. Social members are less likely to have major disputes or conflicts, and can often resolve conflicts through self-mediation, avoiding the escalation of minor issues into major conflicts and serious chaos. This creates a stable and orderly environment for people to live and work in peace.

(2) Observing Social Morality Is the Foundation of the Entire Socialist Ethical System

Social morality plays an important role in promoting the construction of professional ethics and family virtues. Social morality is one of the cornerstones and pillars of general social ethics, and its influence on social moral standards, including professional ethics and family virtues, is stable, profound, extensive and long-lasting.

(3) Observing Social Morality Is an Important Symbol of the Level of Social Civilization

Social morality is a "window" for the civilization of a country or nation. Social morality is an important part of social spiritual civilization, so how people consciously practice it and how popular it is in social life reveal the level of the entire social spiritual civilization. Today, people not only evaluate the level of civilization of a country or region based on its physical environment such as buildings and roads, but also on the level of public morality of its people.

Section Three　Strengthening the Social Morality of International Students in Universities

China's present social morality derives from her fine traditions of social morality and is rooted in socialist economic relations. It develops by highlighting the excellent components of past social morality. The "courtesy", "integrity", "frugality" and emphasis on harmonious coexistence between humans and nature in traditional Chinese morality all belong to the excellent traditional public morality. When setting educational goals, universities should regard moral education for international students as one of the content for their further education. Universities not only attach importance to professional skills education but also constantly enhance the moral literacy of international students. This is not only an important guarantee for international students in China to abide by laws, be friendly in communication, and smoothly study and live, but also a responsibility that Chinese education should undertake to cultivate excellent talents for the world. International students in universities come from all over the world, and they have different cultural backgrounds, living habits, religious beliefs and personal preferences. When they come to a foreign country to study and live, they should pay special attention to learning and understanding the characteristics and requirements of Chinese social morality and public order, strive to adapt to the surrounding environment as soon as possible and integrate themselves into the local society. International students in universities should strengthen the construction of social morality from the following aspects.

1. Respecting Cultural Differences

After enrollment, international students in universities should learn about Chinese laws and regulations, university rules and regulations, moral norms, and public order and customs through the their initial education and personal experiences, and understand the content and characteristics of Chinese social morality.

During their learning process, international students should pay special attention to the differences between Chinese and their own countries in terms of laws and regulations, social morality, public order and civic habits, to avoid inconvenience and trouble caused by misunderstandings. For example, Chinese people are accustomed to nodding their heads to indicate "yes" and shaking their heads to indicate "no", but in some parts of Iran, Bulgaria and Greece, nodding means "no" and shaking means "yes". Chinese people extend their index finger to represent "1", while Europeans and Americans extend their thumbs to represent "1"; Chinese people extend their index and middle fingers to represent "2", while Europeans and Americans extend their thumb and index finger to represent "2". In China, extending the thumb and index finger represents "8". The gesture "OK" means "correct" in India, "no problem" in Thailand, "money" in Japan, Myanmar and South Korea, "insignificant" or "worthless" in France, and is a disgusting and obscene gesture in Brazil, Greece and the island of Sardinia in Italy. Mastering the differences between different cultures will help international students avoid misunderstandings, awkwardness and even legal risks in interpersonal communication, form good interpersonal relationships and interactions, deepen their understanding of social morality and maintain good public order.

2. Practicing Social Morality in China

International students in universities should enhance their awareness of social morality in practice and consciously abide by social moral norms. While it is easy to know what to do, it is difficult to put it into practice consistently. International students need to master the content of Chinese social morality and the knowledge of Chinese laws and regulations, understand cultural differences and consistently regulate their behavior in accordance with social ethical requirements in practice.

There is an old saying in China, "A guest must do as his host does", and in the West, there is also a proverb, "When in Rome, do as the Romans do". But in real life, many international students find it difficult to adjust their behavior in China due to their ingrained habits and beliefs. They cannot integrate smoothly into the surrounding environment. For example, since the outbreak of the COVID-19 pandemic at the end of 2019, Chinese students in various universities have actively responded to the Chinese government's call, consciously followed the school's pandemic prevention and control management regulations, reported their personal travel information as required, strictly followed the rules for entering and leaving the campus, isolated themselves in accordance with the regulations in case of close contact or secondary contact, and regularly took nucleic acid tests. These behaviors are commonplace for Chinese students, but many international students could not understand these regulations. They refused to follow them. They have repeatedly violated school regulations by leaving campus without permission and refusing to report their travel and health status, which have led to troubles in pandemic control and violated social ethical requirements. Some international students are tempted to pursue high-paying jobs illegally. Some international students with religious beliefs engage in illegal religious activities such as preaching in public. These behaviors are not only a violation of social morality but also a violation of Chinese laws. Therefore, international students in universities need to consciously practice social morality, which is not just words in slogans but an issue that demands special attention and vigilance all the time.

3. Starting with Small Things

Social morality regulates behavior, including the smallest details in social life that are often overlooked. When these details are ignored by the majority of people in society, it can lead to negative social trends. Therefore, a high level of public morality must be cultivated in daily life, paying attention to every small matter. As the ancient saying goes, "Do not refrain from doing good because it is small, and do not do evil because it is small".

【Conceptual Analysis】

There are several problems with international students in universities in China. Firstly, there is a poor sense of time. Many international students cannot arrive at the designated place on time, and are often late or absent for meetings with their supervisors. Secondly, there are issues with honesty and integrity. Many international students borrow money and fail to repay it, cheat on exams and go back on their promises, and so on. In fact, it is not difficult to practice social morality, for example, being punctual and not leaving class early, being honest and keeping promises, not lying, greeting teachers and elders, giving up one's seat to those in need on public transport, standing outside the "one-meter line" when queuing in public places such as banks and post offices, turning off the lights when leaving the classroom last, and not carving or vandalizing tourist attractions. Social morality is gradually promoted in these inconspicuous actions.

【Knowledge Expansion】

The Story of Standing in Snow outside Cheng' Door (Cheng Men Lixue)

During the Northern Song Dynasty, Yang Shi and You Zuo came to visit their teacher Cheng Yi and through the window they saw him meditating inside the room. They didn't want to disturb their teacher but also didn't want to miss the opportunity to learn from him. So, they stood quietly outside the door waiting for him to wake up. However, heavy snow started falling, and they remained standing in the snow. When Cheng Yi finally woke up, the snow outside the door had accumulated up to one foot deep. Only then did Yang Shi and You Zuo step inside, treading through the deep snow. Later, Yang Shi became a famous scholar, and this incident became a model of respecting teachers and valuing education. The story passed down throughout the circle of education, evolving into the idiom "Cheng Men Li Xue". Yang Shi's journey to see his teacher and standing in the snow outside Cheng Yi's door is such a famous story that it has been passed down for generations. This idiom tells people that only by being humble and polite can we make progress in our studies and gain the recognition of others. Few people are willing to lend a helping hand to those who are rude and arrogant.

The main purpose of this chapter is to help international students in Chinese universities understand the meaning and content of Chinese social life, public order and social morality. In their study and daily life, they should consciously practice Chinese social morality, observe Chinese laws and regulations, school rules and regulations, and successfully finish their studies in China. International students should turn these expectations into a powerful driving force for improving their own accomplishments, strive to cultivate their own sense of public ethics, and become models in observing public ethics and practicing social morality. They should also take practical actions to promote public ethics in the whole society.

【Questions for Discussion】

1. As an international student in a Chinese university, have you ever engaged in behaviors that violate social morality, such as being late, leaving early, failing to keep promises, or not repaying debts? How do you think you can promote your own understanding of social morality?

2. As an international student studying in China, what are your experiences regarding gender equality and ethnic equality in Chinese society? In comparison to your home country, what progress has China made and what areas still need improvement in these two domains?

第四章　崇尚法治精神　笃行法治生活

　　生活不仅需要秩序,而且更需要法治秩序,从而形成法治生活。法治生活是全人类每一位成员追求的生活环境,每个人都把法治秩序作为自己享受幸福生活的内容之一。法治精神则是每一位成员参与构建法治秩序、享有法治生活的前提。只有人类充满着法治精神,每个人才能生活在法治秩序之中,享受着法治生活。

【思维导图】

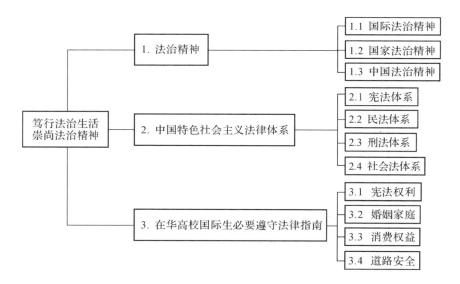

第一节　法治精神

　　法治精神是指人类社会所有成员尊重法律权威、尊崇法治、为法治秩序的形成而充满理性的精神状态。这种精神能够表明人类社会中的每一位成员，对身居其中的法律认知，和对法治的理性追求与价值判断。法治精神可以分为国际法治精神、国家法治精神，以及因工作、学习、生活而停驻在别国形成的他国国家法治精神。国际生到中国高校学习，中国的法治精神就应当成为他们在中国工作、学习、生活过程中应当具备的法治精神。

一、国际法治精神

国际法治精神是指作为全人类中的一员，不分民族、种族、国家、地区等，都应该坚持主体平等、遵守相互间契约、尊重他国（地区）法治状态的国际主义精神。国际法治精神是以国际法为法律渊源，通过国际法调整现实不同政治主体之间的国际关系。国际法又称国际公法，是指适用主权国家之间以及其他具有国际人格的实体之间的法律规则的总体，以区别于国际私法或法律冲突。对于任何人来讲，国际法治精神意味着任何人判断世界上任何政治主体之间的行为标准应以国际法的规定为依据，并且能够依据这些规定处理不同政治主体之间的国际关系。

（一）尊重主权

人类社会正在经历着一个历经漫长文明变迁、年轮积聚无限能量并空前释放的时代。21世纪伴随着经济全球化、网络一体化，国家主权就永远是各个国家和各地区政治主体立足于国际的基础。尽管全人类向前和平发展是任何个人、社会组织和国家阻挡不住的历史潮流，然而，全球化时代国家主权原则仍然有着积极的意义。因此，国际法治精神的价值和意义依然存在，并且是全人类用来解决不同国家、地区之间利益冲突的对话基础。国际法治精神要求每一个人都应坚持国家主权平等，坚持互相尊重主权，这既是作为人类一员的权利，也是维护人类和平发展的义务。21世纪的国际社会，仍然要以国际契约为行为准则，唯有坚持这一原则，国际法治精神才能存续，人类才能形成共筑和平的共同体力量。

（二）平等友好

平等友好是全人类从战争走向和平，从竞争走向合作的前提。真诚友好、平等相待，是不同主体之间关系永葆活力的鲜明底色。全人类自古以来都是命运共同体，人类中每一位成员都应当站在人类命运共同体的视角，同呼吸、共命运，始终尊重对方。平等友好作为全人类发展与团结合作的重要基础,坚持国家不分大小、强弱、贫富一律平等,各国在涉及对方核心利益和重大关切的问题上相互支持,坚定支持每个国家自主解决本地区问题的努力,坚定支持每个国家探索适合本国国情的发展道路。秉持真实亲诚理念和正确义利观,全人类每一位成员应当秉承人类命运共同体精神,不断谱写推动全人类合作高质量发展的辉煌篇章。作为来华留学生,应当以互尊互爱、将心比心的真挚情谊,浇灌出遍布世界各地的合作成果,诠释好朋友、好伙伴、好兄弟的真谛,积极传播国际法治精神,不干预他人探索符合国情的发展道路,不干涉他人内政,不把自己的意志强加于人,实现人类社会大团结。

(三)和平发展

人类是自然界万物的尺度,维护自然与人的关系,维护人类内部的和谐关系,最终目标是实现和平发展,构建人类命运共同体。人们应当反对战争,坚持走和平发展之路。互利是合作的动力,而和平发展则是外部环境的保障。共赢是合作的目的,也是合作的结果,只有共赢的合作才可持续和平发展。每一位来华留学生既是人类命运共同体合作共赢的倡导者,更是积极实践者,既要依靠自身力量和改革创新实现发展,又要坚持对外开放,实现互利共赢、共同发展。一方面人类要支持联合国维护和平,反对任何形式的战争,通过国际法来处理各种争端与利益纠纷,在全人类和平的秩序中达成共识。另一方面,人类社会发展是总体发展,任何人都可对人类社会发展做出大大小小不同的贡献。然而,发展不可能在战乱中实现,只有在和平的环境中才能发展。发展需要每个人安心工作,发挥创新才能,只有团结一致才能实现人类共有家园的发展。

【知识拓展】

国际法的历史与发展

二、国家法治精神

一个国家选择什么样的治理体系是由这个国家的历史传承、文化传统、经济社会发展水平所决定的。每个民族、种族或者国家、地区，都有基于长期历史形成的法治精神，成为现代法治精神的传统基础。人们应当尊重每一个国家的国家法治精神，因为这既是国际法治精神的体现，也是尊重国家主权的体现。任何一个国家，借口所谓的"普世价值"随意指责别国法治精神的行为，都不是国际法治精神的体现。

（一）体现民族习惯

民族风俗习惯是一个民族在其历史发展过程中相延久积而成的喜好、风俗、习惯和禁忌，主要表现在饮食、服饰、居住、婚姻、生育、丧葬、节庆、娱乐、礼节、生产等方面。它具有社会性、规范性、地域性、稳定性、敏感性等特点。任何一个民族的风俗习惯，都是社会历史发展阶段的产物，并或多或少转化为法律内容，体现着法律精神。在人类社会发展过程中，随着生产的发展，社会生活的多样化以及民族共同体的形成，逐渐形成了民族的风俗习惯。在世界范围内，各民族的风俗习惯是在长期社会发展中逐渐形成的。有些民族风俗习惯与一个民族的重大历史事件、重要历史人物有关。还有些风俗习惯是一个民族在一定历史时期的经济文化生活的反映。尊重各民族风俗习惯的实质，就是尊重各民族的平等权利和生活方式，不能因某个民族有某种风俗习惯而歧视或者侮辱它。这些民族习惯随着国家的出现，其中的一些习惯通过立法程序被确认为国家法律，体现着这个民族自古以来的法律精神。

【知识拓展】

民族风俗习惯

（二）传承历史文化

法律是特定地域人群的生存智慧与生活方式，以成文或者不成文作为表现形式的规则体系，其精神源于某一群体的历史文化。人类生活首先而且永远总表现为特定的民族生活，正是本民族内在信念与外在行为方式的历史积淀，决定了该民族法律规范的渊源和精神。在长期的生活中，法治精神促进民族情感和民族意识的逐渐调试与融合，从而赋予法律以民族历史文化作为规范内容的功用与价值。法的功用与价值,正是由于其表现和褒扬民族情感与民族意识,使得民族认同成为法治精神指导下的法治生活。法律的生命力来自民族情感和民族意识,法律精神一如民族的性格和情感,存在于历史之中。法律一旦丧失了与民族风俗习惯的生动联系,也就丧失了该民族法治生活中最为宝贵的部分。所以,民族的存在和性格与法律之间的有机联系,体现了法律内涵的历史文化传承。一旦法律与民族历史文化背离,那么,国家法治精神就失去了历史文化基础。

【知识拓展】

中国特色社会主义法律体系

（三）坚持司法正义

在人类社会漫长的发展过程中,诸多思想家对于驱动人类社会不断进步的动力来自何处进行了多角度的深入思考和论证。然而,在资源日渐减少,人类需求不断增高,个人、社会、国家之间围绕利益的纠纷与争端并没有因为进入现代化而有所减少的时代,谋求纠纷的正义解决,是人们来自内心深处的期待。对于正义的实现,人类社会有着共同的假想和传说,最终形成了以国家司法机构作为居中裁判主体,通过遵循法律实现程序正义与实体正义相统一的司法系统。司法是社会正义的最后一道防线,是人们对正义救赎的最后期盼。法治精神的实质就是权利与权力的对等,是权利之间的平等,一旦对等或者平等发生失衡或者偏颇,那么,司法通过自己刚性的程序,实现权利初始状态的回归。权利对权力的规范性制约,是正义之剑的保障。因此,司法正义不仅是国家维护社会秩序的需要,而且是保护私人权利与约束公权力的需要,满足二者需要的条件就是坚持司法正义。

三、中国的法治精神

中国的法治精神是在中国共产党的领导下,在广大干部人民群众中间养成的以树立中国特色社会主义法律权威,形成"办事依法、遇事找法、解决问题用法、化解矛盾靠法"的法律意识,自觉运用法律,使法治成为铭刻在人们内心的价值准则和行为规范。遵循宪法,始终坚持学法尊法守法用法的法治信念,既是中国法治建设的一条基本经验,又是中国法治精神的基本内涵。

(一)坚持以人为本的理性精神

中国特色社会主义法治是马克思主义中国化的创新发展成果。尊重客观事实,坚持历史唯物主义辩证法是中国法治精神的指导思想和方法论。中国共产党自诞生之日起,就把追求科学与民主作为法治的理性精神,也就是求真务实的科学精神。法治是以和平理性的方式解决社会矛盾的最佳途径。这一理念成为中国特色社会主义法治精神区别于传统封建社会依赖愚昧、无知、迷信、愚忠等非理性因素支撑的人治。法律是全体人民意志的最大公约数,必须经过全体人民的同意,才能成为约束每个人的规定。法律是人民相互之间权利配置、公权力与私权力之间互相制约的规范体系,其深层次的要义在于体现以人为本的理性精神。立法不仅应当从实际出发,科学合理地规定公民、法人和其他组织的权利与义务,而且要科学规范国家机关的权力与责任,推进法治政府建设。以人为本的理性精神在立法中表现为科学立法、民主立法、依法立法。中国特色社会主义法治中以人为本的理性精神,在行政执法领域、司法领域同样以技术理性的形态表现出来,即"以人民为中心"的法治精神。

(二)贯穿诚信守法的精神

自古以来,中华民族就把"诚信"作为一种伟大人格用来检验芸芸众生的道德品质。"人而无信,不知其可",其意义在于一个人如果言行不能一致,就失去了作为一个人应当具有的品质。诚信原则是私法领域中的"帝王原则"。《中华人民共和国民法典》把诚信原则作为民事主体履行民事行为的基本原则之一,把社会公德、职业道德、家庭美德、个人品德中的诚信共性,通过法律化上升为所有平等主体之间必须遵守的基本原则。不仅私法领域要遵守诚信原则,而且公法领域内政府部门同样也要讲究诚信,即信赖原则。因此,无论是公民个人,还是政府部门及其工作人员,都应当遵守法律,严格按照法律规定行使权利、履行义务,或者依法行政,严格行政责任。诚信守法精神包括三个方面:一是每个人都要把遵守法律作为与他人交往的基本准则;二是发生纠纷要运用法律,运用法律是遵守法律的积极表现形式;三是塑造法律信仰,只有在心中树立崇高的法律信仰,才是真正体现守法精神。

【概念解析】

中华民族自古以来就把诚信作为一个人实现伟大理想、铸就伟大人格、成就伟大功业的信仰。"人而无信，不知其可也"是做人的基本要求，是人成为人的根本要求。历经数千年，中华民族的诚信品格不仅内化为每个人的人生观、价值观和世界观，而且转化为中华民族追求富强、文明、民主、和谐、美丽现代化中国的软实力。

（三）尊重法律权威的精神

法律权威来自法律的实施，尊重法律权威，其本质是尊重人民当家作主的权利。《中华人民共和国宪法》第二条规定："中华人民共和国的一切权力属于人民。"尊重法律权威，就是尊重人民的意志，体现了人民意志在国家治理和社会治理过程中的要求。中国特色社会主义国家是人民当家作主的国家，通过法治保护民主，就要在全社会树立起尊重法律权威的精神。邓小平指出："为了保障人民民主，必须加强法制。必须使民主制度化、法律化，使这种制度和法律不因领导人的改变而改变，不因领导人的看法和注意力的改变而改变。"1982年9月修改制定的《中国共产党章程》明确了法律的权威地位，指出"党必须在宪法和法律的范围内活动"。1997年"依法治国"写进《中华人民共和国宪法》。进入21世纪之后，"科学立法、严格执法、公正司法、全民守法"成为新时代尊重我国法治建设的基本方针，体现了中国特色社会主义法治独有的法治精神。

（四）权利与义务对等的精神

人人生而平等，因此，人与人之间的权利义务是对等的。任何社会只要出现任何人不履行义务而享有权利，或者履行义务而不能享有权利，或者履行较少的义务而享有较多的权利，这个社会一定是不公平的。因为人人生而平等，平等的要义之一就是权利义务的统一，即权利义务在量上的统一。然而，由于在社会发展的不同阶段，人们认知客观世界的能力与程度不同，特别是生产力与生产关系发展的程度不同，任何社会的权利都受那个社会当时的社会生产力和生产关系的制约。但是，每个人的权利义务、人与人之间的权利义务不该因为社会提供的物质条件、精神条件不同而存在不对称。在中国主权范围内，任何公民平等地享有宪法和法律规定的各项权利，同时必须履行宪法和法律规定的各项义务。在当代中国,让公权力在宪法和法律规定的范围内运行,把权力关进制度的笼子里,促进权利和义务、权力和责任的对等,是法治国家建设的重要内容。

【知识拓展】

卡尔·马克思讲过:"没有无义务的权利,也没有无权利的义务。"人类社会人人生而有自由的权利,但是,享受这些权利的前提是履行与权利对等的义务。法治精神的核心要义之一,就是人人在法律面前一律平等。这既包括依法享有权利的平等,也包括依法履行义务的平等。

第二节　中国特色社会主义法律体系

法律体系,也称法的体系,是指法律规范以法的部门划分为基础而构成的一个和谐的有机整体。一般认为,中华人民共和国的法律部门可以从三个层次来划分。第一层次是从根本法这一层次划分为宪法部门,这是中华人民共和国的根本大法,是法律体系的统领部门,也是法律体系赖以矗立起来的基础。第二层次是基本法律部门,包括由全国人民代表大会及其常务委员会制定的,包括行政法、民法、经济法、劳动法、刑法、婚姻法、诉讼法等基本法律,以及部分一般法律。第三层次包括各基本法律部门的子部门。概括起来,中华人民共和国法律部门主要有宪法、行政法、民商法、经济法、婚姻法、劳动与社会保障法、刑法、诉讼与非诉讼程序法。2010 年,中国特色社会主义法律体系如期建成。

一、宪法体系

目前,中国特色社会主义法律体系呈现 3 个层次,涵盖 7 大部门,宪法加上 7 大法律部门共 200 多部法律,构成了中国现行法律体系的核心内容。第一层为宪法,第二层次为基本法律和一般法律,第三层次为行政法规、地方性法规等规范性文件。宪法以法律的形式确认了中国各族人民奋斗的成果,规定了国家的根本政治制度和根本任务,是国家的根本法,具有最高的法律效力。全国各族人民、一切国家机关和武装力量、各政党和各社会团体、各企业事业组织,都必须以宪法为根本的活动准则,并且负有维护宪法尊严、保证宪法实施的职责。除此之外，宪法还规定了国家的经济制度、公民的基本权利和义务，具有最高的法律效力。宪法体系包括除宪法以外的各类组织法。如各级人民代表选举法、各级人民法院组织法、各级人民检察院组织法、中华人民共和国地方各级人民代表大会和地方各级人民政府组织法等都属于宪法体系。除却组织法之外，宪法体系还包括一系列行政法，如行政处罚法、行政许可法、行政复议法等。宪法结构体系逻辑严密、布局合理，并与丰富的宪法内容有机地结合起来。中华人民共和国现行宪法的结构体系是序言、总纲、国家机构、公民的基本权利和义务、国旗、国歌、国徽、首都。

【知识拓展】

"五四宪法"：新中国首部具有
基础意义的宪法

二、民法体系

中华人民共和国第十三届全国人民代表大会三次会议审议通过了《中华人民共和国民法典》(以下简称《民法典》)，这是新中国成立以来第一部以"法典"命名的法律，它的颁布标志着中国正式步入民法典时代，是新时代中国特色社会主义法治建设的重大成果。《民法典》开创了中国法典编纂立法的先河，具有里程碑意义。《民法典》被誉为"社会生活的百科全书"，共1260条，分为七编（总则编、物权编、合同编、人格权编、婚姻家庭编、继承编、侵权责任编）及附则，是中国法律体系中条文最多、体量最大、篇章结构最复杂的一部法律。它涵盖了此前颁布实施的《中华人民共和国民法通则》《中华人民共和国民法总则》《中华人民共和国物权法》《中华人民共和国担保法》《中华人民共和国合同法》《中华人民共和国继承法》《中华人民共和国婚姻法》《中华人民共和国收养法》《中华人民共和国侵权责任法》《中华人民共和国人格权法》以及涉外民事关系。除《民法典》内部包括的内容之外，民法体系还包括《中华人民共和国著作权法》《中华人民共和国商标法》《中华人民共和国专利法》等。

【知识拓展】

《中华人民共和国民法典》

三、刑法体系

一般说来,刑法总则是关于犯罪、刑事责任和刑罚的一般原理原则的规范体系,是认定犯罪、确定刑事责任和适用刑罚所必须遵循的共同的规则。刑法分则是关于具体犯罪和具体法定刑的规范体系,是解决具体行为定罪量刑的标准。刑法总则与刑法分则的关系是一般与特殊、抽象与具体的关系。总则指导分则,分则是总则所确定的原理原则的具体体现,二者相辅相成。刑法的体系即是指刑法的组成和结构。中国现行有效的刑法分为总则、分则和附则三部分。其中,总则、分则各为一编。其编之下,根据法律规范的性质和内容有次序地划分为章、节、条、款、项等层次。第一编总则分设五章,即刑法的任务、基本原则和适用范围;犯罪;刑罚;刑罚的具体运用;其他规定。第二编分则分设十章,即危害国家安全罪;危害公共安全罪;破坏社会主义市场经济秩序罪;侵犯公民人身权利、民主权利罪;侵犯财产罪;妨害社会管理秩序罪;危害国防利益罪;贪污贿赂罪;渎职罪;军人违反职责罪。

【知识拓展】

《中华人民共和国刑法》

四、社会法体系

社会法是中国近年来在完善市场经济法律体系,落实科学发展观、构建社会主义和谐社会的历史大潮中应运而生的新兴法律门类和法律学科。社会法是与社会主义制度最为契合的法。社会法在缓和社会矛盾、维护社会稳定方面能够发挥积极作用,和谐社会的建立离不开社会法的发展。随着社会建设和经济建设、政治建设、文化建设被摆在同等重要的位置,社会法的重要性日益凸显。社会法的主旨在于保护公民的社会权利,尤其是保护弱势群体的利益。通过法治途经即制定和完善社会法是改变这种失衡局面的必然选择。在当前中国深化改革而社会法理论与实践又比较薄弱的环境下,完善社会法,保障公民的社会权,使人们实现真正的解放,对构建和谐社会具有重大而深远的理论和现实意义。中国现行的社会法包括《中华人民共和国劳动法》《中华人民共和国劳动合同法》《中华人民共和国工会法》《中华人民共和国未成年人保护法》《中华人民共和国老年人权益保障法》《中华人民共和国妇女权益保障法》《中华人民共和国残疾人保障法》《中华人民共和国矿山安全法》《中华人民共和国红十字会法》《中华人民共和国公益事业捐赠法》《中华人民共和国职业病防治法》等。

【知识拓展】

社会主义是人类历史上迄今为止最为崭新的社会制度,社会主义法律体系是人类历史上最为崭新的法律体系。中国特色社会主义法律体系以宪法为根本大法,国家基本法律、一般法律、法规与自治条例、单行条例,以及地方性法规构成了符合中国国情的法律体系。

第三节 高校国际生必须遵守的法律指南

法律遵守是指国家机关、社会组织和公民个人依照法律规定行使权力和权利以及履行职责和义务的活动。在中国特色社会主义国家,一切组织和个人都是守法的主体。一切国家机关和武装力量,包括各类政党和各种社会团体、各种企业事业组织,必须遵守中华人民共和国法律,依法享有法律权利,依法履行法律义务,在宪法和法律规定的范围内开展活动,其合法权益受到国家法律的平等保护。

一、宪法权利

宪法权利是指由宪法或宪法性法律所确定的权利。这些权利一般都是最重要的权利,所以通常称为公民的基本权利。各国宪法一般都规定公民应享有的权利和自由。宪法规定公民的基本权利,包括公民的平等权、公民的政治权利和自由、公民的宗教信仰自由、公民的人身自由,以及公民的批评、建议、申诉、控告、检举权和取得赔偿权。宪法义务包括依法服兵役的义务、依法纳税的义务、受教育的义务、环境保护的义务、遵守宪法和法律的义务、劳动的义务。其中,教育和劳动既是公民的宪法权利,也是公民的宪法义务,具有双重属性。

二、婚姻家庭

《中华人民共和国民法典》第五编《婚姻家庭》第一章对婚姻家庭关系作了详细的规定。在华外国人应当理解、遵守中国法律关于婚姻家庭生活的主要规定,尊重中国传统关于婚姻家庭积极向上的道德观,遵守中华人民共和国法律法规关于婚姻家庭的规定。在家庭婚姻生活中,孝顺父母、爱护子女、尊重对方、忠诚家庭。双方能够主动承担家庭责任,共同教育子女成长,赡养双方老人。

【知识拓展】

婚姻家庭相关法律

三、消费权益

《中华人民共和国消费者权益保护法》是依法维护消费者权利的一部法律,其宗旨是维护市场秩序,打击违法犯罪的经营活动。在华留学生应当依法保护自己的消费权益,在消费过程中,既要主动通过学习,提高消费权利意识,又要依法依规维护消费权益。同时,中华人民共和国严厉打击恶意消费索赔行为,维护市场经济秩序。在华留学生在消费过程中,如果由于语言交流产生词不达意障碍,应主动通过各种有效方式进行沟通,让服务者深入了解自己消费需求,实现双方公平诚信、合法合规的消费关系。

【知识拓展】

《中华人民共和国消费者权益保护法》

四、道路安全

　　为了维护道路交通秩序,预防和减少交通事故,保障人身安全,保护公民、法人和其他组织的财产安全及其他合法权益,提高通行效率,制定道路交通安全法。我们在日常生活中,应当把自己的生命健康和他人的生命健康放在第一位,遵守交通法规,合理使用交通工具。遇到交通事故时,应当保护现场,联系警察处理。在警察处理的过程中,应当控制情绪,积极配合,按照警察的要求出示有效证件,实事求是地做好笔录。遇到轻微交通事故时,应积极主动与对方沟通,移挪交通工具,确保交通秩序不受影响。根据情况确定是否联系保险公司,积极主动赔偿对方损失或者依法要求对方赔偿自己损失。遇到交通事故造成身体受伤的,应第一时间呼叫 120 急救中心,在第一时间内抢救伤员,最大限度保障人身生命健康。

【知识拓展】

《中华人民共和国道路交通安全法》

【知识拓展】

　　在中华人民共和国内,任何人都必须遵守宪法法律,在宪法法律规定的范围内行动。国家依法保障人权。任何人在遇到困难时,都能够通过有效途径依法获得帮助。遵守中国法律,依法享有中国法律保护的权利,是在华每个外国友人的权利和义务。

【思考题】

1. 如何实现法治精神对于维护当今世界秩序的价值？
2. 为什么诚信原则是法治精神的核心价值？

Chapter Four   Advocating the Spirit of the Rule of Law and Practicing the Rule of Law in Daily Life

Life not only requires order but also requires the rule of law so as to create a life under the rule of law. Life under the rule of law is what every member of humanity pursues, and it also forms part of people's happy life. The spirit of the rule of law is the premise for every member to participate in constructing the rule of law society and enjoying the rule of law life. Only when humanity is full of spirit can everyone live in a society under the rule of law and enjoy a life under the rule of law.

【Mind Map】

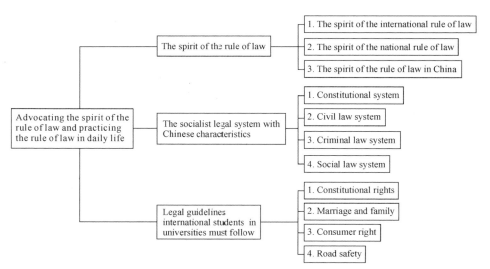

Section One　The Spirit of the Rule of Law

The spirit of the rule of law refers to the rational state of mind in which all members of human society respect the authority of law, uphold the rule of law and are committed to the formation of a legal order. This kind of spirit can demonstrate the legal awareness of each member of human society, as well as their rational pursuit and value judgment on the rule of law. The spirit of the rule of law can be divided into that of the international rule of law, the national rule of law and the rule of law of other countries formed out of one's oversea work, study or life. As international students come to study in Chinese universities, the spirit of the rule of law in China should become one of the legal spirits they should possess in the process of working, studying, and living in China.

1. The Spirit of the International Rule of Law

The spirit of the international rule of law refers to the internationalist spirit that as a member of the human race, regardless of nationality, race, country region, etc., one should uphold the principles of sovereign equality, comply with contracts and respect the rule of law in other countries or regions. The spirit of the international rule of law originates from international law which regulates the international relations between different political entities in reality. International law, also known as public international law, refers to the body of legal rules applicable to sovereign states and other international legal entities, as distinguished from private international law or conflict of laws. For anyone, the spirit of the international rule of law means that he should take the provisions of international law as the behavior standards for any political entity in the world and that the international relations between different political entities should be handled based on these provisions.

(1) Respect for Sovereignty

Human society is experiencing an era of unprecedented energy accumulation and release after a long period of changes in civilization. In the 21st century, with the emergence of economic globalization, network integration and capital globalization, the international community is still dominated by nationalism. As long as states, the political entity, exist in human social life, state sovereignty will always be the foundation on which various countries and regions participate in international affairs. Although the peaceful development of mankind is an unstoppable historical trend for any individual, social organization and country, the principle of state sovereignty still has a positive meaning in the era of globalization. Therefore, the value and significance of the spirit of the international rule of law still exist and serve as the basis for dialogue to resolve conflicts of interest between different countries and regions. The spirit of the international rule of law requires that everyone should uphold the equal sovereignty of states and respect each other's sovereignty. This is not only the right for each member of humanity but also the obligation for them to maintain a peaceful development. In the 21st century, international contracts should still be the standard of behavior in international society, and only by adhering to this principle can the spirit of the international rule of law continue to exist and human beings be community forces to build world peace.

(2) Equality and Friendship

Equality and friendship are the prerequisites for all of humanity to move from war to peace and from competition to cooperation. Sincere friendship and equal treatment are the basis that keeps the relationships between different entities alive. Since ancient times, all humanity has been a community with a shared future, and every member of humanity should take the perspective of the community, breathe together, share the same destiny, and always respect each other. Equality and friendship serve as an important foundation for the development and solidarity of all of humanity. Countries should adhere to the principle of equality regardless of their size, strength, or wealth, and support each other on issues that involve each other's core interests and major concerns. They should also firmly support every country's effort to independently solve regional problems and explore development paths that suit their own national conditions best. Every member of humanity should uphold the spirit of a shared community with a genuine, sincere and just standpoint, and continue to promote high-quality cooperation and development for all of humanity. As a foreign student in China, one should develop sincere friendship through mutual respect and empathy, promote cooperation across the world, and demonstrate the true meaning of being good friends, good partners, and good brothers. One should actively promote the spirit of the international rule of law, not interfere with other countries' efforts to explore development paths that suit their own national conditions, not interfere with their internal affairs and not impose one's own will on others, so as to achieve the great unity of human society.

(3) Peaceful Development

Humanity is the measure of all things in nature. It maintains the relationship between nature and humans and the harmony among humans, and its ultimate goal is to achieve peaceful development and realize a shared future for mankind. People should oppose wars and insist on the path of peaceful development. Mutual benefit is the driving force of cooperation, and peaceful development is the guarantee of the external environment. Win-win cooperation is the purpose and result of collaboration, and only win-win cooperation can achieve sustainable and peaceful development. Each international student in China is not only an advocate of cooperation in building a shared future for humanity, but also an active practitioner who relies on their own strength to achieve development. Furthermore, they adhere to opening up to achieve mutual benefit and common development. On the one hand, humanity should support the United Nations in maintaining world peace, oppose any form of war and reach a consensus through international law to handle various

disputes and conflicts of interest within the framework of global peace. On
the other hand, the social development of humanity is a comprehensive
process, and everyone has made different contributions to the development
of humanity. However, development cannot be achieved in times of war
and conflict. It can only be achieved in a peaceful environment.
Development requires every individual to focus on their work, display
creativity and unite to build a shared home for humanity.

【Knowledge Expansion】

The History and Development of
International Law

2. The Spirit of the National Rule of Law

The choice of governance system by a country is determined by its
historical heritage, cultural traditions, and level of economic and social
development. Every ethnic group, race, country, or region has a spirit of
the national rule of law based on its long history, which becomes the
foundation of the modern rule of law. People should respect the rule of
law spirit of every country, as this is not only a reflection of the
international rule of law spirit but also a manifestation of respect for
national sovereignty. Any country that accuses another country's spirit of
the rule of law under the pretext of so-called universal values is not a
reflection of the international rule of law spirit.

(1) Embodying National Customs

The customs of a nation are the accumulated preferences, habits, and
taboos that have developed over its history. They are primarily manifested
in aspects such as diet, clothing, housing, marriage, childbirth, funerals,
festivals, entertainment, etiquette, and production. They bear

characteristics of sociality, normativity, regionality, stability, sensitivity, etc. The customs and habits of any nation are products of its social and historical development and have been more or less transformed into legal content, reflecting the spirit of the law. In the process of human social development, with the development of production, the diversification of social life and the formation of ethnic communities, ethnic customs and habits gradually formed. Around the world, the customs and habits of different ethnic groups have gradually formed in long-term social development. Some ethnic customs and habits are related to significant historical events or historical figures of a nation, while others are reflections of the economic and cultural life of a nation in a certain historical period. However, the essence of respecting the customs and habits of all ethnic groups is to respect their equal rights and ways of life. Discrimination or insult cannot be directed towards a particular ethnic group because of its customs and habits. With the emergence of the nations, some of these ethnic customs and habits have been confirmed as national laws through legislative procedures, reflecting the legal spirit of the nation since ancient times.

【Knowledge Expansion】

Ethnic Traditions and Customs

(2) Inheriting Historical and Cultural Heritage

Law is a system of rules that represents the survival wisdom and way of life of a specific geographic population. It is expressed in written or unwritten forms, and its spirit originates from the historical culture of a certain community. Human life always and forever manifests as specific ethnic life in the very beginning. It is determined by the historical accumulation of the inner beliefs and external behaviors of that ethnic group, which decide the source and spirit of their legal norms. In the long term, the rule of law promotes the gradual adjustment and integration of national emotions and national consciousness, thereby endowing law with the function and value of using national historical culture as normative content. The function and value of law lie precisely in its expression and praise of national emotions and national consciousness, making national identity the guiding principle of the rule of law. The vitality of law also comes from national emotions and national consciousness, and the spirit of law is just like the character and emotions of a nation and exists throughout history. Once law loses its connection with national customs and habits, it loses the most valuable part of the rule of law in that ethnic group's life. Therefore, the organic connection between the existence and character of a nation and its law reflects the historical and cultural inheritance of the legal connotation in that nation. Once law deviates from a nation's history and culture, the spirit of the rule of law of the country will lose its foundation.

【Knowledge Expansion】

The Legal System of Socialism
with Chinese Characteristics

(3) Adhering to Judicial Justice

In the long course of human development, many thinkers have deeply reflected and argued about the driving force behind the constant progress of human society. However, in an era where resources are dwindling and human demands are increasing, disputes and conflicts over interests between individuals, groups and nations have not decreased with modernization. Seeking justice to resolve disputes, whether for individuals or nations, is an expectation that comes from deep within. For the realization of justice, human has common ideals and many legendary stories, which have ultimately formed a judicial system that takes the state judiciary as the central adjudicator and implements procedural justice and substantive justice in a unified manner through the adherence to procedures. The judiciary is the last line of defense for social justice and the final hope for people's redemption of justice. The essence of the rule of law is the balance between rights and powers as well as the equality among people in rights. Once balance and equality are lost or biased, the judiciary uses its rigid procedures to restore the initial state of rights. The normative constraint of power by rights is the guarantee of justice. Therefore, judicial justice is not only a need for the state to maintain social order, but also a need to protect private rights and constrain public power, both of which demand upholding judicial justice.

3. The Spirit of the Rule of Law in China

The spirit of the rule of law in China, under the leadership of the Communist Party of China, has been well cultivated among all the Chinese people, aiming to establish the legal authority of socialism with Chinese characteristics, and form a legal consciousness of "conducting affairs according to the law, seeking help from law in case of trouble, solving problems through law, and resolving conflicts relying on law". People consciously apply the law, making the rule of law a value criterion and behavioral norm imprinted in their hearts. Following the Constitution and always adhering to the beliefs of learning the law, abiding by the law and using the law are not only a basic experience in the construction of the rule of law in China but also the basic content of its spirit in China.

(1) Adhering to the Human-oriented Rational Spirit

The socialist rule of law with Chinese characteristics is an innovative development of Marxism to the Chinese context that emphasizes respecting objective facts and adhering to the dialectics of Historical Materialism, serving as the guiding ideology and methodology of China's legal system. Since the founding of the Communist Party of China,

pursuing science and democracy has been regarded as the rational spirit of
the rule of law, namely, the spirit of seeking truth and pragmatism. The
rule of law is the best way to resolve social conflicts through peaceful and
rational means. This distinguishes the socialist rule of law with Chinese
characteristics from the traditional rule of man which relies on non-rational
factors such as ignorance, superstition and blind loyalty. Law is the most
important common denominator of the will of all people, and must be
agreed upon by all in order to be a regulation that constrains each
individual. Law is a normative system for the allocation of rights between
people and mutual restraint between public power and private rights, and
its profound essence lies in embodying the human-oriented rational spirit.
Legislation should not only scientifically and reasonably specify the rights
and obligations of citizens, legal persons and other organizations based on
reality, but also scientifically regulate the power and responsibilities of
state organs and promote the construction of a rule-of-law government.
The human-oriented rational spirit in legislation is manifested in scientific
legislation, democratic legislation and legislation according to law. In the
socialist system of the rule of law with Chinese characteristics, the
human-oriented rational spirit is also manifested in judiciary and law
enforcement in the form of technical rationality, namely, the spirit of the
people-centered rule of law.

(2) Upholding the Spirit of Integrity and Law-abidingness

Since ancient times, Chinese people have regarded "integrity" as an
important character trait to test a person's moral qualities. "If a person
lacks integrity, he or she cannot be trusted" means that if a person's
words and actions are inconsistent, he or she loses the basic qualities that
a person should possess. The principle of integrity is the "purple
principle" in the field of private law. *Civil Code of the People's Republic
of China* regards the principle of integrity as one of the basic principles for
civil subjects to perform civil acts, and promote the commonality of
integrity in social morality, professional ethics, family virtues and
personal character to a basic principle that all equal subjects must abide

by. Not only should the principle of integrity be followed in the field of private law, but also the government departments in the field of public law should also pay attention to integrity, that is, the principle of trust. Therefore, an individual citizen should abide by the law, exercise their rights and fulfill their obligations strictly according to the law, and a government department and its staff should also administrate according to law and strictly assume administrative responsibilities. The spirit of integrity and law-abidingness can be seen from three aspects: first, everyone should regard obeying the law as a basic principle of interpersonal communication; second, using the law to resolve disputes is an manifestation of obeying the law; and third, everyone should build up their legal beliefs and only by establishing a lofty legal belief in one's heart can one truly embody the spirit of law-abidingness.

【Conceptual Analysis】

Since ancient times, the Chinese have regarded integrity as a belief for individuals to achieve great ideals, cultivate great character and accomplish great achievements. "If a person lacks integrity, he or she cannot be trusted" demonstrates the basic requirement for being a person. Over thousands of years in China, the quality of integrity has not only been internalized as the worldview, values and life philosophy of every individual, but also been transformed into the soft power of the China in its pursuit of a modern, prosperous, civilized, democratic, harmonious and beautiful country.

(3) Respecting the Spirit of the Authority of Law

The authority of law comes from its implementation. Respecting the authority of law is essentially respecting for the running of the country by the people. Article 2 of *the Constitution of the People's Republic of China* stipulates that "All power in the People's Republic of China belongs to the people". Respecting the authority of law is respecting the will of the people, and it reflects the requirements of the people in the process of

state governance and social governance. China is a socialist country with
Chinese characteristics where the people are the masters of the country.
To protect democracy through the rule of law, it is necessary to establish
the spirit of respecting the authority of law in the whole society. Deng
Xiaoping pointed out: "To guarantee democracy for the people, it is
necessary to strengthen the legal system. It is necessary to institutionalize
and legalize democracy and to make this system and laws do not change
with changes in leadership, nor with changes in the views and attention of
leaders". *The Constitution of the Communist Party of China*, revised and
formulated in September 1982, clarified the authoritative position of the
law, stating that "the Party must operate within the scope of the
Constitution and the law". In 1997, "law-based governance of the
country" was written into *the Constitution of the People's Republic of
China*. After entering the 21st century, "scientific legislation, strict law
enforcement, impartial judiciary and law-abiding by all citizens" have
become the spirit of respecting the authority of law in the new era,
reflecting the unique rule of law spirit of socialism with Chinese
characteristics.

(4) Upholding the Spirit of the Equivalence of Rights and Obligations

All people are born equal, and therefore, the rights and obligations
between individuals are equal. In any society, if someone enjoys rights
without fulfilling their obligations, or fulfills obligations without being
able to enjoy rights, or fulfills fewer obligations but enjoys more rights,
then it must be unfair. The essence of equality is the unity of rights and
obligations, i. e. the unity of rights and obligations in terms of quantity.
However, at different stages of social development, people's ability in
understanding the objective world are different. Rights people could enjoy
are especially related to the degree of development in productivity and the
relations of production, and therefore rights in any society are subject to
the constraints of that society's current level of social productive forces
and production relations. Nevertheless, every person's rights and
obligations, as well as the rights and obligations between individuals, do

not exist in an asymmetric manner due to the different material and spiritual conditions provided by society. Within the sovereign territory of China, every citizen has equal enjoyment of all rights provided by the Constitution and laws, and at the same time must fulfill all obligations stipulated by the Constitution and laws. In contemporary China, it is important to build a rule of law state to ensure that public power operates within the framework of the Constitution and laws, putting power into an Institutional Cage according to the Constitution, and to promote the equivalence of rights and obligations, power and responsibility.

【Knowledge Expansion】

Karl Marx once said, "There are no rights without obligations, and no obligations without rights". Every person in human society has the right to freedom, but enjoying these rights requires fulfilling obligations that are equal in nature to those rights. One of the core tenets of the rule of law is the equality of all individuals before the law, which includes equal rights to enjoy and equal legal obligations to fulfill.

Section Two   The Socialist Legal System with Chinese Characteristics

The legal system, also known as the system of law, refers to a harmonious and organic whole formed by dividing legal norms into different law sections. Generally speaking, the legal system of the People's Republic of China can be divided into three levels. The first level is the Constitution, which is the fundamental law of the People's Republic of China, the commanding section of the legal system and the foundation upon which the legal system is established. The second level is the basic legal section, which includes the basic laws of administrative law, civil law, economic law, labor law, criminal law, marriage law, procedural law and some general laws, enacted by the National People's Congress and

its Standing Committee. The third level includes the branches of each
basic legal section, and the fourth level contains the sub-branches of the
sections in the third level. In summary, the legal sections of the People's
Republic of China mainly include the Constitution, administrative law,
civil and commercial law, economic law, marriage law, labor and social
security law, criminal law, procedural law and non-litigation procedural
law. In 2010, the socialist legal system with Chinese characteristics was
established as scheduled.

1. Constitutional System

The current Chinese socialist legal system has three levels and covers
seven departments, consisting of more than 200 laws which form the core
of China's current legal system. The first level is the Constitution, the
second level includes basic and general laws, and the third level includes
normative documents such as administrative regulations and local
regulations. The Constitution confirms the achievements of the Chinese
people of all ethnic groups and sets forth the fundamental political system
and tasks of the state. It is the fundamental law of the country and has the
highest legal effect. People of all ethnic groups, state organs and armed
forces, political parties, social groups, enterprises and institutions must
take the Constitution as the fundamental guideline for their activities and
have the responsibility to uphold the dignity of the Constitution and to
ensure its implementation. In addition, the Constitution also stipulates
the country's economic system, citizens' basic rights and obligations and
has the highest legal effect. The Constitution system includes various
organizational laws other than the Constitution, such as the election law
of people's representatives at all levels, the organization law of people's
courts at all levels, the organization law of people's procuratorates and the
organization law of local people's congresses and local people's
governments at all levels. In addition to organizational laws, the
Constitution system includes a series of administrative laws, such as
administrative punishment law, administrative license law, administrative

reconsideration law, etc. In terms of its structural system, the Constitution has a logical and reasonable layout and is organically combined with rich constitutional content. The current structure of the Constitution of the People's Republic of China includes a preamble, general provisions, state organs, basic rights and duties of citizens, national flag, national anthem, national emblem and the capital city.

【Knowledge Expansion】

The Constitution of 1954: The First Constitution of China with Fundamental Significance

2. Civil Law System

The 13th National People's Congress of the People's Republic of China approved *the Civil Code of the People's Republic of China* at its third session. It marked the official entry of China into the era of civil code, representing a major achievement in the construction of socialist law system in the new era. *The Civil Code of the People's Republic of China* is the first law named "Code" since the founding of the People's Republic of China and is considered a milestone in China's codification and legislation. *The Civil Code of the People's Republic of China* consists of 1260 articles and is regarded as the "encyclopedia of social life". It is divided into seven parts (general provisions and sections on property, contracts, personality rights, marriage and family, inheritance and torts) and some supplementary provisions. It is the law with the most articles, the largest volume and the most complex structure in the Chinese legal system. It covers the previously issued laws such as *General Principles of Civil Law of the People's Republic of China*, *Property Law of the People's Republic of China*, *Guarantee Law of the People's Republic of China*, *Contract Law of the People's Republic of China*, *Inheritance*

Law of the People's Republic of China, *Marriage Law of the People's Republic of China*, *Adoption Law of the People's Republic of China*, *Tort Liability Law of the People's Republic of China*, *Personality Rights Law of the People's Republic of China*, as well as foreign-related civil relations. In addition to the content included in *The Civil Code of the People's Republic of China*, the civil law system also includes the *Copyright Law of the People's Republic of China*, *Trademark Law of the People's Republic of China*, *Patent Law of the People's Republic of China* and others.

【Knowledge Expansion】

The Civil Code of the People's Republic of China

3. Criminal Law System

Generally speaking, the general provisions of criminal law are a normative system of general principles related to crimes, criminal responsibilities and punishments. They are the common rules that must be followed in determining crimes, determining criminal responsibilities and applying punishments. The specific provisions of criminal law are a normative system related to specific crimes and specific statutory penalties, and are standards for determining the guilt and punishment of specific behaviors. The relationship between the general provisions and the specific provisions of criminal law is one of general and specific, as the name suggested, as well as abstract and concrete. The general provisions guide the specific provisions, and the specific provisions embody the principles established by the general provisions. The two are complementary to each other. The system of criminal law refers to the composition and structure of criminal law. The current criminal law in effect in China is divided into three parts: the general provisions, the specific provisions, and the supplementary provisions. The general provisions and specific provisions each constitute a whole part. Under each part, they are divided into chapters, sections, articles, paragraphs and items in an orderly manner according to the nature and content of the legal norms. The first part containing the general provisions is divided into five chapters, namely, the task, basic principles, and scope of application of criminal law; crimes; punishments; the specific application of punishments; and other provisions. The second part containing the specific provisions is divided into ten chapters, namely, crimes endangering national security; crimes endangering public security; crimes disrupting the socialist market economic order; crimes infringing upon citizens' personal rights and democratic rights; crimes infringing upon property; crimes obstructing social management order; crimes endangering national defense interests; crimes of embezzlement and bribery; crimes of dereliction of duty; and crimes committed by military personnel in violation of their duties.

【Knowledge Expansion】

The Criminal Law of the People's Republic of China

4. Social Law System

Social law is a new category and discipline of law that has emerged in the historical trend of China's improving the legal system of the market economy, implementing the scientific outlook on development and building a socialist harmonious society in recent years. Social law is the law that is most compatible with the socialist system. Social law can play a positive role in alleviating social contradictions and maintaining social stability, and the development of social law is essential for the establishment of a harmonious society. With social construction, economic construction, political construction and cultural construction being placed in equally important positions, social law is increasingly prominent in social life. The main purpose of social law is to protect citizens' social rights, especially the interests of vulnerable groups. The establishment and improvement of social law through the rule of law is an inevitable choice. The theory and practice of social law are relatively weak in the background of deepening reform in China, improving social law, protecting citizens' social rights and achieving true liberation are of great theoretical and practical significance for building a harmonious society. China's current social laws include *the Labor Law of the People's Republic of China*, *the Labor Contract Law of the People's Republic of China*, *the Trade Union Law of the People's Republic of China*, *the Law on the Protection of Minors of the People's Republic of China*, *the Law on the Protection of the Rights and Interests of the Elderly of the People's Republic of China*, *the Law on the Protection of Women's Rights and Interests of the People's Republic of China*, *the Law on the Protection of the Rights and Interests of Disabled Persons of the People's Republic of China*, *the Mining Safety Law of the People's Republic of China*, *the Red Cross Law of the People's Republic of China*, *the Law on Donations for Public Welfare Undertakings of the People's Republic of China*, *the Law on Prevention and Control of Occupational Diseases of the People's Republic of China*, and so on.

【Knowledge Expansion】

Socialism is the most innovative social system in human history, and the socialist legal system is the most innovative legal system in human history. The socialist system of laws with Chinese characteristics is based on the Constitution as the fundamental law, and is composed of basic laws, general laws, regulations and autonomous regulations, separate regulations as well as local regulations. This legal system is in line with China's national conditions.

Section Three   Legal Guidelines International Students in Universities Must Follow

Legal compliance refers to the activities of state organs, social organizations and individual citizens to exercise their powers and rights, fulfill their responsibilities and obligations in accordance with legal provisions. In the socialist country with Chinese characteristics, all organizations and individuals are the subjects of law. All state organs and armed forces, including various political parties, various social organizations and various business entities, must abide by the laws of the People's Republic of China, enjoy legal rights and fulfill legal obligations in accordance with the law, and conduct activities within the scope prescribed by the Constitution and laws. Their legitimate rights and interests are equally protected by national laws.

1. Constitutional Rights

Constitutional rights refer to the rights determined by the Constitution or Constitutional laws. These rights are usually the most important rights, and are therefore commonly referred to as the fundamental rights of citizens. Constitutions of various countries generally provide for the rights and freedoms that citizens should enjoy. The basic Constitutional rights of citizens include the right of equality, political rights and freedoms, freedom of religious belief, personal freedom, the right to criticize, suggest, appeal, accuse and report, and the right to obtain compensation. Constitutional obligations include the obligation to serve in the army, to pay taxes, to receive education, to protect the environment, to abide by the Constitution and laws, and to work. Among them, education and work are both Constitutional rights and obligations of citizens. They are of dual attributes.

2. Marriage and Family

The first chapter in the fifth part of the *Civil Code of the People's Republic of China*, "Marriage and Family", provides detailed provisions on marriage and family relationship. Foreigners in China should understand and comply with the main provisions of Chinese laws regarding marriage and family life, and respect the positive moral views of Chinese traditions regarding marriage and family. In a family life with marriage, the couple should respect and care for parents and children, respect each other and be loyal to the family. They should actively take on family responsibilities, jointly educate their children and support their elderly parents.

【Knowledge Expansion】

Laws Related to Marriage and
Family Life

3. Consumer Rights

Law on the Protection of Consumer Rights and Interests of the People's Republic of China is a legal document that protects the rights of consumers and maintains market order while cracking down on illegal business activities. International students in China should protect their rights in consumption in accordance with the law. During the consuming process, they should not only proactively improve their awareness of consumer rights through learning but also protect their rights in accordance with laws and regulations. At the same time, the People's Republic of China strongly opposes malicious claims for compensation to maintain market order. During the consuming process, international students in China may encounter language barriers. They should effectively communicate through various means to help service providers better understand their needs so as to establish a fair, honest and lawful consumer relationship.

【Knowledge Expansion】

The Consumer Rights Protection Law of the People's Republic of China

4. Road Safety

Road Traffic Safety Law of the People's Republic of China is formulated to maintain road traffic order, prevent and reduce traffic accidents, protect personal safety, protect the property safety and other legitimate rights and interests of citizens, legal persons and other organizations, and improve traffic efficiency. In our daily life, we should put the health and lives of ourselves and others first, comply with traffic regulations and use means of transportation reasonably. In the event of a traffic accident, the accident scene should be protected and the police should be called to handle the case. When the police are handling the case, one should actively cooperate, show valid identification documents as required, truthfully report the incident and try to control their emotions. In the event of a minor traffic accident, one should actively communicate with the other party, move the vehicles to ensure that traffic is not affected. They should determine whether to contact the insurance company according to the situation, and they should also actively compensate for the other party's losses or require the other party to compensate for their own losses in accordance with the law. If a traffic accident causes bodily injury, one should dial 120 for help as soon as possible, rescue the injured and try their best to protect people's life.

【Knowledge Expansion】

*The Road Traffic Safety Law of the
People's Republic of China*

【Knowledge Expansion】

In the People's Republic of China, everyone must abide by the Constitution and laws, and act within the scope provided by the Constitution and laws. The state guarantees human rights in accordance with the law. Anyone encountering difficulties can obtain help through effective legal channels. Abiding by Chinese laws and enjoying the rights protected by Chinese laws are both the right and obligation of every foreign friend in China.

【Questions for Discussion】

1. How does the spirit of the rule of law contribute to maintaining the value of global order today?

2. Why is the principle of integrity the core value of the spirit of the rule of law?

第五章 树立职业意识 规划职业生涯

越来越多的国际生来到中国高校求学,他们中的许多人对于毕业后的发展去向犹豫不定,对于自己的职业生涯充满困惑与迷茫。在来华求学时期,必须树立起职业意识,规划好职业生涯,才能使专业学习更有针对性,才能高质量就业创业,从而获得更好的发展。

【思维导图】

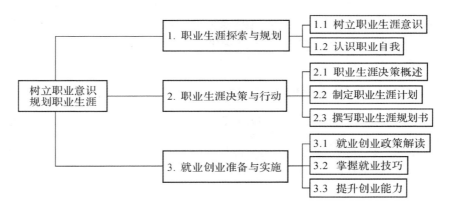

第一节 职业生涯规划与探索

一、树立职业生涯意识

(一)职业生涯规划的概念

职业生涯规划又叫职业生涯设计,是个人结合自身情况以及眼前制约的因素,为实现职业目标而确定的行动方向、行动时间和行动方案。具体来说,职业生涯规划就是在对一个人职业生涯的主、客观条件进行测定、分析、总结的基础上,对其兴趣、爱好、能力、特点进行综合分析与权衡,结合时代特点和个人的职业倾向,确定其最佳的职业奋斗目标,并为实现这一目标做出行之有效的安排。

面向高校国际生的职业生涯规划是指高校国际生在进行自我剖析的基础上进行自我定位,在全面客观地分析环境的基础上解读就业国家的政策,设定自己的职业生涯发展目标,选择实现既定目标的职业,制订相应的计划,并按照一定的时间安排,采取各种积极的行动去达成职业目标的过程。

职业生涯规划是涉及内心及行为的一种动态过程,包含确定与实施两个步骤。每个高校国际生需要明确自己的预期目标,并自觉地按照预期目标的要求,不断努力提高自身的能力和综合素质。

【知识拓展】

职业辅导之父——帕森斯

弗兰克·帕森斯(Frank Parsons),美国波士顿大学教授,被誉为美国"职业辅导之父",于 1908 年在波士顿创设职业局,并在实践中建立了"特质因素理论",他的理论著作《选择一份职业》(*Choosing a Vocation*)提出,人与职业相匹配是职业选择的要素。帕森斯的"特质因素理论"是用于职业选择的经典理论,是最早的职业指导理论。

根据"特质因素理论",假定每种人格模式的人都有相适应的职业,人人都有选择职业的机会,并且每个人的特质都可以进行客观而有效的测量。职业选择要经历以下几个步骤:一是了解个人的特质,包括自己的能力、兴趣、价值观及自身局限等;二是获取职业相关信息,分析各种职业对人的需求;三是实现人和职业的对照,选择出与个人相匹配的职业。这也是职业指导的三大要素。

(二)做好生涯规划,开启黄金人生

职业生涯规划是人对自己一生的思考,需要着眼一生,落实当前。面对国际复杂的就业形势,科学规划自身的职业发展道路,是摆在每一位高校国际生面前紧迫而现实的问题。在留学阶段,从自身实际出发,建构生涯规划的知识和能力是每一位高校国际生成长成才的必经之路。

来华求学阶段是高校国际生人生的黄金阶段,也是职业生涯规划的重要时期。主动协调学习和职业发展的关系,思考职业生涯的意义,能够帮助高校国际生在华求学期间减少漫无目的随波逐流和无所适从的徘徊不前,在错综复杂的国际环境中理清思路,增加自身发展的确定性。

职业生涯规划将伴随人的一生,具有重要意义。第一,正确的职业生涯规划能培养高校国际生树立与就业国家相对应的职业观,树立职业道德、创新意识、竞争意识、协作意识和奉献意识,形成良好的职业素养。第二,正确的职业生涯规划有助于发掘高校国际生的自我潜力,提升个人实力。正确的职业生涯规划能够引导他们认识自我、判断自我,综合分析自己的优势与劣势,对自己的价值进行准确定位,减少跨文化因素的冲击,通过树立明确的职业发展目标,评估目标与社会现实之间的差距,采取科学可行的方式提升自身的竞争力。第三,正确的职业生涯规划能帮助高校国际生增强个人发展的计划性,提升个人竞争力。职业生涯规划都是有计划、有目的的,其有助于高校国际生科学地集中时间和精力尽早准备,并为践行职业目标稳步行动,做有准备的人,无论在哪个国家就业,都能在与他人的竞争中立于不败之地。第四,正确的职业生涯规划能帮助高校国际生实现自我价值,收获有意义的人生。各个阶段职业目标的实现,能激发积极向上的人生态度,为实现人生目标而不断进取。

【观点交流】

1. 你对自己未来的人生有过规划吗?
2. 怎样才能将生命活出自己想要的样子?

二、认知职业自我

(一)职业兴趣认知

兴趣是指人们力求认识某种事物和从事某项活动的意识倾向,呈现为人们对某件事物、某项活动的选择性态度和积极的情绪反应。职业兴趣则是指个体对工作的态度和适应能力,表现为从事相关工作的兴趣和愿望。兴趣对于个人的职业行为有着巨大的推动作用,会影响个人对职业的选择,也是个人获得职业成就感和职业稳定性的重要因素。

美国职业指导专家霍兰德认为,人的兴趣、人格和职业有着非常密切的关系。他在人格类型理论中将人格类型划分为六种(见图 5-1、表 5-1)。该理论也在职业兴趣研究理论方面产生了较大的影响。

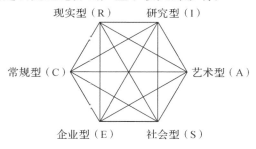

图 5-1　霍兰德六角形模型

表 5-1　霍兰德的六种人格类型划分

类　型	表　现
现实型（realistic）	动手能力强，手脚灵活，喜欢使用工具或者机器从事操作性工作，偏好于明确的、具体的技术性工作。不善言辞，做事保守，不善于与人交往。
研究型（investigative）	善于思考，求知欲强，喜欢独立的、富有创造性的工作。喜欢用智力通过逻辑分析、推理等科学地解决问题。社交要求不高，不善于领导他人。
艺术型（artistic）	想象力丰富，创造力强，喜欢用个性、自由的表现方式抒发丰富的情感，实现自身的价值。做事追求完美，不重实际。缺乏事务性办事能力，不愿服从依赖他人。
社会型（social）	乐于助人，易于合作，善于言谈。喜欢与人交往，愿意服务和教导别人。关心社会问题，责任感强，较注重社会道德和义务。往往缺乏动手能力。
企业型（enterprising）	喜欢竞争，敢冒风险，有领导才能。有较强的自我表现欲望，做事有较强的目的和动机。善于管理和说服他人。缺乏科学研究精神。
常规型（conventional）	注重实际，尊重权威，有较强的规则意识，有较好的耐心和自制力。喜欢按计划办事，喜欢有条理、系统性强的工作。不喜欢冒险和竞争，比较保守谨慎，缺乏创造力。

【知识拓展】

霍兰德人格类型理论

霍兰德(John L. Holland),美国霍普金斯大学心理学教授,也是美国著名的职业指导专家,他提出了具有广泛社会影响的人格类型理论。该理论源自人格心理学概念,是在特质因素理论基础上发展起来的人格与职业类型相匹配的理论。

霍兰德认为职业选择是个人人格的表现和延伸。该理论包含了一系列假设:人根据不同的特质可以归类为六种类型,即现实型(realistic)、研究型(investigative)、艺术型(artistic)、社会型(social)、企业型(enterprising)及常规型(conventional),根据六种类型的英文词的首字母分别简称为 R、I、A、S、E、C 型。而职业环境也可以分为相对应的六种。当人格类型与职业环境的协调性和匹配度较高时,人就能充分发挥自己的积极性,展现能力,实现价值,有较高的工作效率和满意度。

霍兰德还在该理论的基础上,建立了职业兴趣测试,人们根据测评结果,选出适合自己的职业类型。

【知识拓展】

职业兴趣测试量表

(二)职业性格认知

性格是指表现在人对现实的态度和相应的行为方式中比较稳定的、具有核心意义的个性心理特征,主要体现在对自己、对别人、对事物的态度和所采取的言行上。职业性格则是指人在长期特定的职业生活中形成的与职业相关的稳定心理特征。

职业性格会影响职业命运,不同的职业性格适合不同的职业,性格对职业的选择和发展都有着重要影响。每个人的性格不同,不能做到百分之一百匹配某项职业,但可以根据自己的职业倾向,培养和发展相对应的职业性格。科学做好职业性格分析,找出自己的职业倾向,是做好职业生涯规划的关键一环。

影响高校国际生职业性格形成、发展的因素是多方面的,是个人体质、国籍文化背景、社会生活环境、家庭教育、学校教育以及自我教育等共同作用的结果。

随着社会国际化进程的推进,高校国际生的性格也出现了加速发展的现象。为克服跨文化焦虑,不断适应留学环境,他们在对社会、对集体、对他人、对自己的态度和行为方式上迅速打破了单一应对模式,在不断地调整和完善的过程中建立起了多角度、成体系的应对机制。他们性格特征的外部表现变得更为复杂,其职业性格也更加丰富鲜明。

【知识拓展】

MBTI 性格理论

MBTI(myers briggs type indicator)性格理论由美国的心理学家 Katherine Cook Briggs(1875—1968)和她的心理学家女儿 Isabel Briggs Myers 在瑞士著名的心理分析学家 Carl G. Jung(荣格)的心理类型理论基础上,经过对人类性格差异长期观察研究而发展形成。目前 MBTI 已经成为当今全球权威的性格测试工具。

MBTI 从人际互动偏向(外向 E、内向 I),信息获取方式(感觉 S、直觉 N),决策方式(思维 T、情感 F),认知方式(判断 J、知觉 P)等四个维度的差异出发将人的性格类型分为四大类,通过两两组合,可以形成 16 种性格倾向。

【知识拓展】

MBTI 职业性格测试量表

(三)职业能力认知

能力是指顺利完成一项目标或者任务所体现出来的主观条件,是使活动顺利完成的个性心理特征。职业能力则是指在职业活动中人们顺利完成工作所需的能力。一个人的能力水平决定职业的发展成就,是影响职业发展的因素之一。

职业能力包括一般能力和特殊能力。一般能力是人们在各种职业活动中都必须具备的基本能力,如记忆力、观察力、想象力、注意力等,这是人们的基本能力,即智力,这与我们的认识活动密切相关。特殊能力则是指从事某种职业所必须具备的能力,它是判定能否胜任职业的依据,与职业活动有更加直接的联系,如教师的教学能力、司机的操作能力、会计的计算能力等。

中国在强化学生关键能力培养的过程中,则注重培养认知能力(独立思考、逻辑推理、信息加工等)、合作能力(自我管理、与人合作、集体协作等)、创新能力(积极探索、大胆尝试、创新创造等)、职业能力(爱岗敬业、知行合一等)。

不同的职业之间存在差异,不同的职业对于人的职业能力要求也各不相同。人的职业能力在很大程度上会影响人择业的自由度。如果不考虑自身的职业能力,盲目择业就业,就会影响人职业生涯的发展。因此,在择业前务必考虑职业与自己能力的匹配度,根据自己的能力类型选择适合的职业。只有做到扬长避短,方能最大限度发挥个人的作用,实现职业价值。

【知识拓展】

能力倾向和描述对照表见表 5-2。

表 5-2　能力倾向和描述对照

能力倾向	描　述
抽象推理	能够脱离具体事务的存在理解思想的能力,不是词汇和数字,而是用符号或图像表达概念
听觉辨别	区分不同声音(对音乐家尤为重要)的能力
文书能力	记录、复制、存档、校对、识别细节、避免拼写和计算错误的能力
颜色辨别	察觉颜色的相似性与不同以及感知不同深浅的颜色的能力,即观察颜色之间的协调性的能力
眼、手、足协调性	在视野范围内手足协调运动反应的能力

续表

能力倾向	描 述
手指灵活性	手指迅速、敏捷、精确地操纵微小物体的能力
形状感知	进行视觉对比、观察物体和图画的形状及阴影的细小差别的能力
语言使用	使用词汇、语法、标点的能力
机械推理	理解物理定律、机械、工具、机器设备的能力，以及进行建筑、操作、机械维修的能力
记忆	回忆已发生事件或保留学习信息的能力
运动协调性	四肢和身体在保持一定速度、姿势和精确性的情况下，有节奏地精确运动（对运动员和舞蹈演员很重要）
数字能力	迅速、准确地理解数字和进行数学推理的能力
说服能力	提供可信服的理由或劝说他人采纳自己观点的能力
身体力量	运用身体肌肉去完成搬、运、抬举重物的能力和耐力
敏捷	思维敏捷，或身体以一定速度、灵敏度和准确性运动的能力
社会技能（同感）	理解他人和与人相处的能力，感同身受地体会他人处境的能力
空间能力	在头脑中描绘各种形状和大小的三维对象的能力
拼写能力	区别拼写正误的能力
文字推理	理解文字表达的思想或概念的能力，使用文字思维和推理的能力
词汇	理解和准确使用词语含义的能力

（四）职业价值观认知

价值观是人认定事物、辨别是非的一种思维或价值取向，是我们在生活和工作中看重的原则、标准或者品质，是我们在处理价值关系时保持的立场、观点和态度的总和。职业价值观则是人对职业的认识和态度以及对职业目标的追求和向往。价值观在我们的人生和职业生涯中都起到了方向性的作用。

　　因受国别差异、家庭环境、求学经历、兴趣爱好、社会因素等影响,不同个体的职业价值观均存在不同程度的差异,但这也体现了个体的独特性。职业价值观影响着高校国际生的择业地点、择业方向、就业态度、职业行为等。现实中有很多高校国际生不知道自己真正追求的方向,因而无法制定出明确的目标,无法采取有效的行动,只会随波逐流、庸碌一生。

　　探索自己的价值观有助于认清自我,坚定自己的职业选择。人越清楚自己的价值观,职业发展目标也就越清晰,职业发展轨迹也就越顺畅,在陷入迷茫时往往更容易做出选择。了解自身的价值观有助于强化自我行动力。高校国际生可以通过不断审视自己的价值观,强化自己的分析力和判断力,提高自己的决策能力,坚守自己的职业追寻,促进自我的成长和发展,实现生命的价值。

　　无论在哪个国家求职,在进行职业选择时,高校国际生也要树立正确的价值观。一是要正确处理好个人需求与个人欲望之间的关系,切忌盲目追求名利,要搞清自己求职的目的和动机,不可因个人私欲影响职业选择。二是要认清自我,发现自己无可替代的优势,关注自身进步,万勿盲目攀比。三是要处理好自身与就业国的价值观差异,要拥有求同存异、取长补短的心态,做到在尊重他人的基础上实现自我价值。四是要以职业成长的心态面对职业生涯中的机遇和挑战,收获成长道路上的快乐和风景。五是要以社会需求为导向,树立职业无贵贱、行行出状元的思想。

【知识拓展】

罗克奇的价值观

　　米尔敦·罗克奇(Milton Rokeach),美国社会心理学家、精神病学家,密歇根州立大学教授,一生致力于价值观的研究。他将价值观分为两种,一种是终极价值观,即生存的最终状态;还有一种是工具价值观,即我们在日常生活中行动和行为的方式(见表5-3)。

表 5-3　罗克奇的价值观

终极价值观	工具价值观
舒适的生活(富足的生活)	雄心勃勃(辛勤工作、奋发向上)
振奋的生活(刺激的、积极的生活)	心胸开阔(开放)
成就感(持续的贡献)	能干(有能力、有效率)
和平的世界(没有冲突和战争)	欢乐(轻松愉快)
美丽的世界(艺术和自然的美)	清洁(卫生、整洁)
平等(兄弟情谊、机会均等)	勇敢(坚持自己的信仰)
家庭安全(照顾自己所爱的人)	宽容(谅解他人)
自由(独立、自主的选择)	助人为乐(为他人的福利工作)
幸福(满足)	正直(真挚、诚实)
内在和谐(没有内心冲突)	富于想象(大胆、有创造性)
成熟的爱(性和精神上的亲密)	独立(自力更生、自给自足)
国家的安全(免遭攻击)	智慧(有知识、善思考)
快乐(快乐的、休闲的生活)	符合逻辑(理性的)
救世(救世的、永恒的生活)	博爱(温情的、温柔的)
自尊(自重)	顺从(有责任感、尊重的)
社会承认(尊重、赞赏)	礼貌(有礼的、性情好)
真挚的友谊(亲密关系)	负责(可靠的)
睿智(对生活有成熟的理解)	自我控制(自律的、约束的)

第二节　职业生涯决策与行动

一、职业生涯决策概述

(一)职业生涯决策的影响因素

职业生涯决策是指对职业生涯事件做出决定和选择的过程。职业生涯到处充满抉择。认识生涯决策,学习生涯决策,能帮助我们提升解决问题的能力,帮助我们的职业生涯走向成熟。职业生涯决策是一个复杂的认知过程,不同的因素会影响个人的生涯选择和生涯决定,每一个决策都是各种因素共同作用的结果。

第一是个人因素。个人的心理特征和自我认识对职业决策有着定向作用，包括个体的性格、能力、兴趣、价值观等。个体的智力、种族、年龄、性别、学习背景、经历的事件差异也会造成不同的决策结果。此外，做决策时的即时状态也是影响因素之一，包括身体状态、精神状态、情绪状态等。

第二是家庭和成长环境因素。每个人的家庭和成长环境均存在差异，生长的国家、父母的价值观、行为习惯、人生态度、教育方式等都会造成个人认知的差异，会对人的职业决策产生直接或者间接的影响。朋友群体和生活圈的认知方式、行为特点等也会影响个人的职业偏好。

第三是社会因素。国别、历史、政治、经济、文化都会影响个人职业决策的形成。社会主流的职业价值观、用人单位的用工需求都能够干扰个人有效决策的形成。

(二)科学的职业生涯决策的基本原则

可行性。职业生涯决策与规划必须目标清晰、明确、具体化，应该在自我评估和环境评估的基础上进行，要考虑决策是否与自身的能力、性格、兴趣和价值观相匹配。同时，需要预判职业决策的达成度，既要具有挑战性，又要确保可行性，根据职业决策制订科学的行动计划。

发展性。职业决策并不是唯一的，也不是一成不变的。职业生涯发展可分为若干个阶段，需要不停地做出职业决策，需要根据现实效果，不断调整策略，扬长避短，注重优选，遵循效益。

社会性。职业决策必须遵循社会发展规律，考虑职业决策对社会发展的影响，要将个人价值融入社会价值中去，将为国际社会做贡献作为终身目标。

二、制订生涯行动计划

(一)合理划分职业发展阶段

高校国际生在毕业后的职业选择主要可以分为在中国就业、在中国创业以及回国发展等。但是，他们大部分都缺乏职业生涯规划的意识，鲜少有人会制订职业生涯行动计划，常常会随大流。然而，计划是行动的引领，行动是成功的前提。制订科学有效的生涯行动计划可以帮助我们少走弯路，直面成功。

职业生涯发展规划的关键是对将来的立业和发展建立的阶段进行细分，选择适合自己的目标，做出大致合理的规划安排。

不同职业生涯阶段的根本区别在于个性心理特征和职业发展需求不同，这是划分职业生涯发展阶段的主要依据。职业生涯阶段划分因人而异，不仅仅以年龄作为依据。高校国际生需要根据自己的实际，参考职业发展阶段的特征来划分自己的生涯发展阶段。例如，将留学生涯列入职业准备阶段，毕业后三至五年列入职业初期，以后每五年作为一个阶段。

【知识拓展】

舒伯生涯发展理论

舒伯(Donald E. Super)，美国著名的职业生涯规划师，在职业规划与生涯教育领域做出了无与伦比的不朽贡献，在生涯发展理论的推演中，产生了无可替代的影响。帕森斯的特质因素论所关注的焦点集中在职业选择上，而舒伯则更多地关注生涯发展的问题。

舒伯认为职业生涯是一个人长期而又发展的过程，一个人在不同的发展阶段有不同的职业需求，他将人的职业生涯发展划分为五个阶段：成长期、探索期、建立期、维持期、衰退期。

经过不断研究，舒伯还提出了生活广度、生活空间的生涯发展观。在原有的发展阶段理论上，舒伯还增加了角色理论，并将生涯发展阶段与角色间交互的影响绘制成了生涯彩虹图（见图 5-2）。

（二）逐级分解职业发展目标

职业生涯目标是指个人在选定的职业领域内、未来时点上所要达到的具体目标，是人生的指南针。明确的职业目标是获取职业成功的前提。职业生涯的发展是一场持久战，目标分解是将目标清晰化、具体化的过程，是将目标量化成可操作方案的有效手段。

目标分解帮助个体在现实环境和美好愿望之间建立起快速通道。将目标细化和分解是实现目标非常重要的方法。如图 5-3 所示，可以按时间分

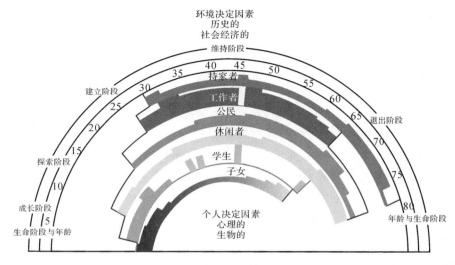

图 5-2　生涯彩虹图

解来分解目标。

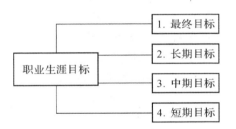

图 5-3　职业生涯目标分解

(三)制订行动计划

制订行动计划可以采用 3W 方法,即回答要做些什么(what)、怎样达到(how)、什么时候完成(when)三个问题,将行动计划逐条落实。

制订行动计划一般包含六个步骤:

(1)明确各阶段具体目标。

(2)确定行动内容、所需的资源和责任。

(3)制订行动时刻表。

(4)预测结果,制订应变方案。

(5)按照时间顺序列出详细的行动计划。

(6)以分阶段的具体目标为基础,实施、监督执行并作出评估。

行动计划可用表格的形式呈现(见表 5-4)。

表 5-4　行动计划

计划名称	总目标	分目标	计划内容
短期计划	毕业时要达到的目标	各个留学阶段要达到的目标或某方面要达到的目标	语言能力、专业学习、职业实践、职业技能培养、熟悉就业国政策等
中期计划	毕业后第五年要达到的目标	毕业后一至五年分别要达到的目标或某方面要达到的目标	就业环境调整、职场适应、资源积累、岗位升迁等
长期计划	中年要达到的目标	毕业后十年,二十年要达到的目标	事业发展、身心健康、家庭生活、子女教育等

留学期间应制订具体详细的计划,包括年计划、学期计划、月计划、周计划等。除了提升专业能力,还应考虑自己整体的学习计划、勤工助学、社会实践活动、技能培训等问题。通过自我剖析、学习训练、竞技竞赛等手段,努力提升职业能力和水平,开发想象力和创造力。在社会交往锻炼中增强自身的情商、自信心、跨文化接受能力、抗压能力和心理承受能力,为行动计划的有效实施注入力量。

【观点交流】

1.你目前处于职业生涯发展的哪个阶段?
2.你现阶段的发展目标和任务是什么?

三、撰写职业生涯规划书

(一)职业生涯规划书的形式和内容

职业生涯规划书是职业生涯规划的书面呈现,有助于更加清晰地理清规划思路,对留学生接下去的职业生涯发展起到指导和鞭策的作用。一份完整的职业生涯规划书需要包含的内容见表 5-5。

表 5-5　职业生涯规划书包含的内容

项目	内容
封面和扉页	包括题目、个人信息、目录、年限等
职业方向和总体目标	确定目标对于职业生涯发展有引导作用,是职业生涯发展的关键。有效的职业生涯规划设计必须要有明确可行的目标
自我分析	主要包括对自身职业兴趣、职业性格、职业能力、职业价值观等方面的测评结果,同时认清自己的跨文化适应能力,了解自己的优势和劣势
环境分析	主要包括对就业国家政治、经济、文化,社会环境,行业发展,企业环境等外部环境的分析,考虑国别差异和文化因素的冲击,以保证职业生涯规划的科学性
角色建议	记录他人对自己的评价以及对自己职业生涯发展影响较大的人的意见和建议
目标分解	将职业生涯中的远大目标分解为有一定时间规定的阶段性分目标
实施方案	找出自身与实现目标之间的差距,制定具体方案,逐步缩小差距,实现各阶段的分目标
评估调整	如果在实施过程中发现目标差距要及时修正和调整实施方案和计划。尤其是对在他国学习、就业的高校国际生来说,更要重点关注阶段目标的实现情况以确保职业计划的可实现性

(二)职业生涯规划书的编写原则和技巧

信息明确。一份有效的职业生涯规划书,首先要确定自己的基本信息,包括姓名(英文＋中文)、国别、年龄、专业、学校、职业最终目标、职业路径、职业规划年限等方面,这些应该在计划书的扉页都能够体现出来,让读者清晰明了,阅读正文之前就心中有数。

完整详细。职业生涯规划书要包括自我评价、环境评估、职业目标、实施方案、评估反馈等多项内容,要求真实完整,充分分析自我,充分认识环境对自己职业的影响,尤其是国际环境对自身发展的影响,且需要具有个人特点,适合自身的发展。

科学有据。要了解测评理论和知识,合理利用测评工具,分析测评结果,根据自身条件和就业环境实际做出职业决策,做到人职匹配。过程要有理有据,图文并茂,增加可信度和说服力。

合理可行。职业目标要高低适宜,要结合社会需要,既要有激励作用,又要合理可行。职业行动计划要具备可操作性,不可空想,脱离现实。确定目标时可以采用生涯人物访谈方式作为参考,通过访谈了解行业内精英的职业发展路径,也可以向和自己有类似经历的国际友人咨询职业发展经验,从而确定自己的职业发展目标,并结合调研了解各个职业阶段的需求,对照自身,合理分解目标,为计划实施做好准备。

评估反馈。评估反馈是生涯规划的计划调整、修正反馈的手段。在评估反馈的内容中,主要撰写方法和手段,在计划实施的过程中遇到阻碍如何解决。对不同时期的目标设定可以提出备选方案,备选方案要和本来的职业目标有一定的关联性。

清晰连贯。全文要行文流畅,用词精准,条理清晰,必要时可以用多语言版本,围绕职业目标这条主线层层展开,体现论述的逻辑连贯性。

创意新颖。要充分体现个性,反映自身的精神面貌,不能依样画瓢、千篇一律。

【模板范本】

职业生涯规划书范本

第三节　就业创业准备与实施

一、就业创业政策解读

(一)国家层面

作为引导高校国际生毕业去向的风向标,就业政策直接影响着高校国际生的职业选择。近年来,越来越多的高校国际生选择来到中国求学。随着国家综合实力的增强,中国以更积极主动、灵活包容、开放自信的态度,解决高校国际生毕业后在华就业问题。

2016 年 2 月,中共中央办公厅、国务院办公厅印发《关于加强外国人永久居留服务管理的意见》,提出要"放宽外国优秀留学生在华工作限制,为其毕业后在中国境内工作和申请永久居留提供渠道"。

2016 年 3 月,中共中央印发《关于深化人才发展体制机制改革的意见》,提出要充分开发利用国内国际人才资源,主动参与国际人才竞争,完善更加开放、更加灵活的人才培养、吸引和使用机制,同时提出要对外国人才来华签证、居留,放宽条件,简化程序,落实相关待遇等。

2017 年 1 月,人力资源和社会保障部、外交部、教育部《关于允许优秀外籍高校毕业生在华就业有关事项的通知》明确规定,在中国境内高校取得硕士及以上学位且毕业一年以内的外国留学生,以及在境外知名高校取得硕士及以上学位且毕业一年以内的外籍毕业生,凡年满 18 周岁,身体健康,无犯罪记录,学习成绩优秀,平均成绩不低于 80 分(百分制,其他分制换算成百分制处理)或 B+/B(等级制)及以上,毕业后所从事的工作与所学专业对口,均可申请外国人就业许可证。

2017 年 7 月,《外国人来华工作分类标准(试行)》(外专发〔2017〕40 号文)规定,40 岁以下在国(境)外高水平大学或中国境内高校从事博士后研究的青年人才可认定为"优秀青年人才",列入"外国高端人才(A 类)",实行"绿色通道"和"容缺受理"服务,可以先申请人才签证,入境后凭人才签证办理外国人来华工作许可。

2019 年 7 月,《公安部 12 条移民与出入境便利政策》规定,国内重点高等院校本科及以上学历的优秀留学生,毕业后在中国从事创新创业活动的,可凭毕业证和创新创业证明材料,向公安机关出入境管理部门申请有效期为 2 至 5 年的居住证。

2022 年 8 月,根据国家移民管理局消息,具有博士学位、在中国境内工作的外籍华人,可向公安机关出入境管理部门申请在华永久居留,其外籍配偶和未成年子女可随同申请。该政策在全国范围内实施,无地域限制。

(二)地方层面

随着来华留学教育的不断发展,各个地区积极响应国家政策,北京和上海作为高校国际生最多、经济发展对外籍人才的需求较大的代表型城市,在 2015 年就开始探索外籍人才的就业创业政策,引领了高校国际生在华就业创业新局面。

2015 年 7 月,公安部推出支持上海科技创新中心建设系列出入境政策措施。政策支持外国留学生在我国高等院校应届毕业后直接在上海创新创业，吸引在华外籍优秀高校毕业生的智力资源；进一步简化来上海创新创业外国人的入境和居留手续，从境外吸引外国人才资源；扩大长期居留许可签发范围，使在上海工作的外国人享受更为稳定的长期居留预期。通过以上措施，放宽外籍创新创业人员停留居留期限，扩大停留居留证件签发范围，给其创业创新以充分的空间和时间。

2016 年 1 月，公安部又发布了支持北京创新发展的 20 项出入境政策措施（简称"中关村新政 20 条"）。为了更好地吸纳全球优秀青年人才，政策提出吸引国际知名高校外籍优秀毕业生来京创新创业，为其提供签证等便利化服务。

2020 年 7 月 1 日，上海市人力资源和社会保障局发布了《关于做好优秀外籍高校毕业生来沪工作等有关事项的通知》（简称"沪 2020"），支持在上海地区高校取得本科及以上学历的国际生可在中国（上海）自由贸易试验区、中国（上海）自由贸易试验区临港新片区、虹桥商务区、张江国家自主创新示范区，以及"上海科技创新职业清单"内用人单位工作。在中国境内高校取得硕士及以上学位的优秀高校国际生可在本市直接工作。

（三）政策落地

随着中央文件的出台和地方政策的颁布，高校国际生在中国就业的渠道不断拓宽，各地通过举办招聘会鼓励优秀高校国际生在华就业，高校也纷纷成立高校国际生就业指导中心来推进高校国际生的在华就业工作。

教育部留学服务中心于 2016 年在北京大学举办了首届来华留学人才招聘会。招聘会得到了用人单位和高校国际生的积极响应。自此开始，教育部留学服务中心先后举办了多场面向来华高校国际生的人才招聘会，前来应聘的高校国际生人数也呈逐年增加的态势，中国已经成为高校国际生工作的重要目的地之一。

国际青年创新创业计划（简称"藤蔓计划"）自 2017 年在北京启动至今，参加活动的国际青年已经有上万人次。这个项目发挥了中国的创新科技产业优势，帮助各国青年人对接实习考察，孵化创业项目，帮助和培养了一大批国际青年企业家，大大激发了各国青年人创新创业的热情。

【知识拓展】

藤蔓计划

"藤蔓计划"是由中关村"一带一路"产业促进会策划实施的一项服务于国际青年的国际创新创业项目。其宗旨是为发挥各类人才智慧,聚天下英才而用之。"藤蔓计划"有一个愿景叫"百千万",未来希望能够有超过一万名国际青年在"一带一路"合作交流当中真正发挥作用,像藤蔓一样在各国衍生。

通过实习对接、精准派送、考察培训、创业孵化、国际青年企业家培养计划等方式,"藤蔓计划"为高校国际生创造了与中国创新科技企业面对面沟通和交流的机会,帮助他们与相关企业建立起了紧密的工作关系。既为中国企业快速找到了"一带一路"建设的国际化人才,也让高校国际生近距离融入"一带一路"建设当中,为高校国际生在华创新发展提供了支持。

【观点交流】

你如何看待中国的就业政策?

二、掌握就业技巧

(一)收集就业信息

受全球经济形势影响,就业形势日渐严峻,就业压力不断增加。对于毫无就业经历且不熟悉就业国家政策的高校国际生来说,由于缺乏正确的求职方法和技巧,往往会在求职的过程中感到迷茫和手足无措。

获取求职信息是完成就业的基础条件和必要途径。真实可靠、种类丰富的求职信息能够帮助高校国际生在求职过程中少走弯路,做出合理的定位和选择。就业竞争很多时候就是信息的竞争,对于高校国际生来说,及时了解和掌握就业国家的就业政策和就业管理工作流程对于提高就业成功率有很大影响。

高校国际生必须清楚的求职信息主要有:当地就业政策,用人单位的业务范围和地理分布、企业文化、组织架构、员工规模、薪酬体系,以及具体的工作岗位、语言需求和能力要求,为员工提供的培训和发展空间等。只有全面了解上述信息,才能结合自己的优势和特长找到匹配度更高的工作岗位。

高校国际生要牢牢把握毕业阶段的黄金时机,通过各种渠道收集求职信息,做好充分的就业准备(见图 5-4)。

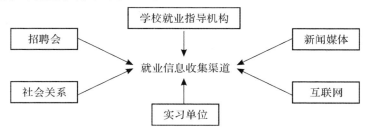

图 5-4 就业信息收集渠道

(二)准备就业材料

准备就业材料是求职过程中必不可少的一环,是用人单位了解求职人员情况的第一渠道,会在很大程度上影响求职的成败。我们需要做好以下几方面的材料准备。

(1)个人简历。个人简历的撰写要做到思路清晰、简单明了、实事求是,需要包括个人基本信息、教育背景、个人特长、所获荣誉、技能证书、实习实践经历、求职意向、自我评价等。此外,还需根据就业国情况,准备多语言版本的简历。

(2)求职信。求职信是求职人员为了获得心仪的岗位有目的地对用人单位表达求职愿望的信函,它需要包含两个要素:一是岗位意向;二是自己竞争这个岗位的优势。要尽可能做到言辞贴切,真诚感人。

(3)成绩单。成绩单是反映高校国际生在校期间学习状况的有效材料,是展现高校国际生学习能力的重要证明。高校国际生成绩单应有中英文两个版本,由学校教务部门出具并盖章。

(4)各类证书。这包括高校国际生在校期间获取的各类竞赛获奖证书、语言能力证书、职业技能证书和各类从业资格证,担任学生干部的证明,研究成果证明,论文发表证明等。

(5)社会实践证明。这里包括高校国际生参加相关社会实践和单位实习的相关材料等。实习实践材料可以帮助用人单位审查高校国际生相关工作能力,不可或缺。

【模板范本】

求职简历范本

三、提升创业能力

（一）创业计划书的撰写

创业计划书也叫商业计划书，是对创业项目有关事项进行全方位统筹的书面材料，全面介绍了企业和项目运作情况、经营思想、商业战略、前景展望、人力财力、营销策略等。创业计划书的制定为创业项目提供了完整详细、具体深入的行动指南。

一份完整的创业计划书一般包含以下的基本内容：计划摘要、项目背景、公司及其产品或服务、团队介绍、市场调研和分析、发展规划、风险应对等。

（1）摘要。应当包括对企业理念、商业战略、目标市场、优势分析等多要点的概括。

（2）立项背景。主要包括行业背景、市场发展趋势和市场空间、时机与机遇。

（3）项目概况（产品与服务）。主要包括项目介绍、消费人群、关键技术、客户价值、核心优势、品牌专利、行业认可、发展方向等。

（4）团队优势与组织架构。主要包括关键管理人员介绍（权利和义务、职责和才能），团队组建的优势（成员教育、实践、工作背景、创新能力、价值观念、互补情况等）。

（5）市场分析。主要包括市场容量分析（客户数量、单位销售额以及总销售额等）、竞争分析（竞争对手的优势和不足）、市场调研及前景分析（目标客户和所规划的市场前景、销售量、销售收入、市场份额和利润等）、营销策略（制定产品、定价、促销、渠道等问题的发展战略和实施计划）。

（6）发展规划及社会效益。主要包括创业以来不同阶段的发展情况、未来发展目标、社会效益及带动就业情况。

（7）财务分析与融资计划。主要包括项目预算、预计收益、融资计划。

（8）风险与对策。主要包括各种潜在风险的预判和应对措施。

（9）项目附件材料及其他。主要包括营业执照副本、组织机构代码扫描件、政府批文、公司章程、专利证书、市场调研资料等。

【知识拓展】

第九届中国国际"互联网＋"大学生创新创业大赛
赛事通知、评审标准

中国"互联网＋"大学生创新创业大赛是由李克强总理在 2015 年倡导发起，由教育部等 12 个中央部委和地方省级人民政府共同主办的重大创新创业赛事。大赛旨在深化高等教育综合改革，激发大学生的创造力，培养造就"大众创业、万众创新"的生力军，推动赛事成果转化，促进"互联网＋"新业态形成，主动服务经济提质增效升级，以创新引领创业、创业带动就业，推动高校毕业生更高质量创业就业。

2020 年大赛更名为中国国际"互联网＋"大学生创新创业大赛。大赛以赛促学，培养创新创业生力军，旨在激发学生的创造力，激励广大青年扎根中国大地了解国情民情，锤炼意志品质，开拓国际视野，在创新创业中增长智慧才干，把激昂的青春梦融入伟大的中国梦，努力成长为德才兼备的有为人才。以赛促教，探索素质教育新途径。把大赛作为深化创新创业教育改革的重要抓手，引导各类学校主动服务国家战略和区域发展，深化人才培养综合改革，全面推进素质教育，切实提高学生的创新精神、创业意识和创新创业能力。推动人才培养范式深刻变革，形成新的人才质量观、教学质量观、质量文化观。以赛促创，搭建成果转化新平台。推动赛事成果转化和产学研用紧密结合，促进"互联网＋"新业态形成，服务经济高质量发展，努力形成高校毕业生更高质量创业就业的新局面。

第九届中国国际"互联网"大学生
创新创业大赛通知

（二）新企业的设立

一个新企业需要获取合法的身份才能开展生产经营活动。高校国际生要在中国创建公司，必须详细了解公司注册的法定程序和工作流程，并且针对每一个流程做好相关准备工作，以保证企业申办的顺利进行。

注册公司需要准备以下材料：个人资料，注册资金，拟定注册公司名称若干，公司经营范围，租房房产证、租赁合同，公司住所，股东名册及联系电话、地址，公司机构及其产生办法、职权、议事规则，公司章程。

公司注册登记开办流程如图 5-5 所示。

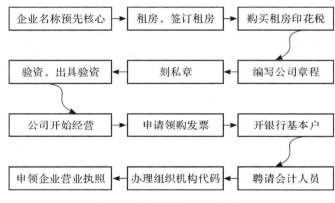

图 5-5　公司注册登记开办流程

【知识拓展】

公司注册时的命名

按照《工商总局关于提高登记效率积极推进企业名称登记管理改革的意见》（工商企注字〔2017〕54 号）的相关规定，根据禁止性规范，企业名称不得与同一企业登记机关已登记注册、核准的同行业企业名称相同；企业名称不得含有有损于国家、社会公共利益的内容和文字；企业名称不得含有可能对公众造成欺骗或者误解的内容和文字；企业名称不得含有外国国家（地区）名称、国际组织名称；企业名称不得含有政党名称、党政军机关名称、群团组织名称、社会组织名称及部队番号；企业名称应当使用符合国家规范的汉字，不得使用外文、字母和阿拉伯数字等；根据限制性规则，企业名称不得与同一企业登记机关已登记注册、核准的同行业企业名称近似,但有投资关系的除外;企业法人名称中不得含有其他非营利法人的名称,但有投资关系或者经该法人授权,且使用该法人简称或者特定称谓的除外。该法人的简称或者特定称谓有其他含义或者指向不确定的,可以不经授权;企业名称中不得含有另一个企业名称,但有投资关系或者经该企业授权,且使用该企业的简称或者特定称谓的除外;企业名称不得明示或者暗示为非营利组织或者超出企业设立的目的,但有其他含义或者法律、法规以及国务院决定另有规定的除外;除国务院决定设立的企业外,企业名称不得冠以"中国""中华""全国""国家""国际"等字样;在企业名称中间使用"中国""中华""全国""国家""国际"等字样的,该字样应是行业的限定语;使用外国(地区)出资企业字号的外商独资企业、外方控股的外商投资企业,可以在名称中间使用"(中国)"字样。以上三类企业名称须经工商总局核准,但在企业名称中间使用"国际"字样的除外等。

【案例分析】

阿里巴巴的诞生与马云

1995 年年初,阿里巴巴集团创始人马云去美国首次接触到互联网。对电脑一窍不通的马云,在朋友的帮助和介绍下开始认识互联网。1999 年 3 月,马云正式辞去公职,和他的团队回杭州,决定创办一家能为全世界中小企业服务的电子商务站点。他们以 50 万元人民币开始了新一轮创业,开发阿里巴巴网站。

阿里巴巴成立初期,公司小到不能再小。他们没有租写字楼,就在马云家里办公,最多的时候一个房间里坐了 35 个人。马云规定,每个员工必须把房子租在离他家五分钟可以到达的路程之内。他们每天花费 16～18 个小时野兽一般在马云家里疯狂工作,日夜不停地设计网页,讨论网页和构思,困了就席地而卧。马云不断鼓动员工,"发令枪一响,你可不会有时间去看对手是怎么跑的,你只有一路狂奔"。他又告诫员工"最大的失败是放弃,最大的敌人是自己,最大的对手是时间"。阿里巴巴就这样孕育、诞生在马云家中。

从 1995 年接触网络到 1999 年阿里巴巴问世,马云用了五年的时间,经历了两次失败才获得了第一阶段的成功。面对困境应该如何生存,马云的回答是"靠毅力取得最大的成功"。回首过去的经历,马云坦言,第一你要相信你能存活,第二你要相信你有坚强的存活毅力。阿里巴巴跟任何中小企业一样,在1999年、2000年、2001年也曾面临发不出工资的困境,当时他们没有什么收入,但要活下去,马云告诉自己和他的员工们,就是半跪着也要坚持,坚持到底就是胜利,让自己做最后一个倒下的人。

【思考题】

1. 职业生涯发展的主要影响因素有哪些? 结合自己的实际谈谈在职业生涯发展中如何发挥主观因素的作用。

2. 想一想,接下来你将如何全面提升自身的就业综合实力?

3. 假如你决定创业,你选择什么样的项目作为你的经营内容,为什么?

Chapter Five　Establishing Vocational Consciousness and Planning Career Path

More and more international students come to study in Chinese universities, and many of them are uncertain about their career path after graduation. They are full of confusion and bewilderment about their professional development. During their studies in China, it is necessary for them to establish a professional consciousness and plan their career path in order to make their professional learning more targeted, and help them to achieve high-quality employment and entrepreneurship and thereby obtain better development in the future.

【Mind Map】

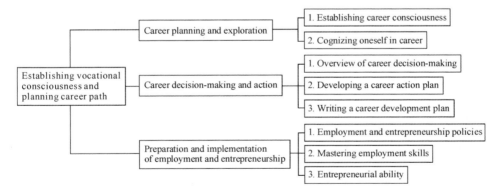

Section One　Career Planning and Exploration

1. Establishing Career Consciousness

(1) The Concept of Career Planning

Career planning, also known as career design, is an action plan developed by individuals based on their own situation and constraints to achieve their career goals. Specifically, career planning refers to deciding one's optimal career goal and making effective arrangements to achieve this goal based on the subjective and objective conditions of an individual's career. Career planning demands comprehensively analyzing and weighing one's interests, hobbies, abilities and characteristics and combining personal career preferences with the characteristics of the era.

Career planning for international students in universities is a goal-oriented process including the following steps: self-positioning based on self-analysis, comprehensively and objectively analyzing the environment, interpreting the country's policies of employment, setting career development goals, selecting careers to achieve the set goals, devising corresponding plans, and taking positive actions to achieve career goals within a set time frame.

Career planning is a dynamic process that involves both determination and implementation. Each international student in universities needs to have clear goals and consciously work to improve their abilities and overall quality according to the requirements of these goals.

【Knowledge Expansion】

Father of Career Counseling—Parsons

Frank Parsons, a professor at Boston University in the United States, is known as the "father of career counseling". In 1908, he founded the

Vocational Bureau in Boston and developed the "Trait-and-Factor Theory" in practice. His book *Choosing a Vocation* proposed that the match between individuals and their chosen profession is a key factor in career selection. Parsons' "Trait-and-Factor Theory" has been a classic theory for career selection and the earliest career guidance theory.

According to the "Trait-and-Factor Theory", it is assumed that each type of personality is suitable for certain professions, everyone has the opportunity to choose a career and each person's traits can be objectively and effectively measured. The career selection process involves several steps: first, understanding one's own traits, including abilities, interests, values and limitations; second, obtaining career-related information and analyzing the needs of various professions; and third, comparing individuals with professions and selecting a profession that matches their traits. These are the three main elements of career guidance.

(2) Making a Good Career Plan and Opening up a Golden Life

Career planning is a lifetime reflection on oneself, requiring one to focus on the long-term while to implement in the present. In face of the complex international job market, scientifically planning one's own career development path is an urgent and practical issue for every international student in universities. During the stage of studying abroad, obtaining the knowledge and skills of career planning based on one's own condition is a necessary path for every international student to grow and succeed.

The stage of studying in China is the golden age of life for international students and an important period for career planning. Actively coordinating the relationship between learning and career development and thinking about the significance of one's career can help international students reduce aimless wandering, clarify their thoughts in the complex international environment and increase the certainty of their own development.

Career activities will accompany a person throughout their life and are of great significance. Firstly, a correct career planning can help the international students to establish a professional concept corresponding to the country they wish to work in, establish professional consciousness of ethics, innovation, competition, cooperation and dedication, and build up good professional qualification. Secondly, it helps to tap into the potential of international students and enhance their personal strength. Correct career planning can guide them to understand and judge themselves, analyze their own strengths and weaknesses comprehensively, accurately locate their own value, reduce the impact of cross-cultural factors, evaluate the gap between their goals and social reality, and adopt scientific and feasible ways to enhance their competitiveness. Thirdly, it helps international students enhance their personal development planning and their competitiveness. Career planning is thoughtful and purposeful, which helps one to concentrate time and energy so as to prepare early and take steady action to achieve career goals. No matter where they work, they can stand undefeated in the competition with others. Fourthly, it helps international students realize their own value and gain a meaningful life. Achieving career goals in each stage can inspire a positive and upward attitude towards life and encourage international students to strive to achieve their life goals.

【Opinion Exchange】

1. Have you made plans for your future life?
2. How can you live your life the way you want it to be?

2. Recognizing Oneself in Career

(1)Career Interest Cognition

Interests refer to the conscious tendency of individuals to seek knowledge of something and engage in certain activities, manifested as their selective attitudes and positive emotional responses towards certain things or activities. Career interests refer to an individual's attitude and adaptability to work, manifested as their interest and desire to engage in related work. Interests play a huge role in an individual's career behavior, affecting their career choices and serving as important factors for achieving career satisfaction and stability.

According to American career guidance expert John Holland, interests, personality and careers are closely related. He classified personality into six categories (see Fig. 5-1 and Tab. 5-1). His theory has had a significant impact on the research of career interests.

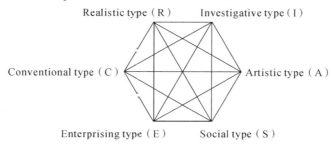

Fig. 5-1   Holland's Hexagon Model

Table 5-1   Holland's Six Categories of Personality

Types	Manifestations
Realistic	Strong hands-on ability, flexible hands and feet, like to use tools or machines for operational work, and prefer clear and specific technical work. Not good at words, conservative in actions, not good at socializing with others.
Investigative	Good at thinking, with a strong thirst for knowledge, and enjoy independent and creative work. Enjoy using intelligence to scientifically solve problems through logical analysis, reasoning, etc. Not having high social demands and not being good at leading others.
Artistic	Rich imagination, strong creativity, like to express rich emotions with personality and freedom of expression emotion, realizing one's own value. Pursue perfection in doing things, not practicality. Lack of transactional skills, unwilling to obey and rely on others.

continued

Types	Manifestations
Social	Willing to help others, easy to cooperate, and good at speaking. Enjoy socializing with people and am willing to serve and teach others. Concerned about social issues, with a strong sense of responsibility, and a greater emphasis on social morality and obligations. Often lacking hands-on skills.
Enterprising	Like competition, dare to take risks, and have leadership skills. Have a strong desire for self-expression, and have a strong purpose and motivation for doing things. Good at managing and persuading others. Lack of scientific research spirit.
Conventional	Pay attention to reality, respect authority, have a strong sense of rules, have good patience and self-control. Enjoy working according to plans and enjoy organized and systematic work. Not fond of adventure and competition, relatively conservative and cautious, lacking creativity.

【Knowledge Expansion】

Holland's Personality Type Theory

John L. Holland, a psychology professor at Johns Hopkins University in the United States and a well-known career guidance expert, proposed a personality type theory that has had a broad social impact. The theory originates from the concept of personality psychology. It is theory that matches personality with occupational types on the basis of the "Trait-and-Factor Theory".

Holland believes that career choice is an expression and extension of an individual's personality. The theory includes a series of assumptions. People can be classified into six types based on different traits: realistic, investigative, artistic, social, enterprising, and conventional, abbreviated as R, I, A, S, E, and C types respectively. The occupational environment can also be divided into the corresponding six types. When the coordination and matching between personality type and occupational environment are high in degree, individuals can fully display their enthusiasm, demonstrate their abilities, realize their vaue and have higher work efficiency and satisfaction.

Based on this theory, Holland also developed a career interest test, which enables people to choose the appropriate occupational type based on the test results.

【Knowledge Expansion】

Professional Interest Assessment Scale

(2)Career Personality Cognition

Personality refers to the relatively stable core personal traits revealed in one's attitude towards reality and their behavior patterns. It can be seen in a person's attitudes and corresponding behavior towards oneself, others and things. Career personality refers to the stable psychological characteristics related to a specific career that a person has developed over long-term work experience.

Career personality can affect one's career development, and different career personalities are suitable for different occupations. Personality has an important influence on career choice and development. Although each person's personality is different, they can cultivate and develop a corresponding career personality based on their career tendencies. Conducting a scientific analysis of career personality and identifying one's career tendencies is a key part of career planning.

There are many factors that influence the formation and development of international students' career personalities, including individual physical condition, national cultural background, social life environment, family education, school education and self-education, etc.

With the advancement of globalization, international students' personalities have also accelerated in development. To overcome cross-cultural anxiety and constantly adapt to the study environment abroad, they have rapidly broken through the single response mode in their attitudes and behaviors towards society, groups, others and themselves. In the continuous process of adjustment and improvement, they have established a multi-angle, systematic coping mechanism. The external manifestations of their personality traits have become more complex, and their career personalities have become richer and more distinctive.

【Knowledge Expansion】

The MBTI (Myers Briggs Type Indicator) Personality Theory

The Myers Briggs Type Indicator (MBTI) personality theory was developed by American psychologists Katherine Cook Briggs (1875—1968) and her daughter, psychologist Isabel Briggs Myers, based on the psychological type theory put forward by the famous Swiss psychoanalyst Carl G. Jung. The theory was developed through long-term observation and research on human personality differences. MBTI has become a globally recognized personality testing tool.

MBTI divides personality into four main categories based on differences in interpersonal interaction preferences (Extraverted E, Introverted I), information gathering methods (Sensing S, Intuition N), decision-making styles (Thinking T, Feeling F), and cognitive styles (Judging J, Perceiving P). By combining these four dimensions in pairs, 16 types pf personality can be identified.

【Knowledge Expansion】

MBTI Occupational Personality Test Questions

(3)Career Ability Cognition

Ability refers to the subjective conditions reflected in successfully achieving a goal or completing task, and it is a personal psychological characteristic that enables activities to be carried out smoothly. Career ability refers to the ability required for people to successfully complete their work in their profession. A person's ability determines their career development achievements.

Career ability includes general abilities and specific abilities. General abilities are basic abilities that people must possess in various professional activities, such as memory, observation, imagination and attention. These are people's basic abilities, i. e. , intelligence, which is closely related to our cognitive activities. Specific abilities refer to the ability required for a certain profession, and it is the basis for judging whether one is qualified for the profession and it has a more direct connection with career activities. Examples of specific abilities include teaching ability for teachers, operational ability for drivers and calculation ability for accountants.

In the process of promoting students' key abilities, China emphasizes the cultivation of cognitive abilities (independent thinking, logical reasoning, information processing, etc.), cooperation abilities (self-management, collaboration with others, collective cooperation, etc.), innovation abilities (active exploration, bold experimentation, innovative creation, etc.), and professional abilities (dedication to work, integration of knowledge and action, etc.).

There are differences among different professions, and the

requirements for career abilities for different professions are also different. A person's career abilities will greatly affect their freedom in choosing a career. If one blindly chooses a career without considering their own career abilities, it will affect the development of their career. Therefore, before choosing a career, it is necessary to consider the degree of matching between the profession and one's own abilities, and choose a suitable career based on one's own ability type, to give play to one's strengths and avoid weaknesses, and thus maximize one's personal effectiveness and achieve career value.

【Knowledge Expansion】

The Treatment aptitude and its descriptions are as shown in Tab. 5-2.

Table 5-2　Treatment Aptitude and Its Descriptions

Abilities	Descriptions
Abstract reasoning	The ability to understand ideas away from the existence of specific affairs, to express concepts in symbols or images but not with words and numbers
Auditory discrimination	The ability to distinguish between different sounds (especially important for musicians)
Instrument ability	The ability to record, copy, archive, proofread, identify details, and avoid spelling and calculation errors
Color discrimination	The ability to detect color similarities and differences and the ability to perceive different shades of color; the ability to detect the coordination between the colors.
Eye-hand-food coordination	Ability of the hand and foot to coordinate motor responses within the view.
Finger flexibility	The ability of the fingers to manipulate tiny objects quickly, swiftly and precisely.

continued

Abilities	Descriptions
Shape perception	The ability to observe and compare minute differences in the shapes of objects and pictures as well as in their shadows
Language use	The ability to use vocabulary, grammar and punctuation.
Mechanical reasoning	Ability to understand the principles of physics, machinery, tools and equipment. Understand the construction, operation and repair of machinery.
Memory	The ability to recall existing events or to retain learnt information.
Motor coordination	The ability to move with certain speed, precision and posture (important for athletes and dancers)
Digital ability	The ability to understand numbers and do mathematical reasoning
Conductive ability	The ability to provide compelling reasons or persuade others to adopt one's views.
Body strength	The ability to move, transport, lift and endure heavy weights.
Agility	The ability to move at a certain speed, sensitivity and accuracy.
Social skills (empathy)	The ability to understand and get along with others, and the ability to empathize with them.
Spacial ability	The ability to depict three-dimensional objects of various shapes and sizes in the mind.
Spelling ability	The ability to distinguish misspelling.
Text reasoning	The ability to understand the ideas or concepts expressed in words, and the ability to think and reason by using written words.
Vocabulary	Ability to understand and use the meaning of the words accurately.

(4)Career Values Cognition

Values are a type of thinking pattern or value orientation that people use to cognize things and make judgments. They are the principles, standards or qualities that we value in our lives and work. They are the sum of the positions, views and attitudes we maintain when dealing with value relationships. Career values are the perceptions, attitudes, pursuits and aspirations that people have toward their career goals. Values play a directional role in our lives and careers.

Due to differences in nationality, family environment, educational background, interests and hobbies, social factors, etc., there are differences in the career values of different individuals. Career values affect international students in their choice of jobs in terms of location, direction, attitude and career behavior. In reality, many international students do not know the direction they truly seek and thus cannot set clear goals and take effective action. Instead, they follow the tide and lead mediocre lives.

Exploring one's values can help to recognize oneself and solidify one's career choices. The clearer one's values, the clearer one's career development goals, and the smoother one's career development. One tends to make wrong choices when they are in a state of confusion. Understanding one's own values helps to strengthen one's self-motivation. Through constantly examining their values, international students can improve their analytical and judgmental abilities, improve their decision-making abilities, adhere to their career pursuits, promote their own growth and development and realize the value of their lives.

Regardless of where one is seeking employment, international students in universities must establish the correct values. Firstly, it is important to handle the relationship between personal needs and personal desires correctly, avoiding blindly pursuing fame and fortune. It is also important to understand the purpose and motivation of one's job choice, avoiding being affected by personal desires. Secondly, it is important to recognize oneself, discover one's irreplaceable advantages, focus on one's own progress and avoid blindly comparing oneself to others. Thirdly, it is important to handle the value differences between oneself and the employment country, and to have a mentality of seeking common ground while respecting differences, realizing one's own value on the basis of respecting others. Fourthly, it is important to face opportunities and challenges in one's career path with a mentality of growth and development, and to enjoy the happiness and "scenery" along the way. Finally, it is important to be guided by social needs. One should establish the idea that every profession is equally important and everyone has the potential to excel in their chosen field.

【Knowledge Expansion】

Rokeach Values

Milton Rokeach was an American social psychologist and psychiatrist, and was a professor at Michigan State University. He dedicated his life to the study of values and divided values into two types: terminal values which are the terminal states of existence, and instrumental values which are the ways in which we act and behave in our daily lives (see Tab. 5-3).

Table 5-3   Rokeach Values

Terminal values	Instrumental values
Comfortable life (abundance)	Ambitious (working hard and striving for success)
Uplifting life (stimulating, positive life)	
Sense of accomplishment (sustained contribution)	Open-minded (open to new ideas and perspectives)
Peaceful world (absence of conflict and war)	Competent (capable and efficient)
	Joyful (happy and cheerful)
Beautiful world (artistic and natural beauty)	Clean (hygienic and tidy)
	Courageous (standing up for one's beliefs)
Equality (brotherhood, equal opportunity)	
Family security (taking care of loved ones)	Tolerant (understanding and accepting of others)
Freedom (independent, personal choice)	
Happiness (satisfaction)	Helpful (working for the welfare of others)
Inner harmony (absence of internal conflict)	
	Honest (genuine and truthful)

continued

Terminal values	Instrumental values
Mature love (sexual and spiritual intimacy) National security (protection from attack) Joy (happy, leisurely life) Salvation (eternal life) Self-esteem (self-respect) Social recognition (respect, appreciation) Genuine friendship (intimate relationship) Wisdom (mature understanding of life)	Imaginative (bold and creative) Independent (self-reliant and self-sufficient) Intelligent (knowledgeable and thoughtful) Logical (rational and reasonable) Loving (warm and gentle) Obedient (responsible and respectable) Politeness (polite and good-tempered) Responsible (reliable and dependable) Self-controlled (disciplined and restrained)

Section Two Career Decision-Making and Action

1. An Overview of Career Decision-Making

(1) Factors Influencing Career Decision-Making

Career decision-making refers to the process of making decisions and choices about career events. Career paths are full of choices. Understanding and learning about career decision-making can help us improve problem-solving skills and guide our career paths towards maturity. Career decision-making is a complex cognitive process, where various factors influence an individual's career choices and decisions. Each decision is the result of various factors working together.

The first factor is personal factors. An individual's psychological characteristics and self-awareness, including personality, abilities, interests, values, etc. play a directional role in career decision-making. Differences in an individual's intelligence, ethnicity, age, gender,

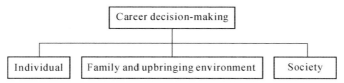

educational background and life experiences can also result in different decision-making outcomes. In addition, an individual's immediate state, including physical state, mental state, emotional state, etc., is also a contributing factor.

The second factor is family and environmental factors. Every individual's family and environmental background is unique. Differences in nationality, parental values, behavioral habits, life attitudes, education methods, etc., can lead to differences in an individual's perception, directly or indirectly impacting their career decisions. Perception and behavioral characteristics of friends and living environment can also affect an individual's career preferences.

The third factor is social factors. Nationality, history, politics, economy and culture can all influence an individual's career decision-making. The mainstream career values of society and the demands of employers can also interfere with an individual's effective decision-making.

(2)Basic Principles of Scientific Career Decision-Making

The basic principles of scientific career decision-making include feasibility, developmental potential and social responsibility.

Career decision-making and planning must have clear, specific goals that are based on self-assessment and environmental assessment. It is important to consider whether the decision aligns with one's abilities, personality, interests and values. Meanwhile, one should also consider whether the decision is achievable. It should bear challenges as well as feasibility. A scientifically-based action plan should be developed based on the career decision.

Career development is not a one-time decision, but a continuous process that involves multiple stages. It is important to continuously adjust strategies based on real-world outcomes, focus on strengths and pursue optimal choices that align with one's goals.

Career decision-making must also follow the laws of social development and consider its impact on society. It is important to integrate personal values into social values and strive to contribute to society as a lifelong goal.

2. Developing a Career Action Plan

(1)Dividing career development stages reasonably

International students in universities have various career choices after graduation, including seeking employment in China, starting a business in China, or returning to their home country for development. However, most of them lack awareness of career planning and tend to follow the crowd, with few making career action plans. Nevertheless, planning leads to action, and action is the prerequisite for success. Developing a scientific and effective career action plan can help us avoid detours and face success directly.

The key to career development planning is to divide the establishment and development of one's career into stages, set suitable goals and make reasonable plans. Different careers have fundamental differences in personality traits and career development needs, which is the main basis for dividing career development stages. The division of career stages varies from person to person and is not solely based on age. International students in universities need to divide their career development based on their actual situations and the characteristics of each career development stage. For example, they can classify their study abroad as a career preparation stage, the first three to five years after graduation as the early career stage, and every five years after that as a new stage.

【Knowledge Expansion】

Super's Career Development Theory

Donald E. Super is a renowned American career counselor who made unparalleled and enduring contributions in the field of career planning and education. In the development of career development theory, he has had an irreplaceable influence. While Parsons' "Trait-and-Factor Theory" focused on career choice, Super's theory focused more on career development.

Super believes that a person's career is a long-term and evolving process, and a person has different career needs at different stages of development. He divides a person's career development into five stages: growth stage, exploration stage, establishment stage, maintenance stage, and decline stage.

Through continuous research, Super also proposed a career development view of life breadth and life space. In addition to the developmental stage theory, Super also put forward the role theory and depicted the interaction between stages and roles as a career rainbow (see Fig. 5-2).

(2)Breaking down Career Development Goals Step by Step

Career goals refer to the specific objectives that an individual aims to achieve within a chosen career and at a future point in time. They serve as a compass for one's life, and having clear career goals is essential to achieving professional success. Career development is a long-term process, and breaking down goals is the process of making goals clear and specific, quantifying them into actionable plans.

Breaking down goals helps individuals establish a fast track between their current reality and their aspirations. Breaking down goals into smaller, manageable steps is a critical method for achieving them. One way to break down goals is to do it based on time(see Fig. 5-3).

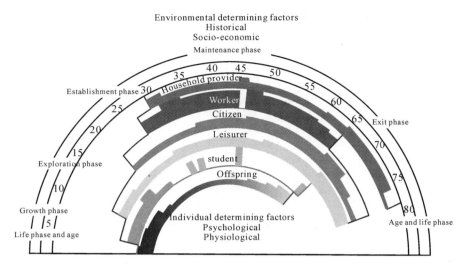

Fig. 5-2　Career rainbow

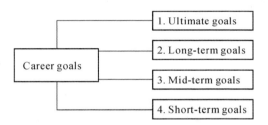

Fig. 5-3　Breaking down career development

(3)Developing an Action Plan

Developing an action plan can use the 3W method, which involves answering the three questions of what to do, how to achieve it and when to complete it. Then implement the action plan step by step.

Generally, developing an action plan involves six steps:

(1) Clarifying specific goals for each stage.

(2) Determining the content of action, required resources and responsibilities.

(3) Developing a timeline for action.

(4) Predicting results and developing contingency plans.

(5) Listing detailed action plans in chronological order.

(6) Implementing, monitoring and evaluating the action plan based on specific goals for each stage.

An action plan can be presented in the form of a table (see Tab. 5-4).

Table 5-4   Action Plan

Name	Overall Goal	Sub-goals	Plan Content
Short-term plan	Goals to achieve upon graduation	Goals to be achieved at each stage of study abroad or in a specific area	Language proficiency, academic learning, professional practice, vocational skill development, familiarity with policies of the employment country, etc.
Medium-term plan	Goals to achieve in the fifth year after graduation	Goals to be achieved in each of the first five years after graduation or in a specific area	Adjustment to the employment environment, adaptation to the workplace, accumulation of resources, job promotion, etc.
Long-term plan	Goals to achieve in middle age	Goals to be achieved in ten and twenty years after graduation respectively	Career development, physical and mental health, family life, children's education, etc.

During the period of studying abroad, specific and detailed plans should be made, including annual plans, semester plans, monthly plans and weekly plans. In addition to improving professional abilities, overall learning plans, part-time work, social practice activities and skills training should also be considered. Through self-analysis, learning, training, competitive activities, etc. , international students in China should make efforts to improve their professional skills, and develop imagination and creativity. They should enhance their emotional intelligence, self-confidence, cross-cultural tolerance, pressure resistance and psychological endurance in social communication, so as to provide strength to the effective implementation of action plans.

【Opinion Exchange】

1. What stage are you currently at in your career development?

2. What are your current developmental goals and tasks?

3. Writing a Career Development Plan

(1) The Form and Content of a Career Development Plan

A career development plan is a written document that presents one's career planning. It can help clarify and organize one's career plans and serve as a guide and motivation for future career development. A complete career development plan should include the following content, see Tab. 5-5.

Table 5-5　The Content of a Career Development Plan

Items	Content
Cover and title page	Including title, personal information, table of contents, timeline, etc.
Career direction and overall goal	Setting goals plays a guiding role in career development and is crucial for effective career planning. A well-designed career plan must have clear and achievable goals
Self-analysis	Including the assessment results of one's career interest, personality, skills and values, as well as the recognition of one's cross-cultural adaptability and the understanding of personal strengths and weaknesses
Environmental analysis	Analyzing the external environment of the employment country, including political, economic, cultural and social factors, industry development and corporate environment, considering the impact of national differences and cultural factors to ensure the scientific nature of career planning
Role recommendation	Recording the evaluation of oneself by others, and recording the opinions and suggestions of others who have a significant impact on one's own career development
Goal decomposition	Breaking down long-term career goals into phased sub-goals with a defined timeline

continued

Items	Content
Implementation plan	Identifying the gaps between oneself and the goals, developing specific plans, gradually narrowing the gaps and achieving phased sub-goals
Evaluation and adjustment	If gaps in the goals are found during the implementation process, the implementation plan and schedule should be promptly corrected and adjusted. Especially for international students studying and working in foreign countries, particular attention should be paid to the achievement of phased goals to ensure the feasibility of their career plans

(2)Principles and Techniques for Writing a Career Development Plan

Explicit in information. An effective career plan should first clarify basic information, including name (in English and Chinese), nationality, age, major, university, ultimate career goal, career path and career planning timeline. These should be reflected on the cover page of the plan to give readers a clear understanding before reading the main content.

Detailed and comprehensive. The plan should include multiple sections such as self-assessment, environmental evaluation, career objectives, implementation plans and feedback evaluations. It should be truthful and comprehensive, fully analyzing oneself and understanding the impact of the environment on one's career, especially the impact of the international environment on personal development. The plan should also bear personal characteristics that are suitable for self-development.

Scientific and evidence based. One should understand the theories and knowledge of assessments, use assessment tools reasonably, analyze assessment results and make career decisions based on personal conditions and actual employment environments to achieve a good match between individuals and their jobs. The process should be well-reasoned and supported by images and data to increase credibility and persuasiveness.

Reasonable and feasible. Career goals should be appropriate and responsive to societal needs. They should be both motivating and reasonable. Career action plans should be practical and actionable, avoiding unrealistic goals that are detached from reality. To determine goals, one can conduct interviews with career models as a reference, understand the career development paths of elites in the industry and consult international friends with similar experiences. They can conduct research to understand the needs of each career stage, and based on their own situation, break down their goals reasonably and prepare for plan implementation.

Evaluative and reflective. Evaluation and feedback are means to adjust and revise the career plan. Evaluation and feedback mainly involve methods and designs, as well as solutions to obstacles encountered during plan implementation. Alternative plans should be provided in different periods according to the newly set goals. The alternative plans should have a certain relevance to the original career objectives.

Clear and coherent. The entire plan should be fluent in expression, accurate in wording and well-organized in structure. If necessary, multiple language versions can be used. The plan should be developed around the career goals and be logically coherent in the exposition.

Innovative and original. The plan should fully reflect personal characteristics and reveal one's spiritual outlook. Copying or imitation should be forbidden.

【Template Example】

Basic Information and Career Experience Reflection Form for Career Planning

Section Three   Preparation and Implementation of Employment and Entrepreneurship

1. Employment and Entrepreneurship Policies

(1)National Policies

As a guiding beacon for the career choices of international students, employment policies have a direct impact on the career choices of international students in Chinese universities. In recent years, an increasing number of international students have chosen to study in China. With the improvement of China's comprehensive national strength, China has taken a more proactive, flexible and open-minded attitude to solving the problem of employment for international students after graduation.

In February 2016, the General Office of the Communist Party of China Central Committee and the General Office of the State Council issued the *Opinions on Strengthening the Management of Permanent Residency System for foreigners*, proposing to "relax the work restrictions on outstanding foreign students in China and provide them with channels for working and applying for permanent residence in China after graduation".

In March 2016, the Central Committee of the Communist Party of China issued the *Opinions on Deepening the Reform of the Talent Development System and Mechanism*, proposing to fully develop and utilize domestic and international talent resources, actively participate in the international talent competition, and build up more open and flexible mechanisms for talent cultivation, attraction and utilization. It also proposes to relax visa and residence requirements for foreign talents coming to China, simplify procedures and provide other necessary conditions.

In January 2017, the Ministry of Human Resources and Social Security, the Ministry of Foreign Affairs, and the Ministry of Education issued the *Notice on matters related to allowing outstanding foreign college graduates to work in China*, which clearly stipulated that foreign students who have obtained a master's degree or above from a Chinese university within one year of graduation, as well as foreign graduates who have obtained a master's degree or above from a well-known overseas university within one year of graduation and who are over 18 years old, healthy, with excellent academic performance, an average score of not less than 80 (in the percentage system, converted to the percentage system for other scoring systems), or B+/B(in the grade system) or above, without criminal record, and whose post-graduation work is related to their major, can apply for a foreigner's employment permit. Notice on matters related to allowing outstanding foreign college graduates to work in China.

In July 2017, the *Categorization Criteria for Work of Foreigners in China (Trial)*(Waizhuanfa [2017] No. 40) stipulated that young talents under the age of 40 who have engaged in post-doctoral research in high-level universities overseas or Chinese universities can be recognized as "outstanding young talents" and listed as "foreign high-end talents (Class A)". They can enjoy "Green Channel" and "Tolerance for Deficiencies" services, and can apply for a talent visa first, and then apply for a foreigner's work permit after entering China.

In July 2019, the 12 *Policies on Immigration and Entry-Exit Convenience of the Ministry of Public Security* stipulated that outstanding foreign students with undergraduate or higher degrees from key domestic universities who engage in innovative and entrepreneurial activities in China after graduation, can apply for a residence permit valid for 2 to 5 years with a college diploma and proof of innovation and entrepreneurship to the immigration management department of the public security organ.

In August 2022, according to the National Immigration Administration, foreign Chinese people with a doctoral degree who work in China can apply for permanent residence in China from the immigration management department of the public security organ, and their foreign spouses and minor children can apply together. This policy is implemented nationwide without territorial restrictions.

(2)Local Policies

With the continuous development of oversea education in China, many provinces and regions actively respond to national policies. Beijing and Shanghai, as representative cities with the largest number of international students in universities and a great demand for foreign talents in economic development, began to explore employment and entrepreneurship policies for foreign talents in 2015, starting a new era of employment and entrepreneurship for international students in China.

In July 2015, the Ministry of Public Security launched a series of entry and exit policy measures to support the construction of Shanghai Science and Technology Innovation Center. The policy supports foreign students to directly start innovation and entrepreneurship in Shanghai after graduating from Chinese universities, in hope of attracting intellectual resources of outstanding foreign graduates in China. It further simplifies the entry and residence procedures for foreigners who come to Shanghai for innovation and entrepreneurship to attract foreign talent resources from abroad. It also expands the scope of long-term residence permit issuance, enabling foreigners working in Shanghai to enjoy more stable long-term residence expectations. Through the above measures, the stay and residence period for foreign innovation and entrepreneurship personnel has been prolonged, and the range of stay and residence documents issuance has been expanded, providing sufficient space and time for their entrepreneurship and innovation.

In January 2016, the Ministry of Public Security issued 20 entry and exit policy measures to support Beijing's innovation and development (also known as "Zhongguancun 20 New Policies"). In order to better attract outstanding young talents from around the world, the policy proposes to attract outstanding foreign graduates from internationally renowned universities to come to Beijing for innovation and entrepreneurship, and to provide them with convenient visa services.

On July 1, 2020, the Shanghai Human Resources and Social Security Bureau issued a notice on "Measures for Excellent Foreign Graduates to Work in Shanghai and Other Related Matters" ("Shanghai 2020"). The policy supports international students who have obtained undergraduate and above degrees from universities in the Shanghai to work in the China (Shanghai) Pilot Free Trade Zone, China (Shanghai) Pilot Free Trade Zone Lingang New Area, Hongqiao Business District, Zhangjiang National Innovation Demonstration Zone, and supports international students to work in companies listed in the "Shanghai Science and Technology Innovation Vocational List". Outstanding international students who have obtained a master's degree or above from Chinese universities can work directly in this city.

(3) Implementation of Policies

With the issuance of central government documents and the promulgation of local policies, the channels for international students to work in China have been continuously expanded. Many provinces and regions encourage excellent international students to work in China by holding job fairs, and universities have established international student employment guidance centers to promote the employment of international students in China.

In 2016, Ministry of Education for Study Abroad Service Center held the first China International Student Talent Recruitment Conference at Peking University, which received positive responses from employers and international students. Since then, the Chinese Service Center for Scholarly Exchange has held several talent recruitment conferences for international students in China, and the number of international students attending these events has increased year by year. China has become one of the important destinations for international students to work after graduation.

Since its launch in Beijing in 2017, the "Tengman Plan", an international youth innovation and entrepreneurship program, has attracted tens of thousands of international participants. This program has leveraged China's advantages in innovation and technology industries, and helped young people from various countries to find internships and incubate entrepreneurial projects, cultivating a large number of international young entrepreneurs and inspiring their enthusiasm for innovation and entrepreneurship.

【Knowledge Expansion】

The "Tengman Plan" (The Vine Plan)

The "Tengman Plan" is an international innovation and entrepreneurship program for international youth, planned and implemented by the Zhongguancun "Belt and Road" Industrial Promotion Association. Its aim is to harness the wisdom of all kinds of talents and gather talents from all over the world. The "Tengman Plan" has a vision called "Hundred, Thousand, Ten Thousand", hoping that in the future, more than 10,000 international young people can truly play a role in cooperation and exchange in "the Belt and Road" initiative, just like vine spreading in various countries.

Through internship, position-matching, training, entrepreneurship incubation, and international young entrepreneur training programs, the "Tengman Plan" has created opportunities for international students to communicate and exchange face-to-face with Chinese innovation and technology companies, helping them establish close working relationships with relevant companies. It has not only helped Chinese companies find international talents for "the Belt and Road" construction quickly, but also allowed international students to get involved in the construction of the "Belt and Road" initiative, providing support for their innovation and development in China.

【Opinion Exchange】

What is your opinions on China's employment policies?

2. Mastering Employment Skills

(1)Collecting Employment Information

Due to the influence of the global economy, the job market is becoming increasingly challenging and the pressure to find employment is constantly rising. For international students in universities who have no work experience and are unfamiliar with the job market policies of the country they are in, they may often feel lost and helpless during the job search process due to a lack of correct methods and skills.

Obtaining employment information is a fundamental condition and necessary means to secure employment. Access to a wide variety of reliable employment information can assist international students in finding suitable jobs and making informed choices. Often, the competition for employment is a competition for information. For international students, timely understanding and mastering of job market policies and management procedures of the target employment country can significantly increase their chances of employment.

International students should be aware of employment information such as local job market policies, the scope and geographic distribution of business of potential employers, organizational structure, number of employees, salary systems, specific job positions, language requirements, skill requirements, training and development opportunities, among other things. Only with a comprehensive understanding of this information, and by combining it with their own strengths and abilities, can international students find more suitable job positions. International students must take full advantage of the golden opportunity provided in their graduation phase, collect employment information through various channels and make adequate employment preparations(See Fig. 5-4).

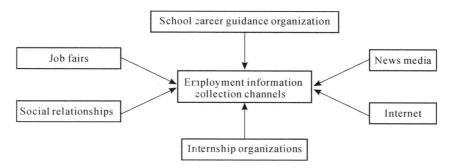

Fig. 5-4 Channels of collection employment information

(2)Preparing Job Application Materials

Preparing job application materials is an essential part of the job search process and is the first way for employers to understand job seekers. It can greatly influence the success or failure of a job hunting. We need to prepare the following materials.

1) Resume. A well-written resume should be clear, concise, and truthful. It should include personal information, education background, skills and abilities, honors and awards, certificates, internship and practical experience, job search intentions, and self-evaluation. In addition, multiple language versions of the resume should be prepared according to the employment situation.

2) Cover letter. A cover letter is a letter that job seekers write to express their job-seeking intentions to employers in order to obtain a desired position. It should contain two elements: job position intention and competitive advantages. The language used should be appropriate, sincere, and compelling.

3) Transcript. A transcript reflects the academic performance of international students in university and is an important proof of their academic ability. The transcript should have two versions in Chinese and English, issued and stamped by the Academic Affairs Department of the university.

4) Certificates. This part covers certificates of various competition

awards, language proficiency certificates, occupational skill certificates, and various professional qualifications that international students have obtained during their studies. It also includes proof of being a student leader, research achievements, and published papers.

5) Transcript of social practice. A transcript also includes other relevant materials such as social practice and internships that international students have participated in. Internship and practical materials can help employers review the relevant work abilities of international students and are indispensable.

【Template Sample】

Template for Job Application Resume

3. Entrepreneurial Ability

(1)Writing a Business Plan

Entrepreneurship plan, also known as a business plan, is a comprehensive written material that coordinates all aspects of a start-up project. It provides a detailed guide on the operation of the enterprise and project, business ideas, commercial strategy, prospect outlook, human and financial resources, marketing strategy, etc.

A complete entrepreneurship plan usually contains the following basic contents: plan summary, project background, company and its products or services, team introduction, market research and analysis, development plan, risk response, etc.

1) Summary. This should include a summary of key points related to the business idea, commercial strategy, target market, competitive advantages, etc.

2) Project background. This mainly includes the industry

background, market development trends, market space, timing, and opportunities.

3) Project overview (products and services). This mainly includes project introduction, target consumers, key technologies, customer value, core advantages, brand patents, industry recognition, development direction, etc.

4) Team advantages and organizational structure. This mainly includes key management personnel introduction (rights and obligations, responsibilities and capabilities), team building advantages (member education, practice, work background, innovation ability, values, complementary situation, etc.).

5) Market analysis. This mainly includes market capacity analysis (customer number, unit sales volume, and total sales volume, etc.), competitive analysis (competitors' advantages and disadvantages), market research and prospect analysis (target customers and planned market prospects, sales volume, sales revenue, market share, and profit, etc.), marketing strategy (developing strategies and implementation plans for product, pricing, promotion, channels, etc.).

6) Development plan and social benefits. This mainly includes the development situation of different stages after the entrepreneurship, future development goals, social benefits, and employment promotion situation.

7) Financial analysis and financing plan. This mainly includes project budget, expected income, and financing plan.

8) Risks and countermeasures. This mainly includes the prediction of various potential risks and corresponding response measures.

9) Project attachment materials and others. This mainly includes a copy of the business license, organization code, government approval, company articles of association, patent certificate, market research materials, etc.

【Knowledge Expansion】

Notice from the Ministry of Education on Hosting The 9th China International " Internet + " College Students Innovation and Entrepreneurship Competition

Notice of the 8th China International "Internet Plus" College Students Innovation and Entrepreneurship Competition and Evaluation Criteria

The China International "Internet plus" College Student Innovation and Entrepreneurship Competition is a major innovation and entrepreneurship event initiated and launched by Premier Li Keqiang in 2015, jointly sponsored by 12 central ministries and commissions, local provincial-level governments, and the Ministry of Education. The competition aims to deepen the comprehensive reform of higher education, stimulate the creativity of college students, cultivate a strong force for "widespread entrepreneurship and innovation," promote the transformation of competition results, promote the formation of new "Internet plus" business models, actively serve the upgrading of the economy, lead innovation with entrepreneurship, boost employment with entrepreneurship, and promote higher quality entrepreneurship and employment for college graduates.

In 2020, the competition was renamed as the China International "Internet plus" College Student Innovation and Entrepreneurship Competition. The competition uses competition to promote learning and cultivate innovative and entrepreneurial talents, aiming to stimulate students' creativity, inspire young people to understand the national situation and the people's sentiments, temper their willpower and quality, broaden their international horizons, and add to their wisdom and ability through innovation and entrepreneurship. The competition serves as a new way to explore quality education, promoting innovation and entrepreneurship education reform, guiding all types of schools to actively serve national strategies and regional development, deepening comprehensive talent training reform, comprehensively promoting quality education, and effectively improving students' innovative spirit, entrepreneurial awareness, and innovation and entrepreneurship capabilities. The competition also builds a new platform for the transformation of competition results, promoting the close integration of industry, academia, and research, and promoting the formation of new "Internet plus" business models, serving the high-quality development of the economy, and striving to create a new situation of higher quality entrepreneurship and employment for college graduates.

(2)Establishment of a New Enterprise

To operate a new business, it is necessary to obtain a legal identity. International students who want to establish a company in China must have a detailed understanding of the legal procedures and workflow for company registration, and prepare relevant documents for each process to ensure the smooth application progress of the company.

The following documents are required for company registration: personal information, registered capital, several proposed company names, business scope, property ownership certificate or leasing agreement, company domicile, shareholder roster with contact phone numbers and addresses, company organization and its establishment method, powers and rules of procedure, and company bylaws.

The process for registering and starting a company is shown as Fig. 5-5.

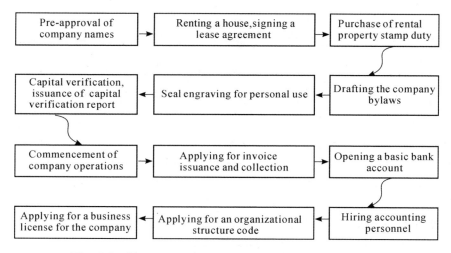

Fig. 5-5 The process for registering and staring a company

【Knowledge Expansion】

Naming during Company Registration

According to the *Opinions of the State Administration for Industry and Commerce on Improving the Efficiency of Registration and Actively Promoting the Reform of Enterprise Name Registration Management* (Industry and Commerce Enterprise Registration [2017] No. 54), when registering a company, the name must comply with certain prohibitive and restrictive rules. Prohibitive rules include: the name cannot be the same as names already registered by another company in the same industry with the same registration authority; the name cannot contain content or words that are harmful to the national or public interests; the name cannot contain content or words that may deceive or mislead the public; the name cannot contain the names of foreign countries or regions, international organizations, political parties, government and military agencies, social organizations, and military numbers. The name must use standard Chinese characters and cannot use foreign languages, letters, or Arabic numerals. Restrictive rules include: the name cannot be similar to a name already registered by another company in the same industry with the same registration authority, unless there is an investment relationship between the two companies; the legal name of the company cannot contain the name of another non-profit organization, unless there is an investment relationship between the two or the non-profit organization authorizes the use of its name or specific title; the name cannot contain the name of another company, unless there is an investment relationship between the two or the company authorizes the use of its name or specific title. The name cannot imply that the company is a non-profit organization or beyond the scope of the company's establishment purpose, unless there are other meanings or there are specific provisions in laws, regulations, or decisions of the State Council. Except for companies established by the State Council, company names cannot include the words "China," "Chinese, " "National, " "International, " etc. If these words are used, they must be limited to the industry. Foreign-invested enterprises using foreign investment enterprise names and foreign-controlled foreign-invested enterprises can use the "China " in the middle of their name. Names that contain the word "International" in the middle do not need to be approved by the State Administration for Industry and Commerce.

【Case Analysis】

The Birth of Alibaba and Jack Ma

In early 1995, Alibaba Group founder Jack Ma first encountered the Internet during his trip to the United States. With no computer knowledge, he began to learn about the Internet with the help of his friends. In March 1999, Jack Ma resigned from his position in the government and returned to Hangzhou with his team to start a new venture—an e-commerce website that could serve small and medium-sized enterprises worldwide. They started with a capital of RMB 500,000 and developed the Alibaba website.

In the early days of Alibaba, the company was so small that they couldn't get an office. They worked in Jack Ma's house, and at most 35 people sat in one room. Jack Ma stipulated that each employee must rent a house within five minutes' walk from his home. They spent $16 \sim 18$ hours a day working hard like "beasts" in Jack Ma's house, tirelessly designing web pages, discussing and brainstorming ideas, and sleeping on the floor when they were tired. Jack Ma kept urging his employees, "When the starting gun goes off, you can't take the time to watch how your opponents are running, you have to run like crazy all the way." He also warned them that "the biggest failure is giving up, the biggest enemy is oneself, and the biggest opponent is time." Thus, Alibaba was born and nurtured in Jack Ma's home.

From encountering the Internet in 1995 to the birth of Alibaba in 1999, Jack Ma took five years and experienced two failures before achieving the first stage of success. In the face of adversity, Jack Ma's answer was to "rely on perseverance to achieve the greatest success." Looking back on his experience, Jack Ma admitted that the first step was to believe that you can survive, and the second step is to believe that you have strong perseverance to survive. Like any small and medium-sized enterprise, Alibaba also faced difficulties in paying salaries in 1999, 2000 and 2001 when they had little income. However, to survive, Jack Ma told himself and his employees that they must persist, even if they have to half-kneel, and persist until the end, for persistence is victory and they would be the last ones standing.

【Questions for Discussion】

1. What are the main factors that influence career development? Discuss how to leverage subjective factors in your own career development.

2. How will you comprehensively improve your employability skills in the future?

3. If you decide to start a business, what kind of project would you choose and why?

第六章　保持心理健康　增强适应能力

　　21世纪是一个科技高度发达又充满压力的时代,这既为现代人的心理健康提供了实现可能,又对现代人的心理素质提出了更高要求。健康的心理是人类全面发展必须具备的条件和基础,尤其是对于离开自身熟悉的文化环境跨国求学的高校国际生而言,具备良好的心理素质和较强的适应能力是学业事业迈向成功的保障。

【思维导图】

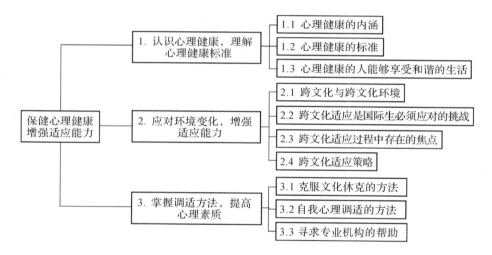

第一节　认识心理健康　理解心理健康标准

一、心理健康的内涵

(一)健康的概念在不断演变

健康,是一个随着时代的推移,在社会和文化因素影响下不断演变的概念。

1948 年联合国世界卫生组织(WHO)宪章认为,"健康,不仅是指没有疾病或不虚弱,还指在身体上、心理上和社会适应上应达到一个完善的状态"。

1989 年世界卫生组织进一步发展了健康的概念,认为健康应该包括身体健康、良好的社会适应能力、道德健康、心理健康等四个方面。

(二)现代健康概念强调生理健康和心理健康的完整统一

与传统健康观念相比,现代健康概念,不仅指生物医学模式下的生理健康,还包括心理和社会适应等方面的完好状态。我们知道,人类同时具有生理活动和心理活动,身心作为一个统一体,共同对外界环境产生反应。

当人的身体状态不佳时,相应的心理健康会受到影响,人可能会出现注意力降低、情绪低落、烦躁易怒,甚至可能出现不同程度的心理障碍;反之,当人的心理健康受到威胁时,例如长期饱受抑郁情绪困扰、压力过大的人更容易产生一系列身体症状。因此,生理健康和心理健康相互依赖,互为一体。

(三)心理健康的定义

在 1946 年召开的第三届国际心理卫生大会上,心理健康被定义为"人能在身体、智能以及情感上与他人的心理不相矛盾的范围内,将个人心境发展成最佳的状态"。

具体而言,心理健康是一种生活适应良好的状态,它既指个体在心理上自我感觉良好的健康状态,同时也指个体能够采取维持心理健康状态的行为手段,例如通过与朋友倾诉缓解内心焦虑等情绪问题。

心理健康可从狭义和广义的角度进行区分。狭义的心理健康,主要目的在于预防或缓解各种心理障碍或行为问题。广义的心理健康,则是以个人的最佳生活状态为目标,即人们在环境中不断提高个体心理健康水平,从而更好地适应社会生活。

【知识拓展】

5.25 中国的大学生心理健康日

每年 5 月 4 日是中国的青年节。长久以来,五月本身就被中国人赋予了和年轻人一样的活力和激情。1999 年四川大学生首创在 5 月 25 日设立大学生心理健康日,谐音"我爱我"(同汉语中"525"音近),意在倡导大学生关爱他人先从关爱自我开始,爱自己才能更好地爱他人。2000 年由北京师范大学倡议,确定 5 月 25 日为驻京各大高校学生的心理健康日,提出了"我爱我,给心理一片晴空!"的口号。2004 年,中华全国青年联合会、全国学生联合会把 5 月 25 日正式确定为全国大中学生心理健康日。

心理健康日的活动目的,旨在倡导大学生爱自己,珍爱生命,把握机会,为自己创造更好的成才之路,同时从珍爱自己出发,做到关爱他人、关爱社会。心理健康的人,首先就是能认识自我、接纳自我,能体验到自己的存在价值,乐观自信;同时也能用尊重、信任、友爱、宽容的态度与人相处,能分享、接受、给予爱和友谊,能与他人同心协力,创造美好生活。

二、心理健康的标准

(一)心理健康的评判标准受具体因素影响

由于心理健康并非一种固定不变的状态,而是处在不断发展变化的过程之中,同时它的状态还受到社会环境、文化背景等因素的影响,因此,制定统一的心理健康评判标准是一个较为复杂的问题,心理学界的专家学者们会采用不同的视角来分析。

【知识拓展】

关于何为心理健康,美国著名人本主义心理学家马斯洛(Abraham H. Maslow)提出了心理健康的 10 个标准:

1. 有足够的自我安全感;

2. 能充分地了解自己,并对自己的能力作适当的估价;

3. 生活理想切合实际；

4. 不脱离周围现实环境；

5. 能保持人格的完整与和谐；

6. 善于从经验中学习；

7. 能保持良好的人际关系；

8. 能适度地发泄情绪和控制情绪；

9. 在符合集体要求的条件下，能有限度地发挥个性；

10. 在不违背社会规范的前提下，能恰当地满足个人的基本需求。

结合心理学家的研究和中国高校学生群体的现实情况，我们判断学生心理健康状态一般依据以下评价标准。

（1）智力发展正常，在学习过程中有较好的表现。智力，主要包括注意力、记忆力、思维力、想象力等能力在内的一种综合能力。智力正常是学生学习、生活、工作最基本的心理条件，也是高校国际生适应环境谋求自身发展的首要条件。

（2）情绪积极稳定，情感协调深刻。情绪，是指个体因为环境满足自身需要程度的不同而产生积极或消极的体验。积极的情绪能够提高人的活动水平，因而有利于人的心理健康；消极的情绪容易降低人的活动水平，从而不利于人的心理健康。一般来说，心理健康的学生往往能体验到更多的积极情绪。情感，属于更高等级的社会性情感，它是和人的社会需要联系在一起的。心理健康的学生往往具有良好的人际关系和较强的社会责任感。

（3）意志品质健全，行为协调一致。心理健康的学生意志的自觉性、果断性、坚韧性和自制性都有较好的发展。他们能根据现实的需要自觉地调整自己的行为；能果断地做出决定并执行；能在目标的指引下坚持不懈地努力直到达到目标；能自觉抵制不合理欲望，有效约束自己的行为。

（4）个性和谐统一，人格完整独立。人格，指一个人的各种重要的、持久的心理特征的总和。心理健康的人在人格结构的各方面均保持着一定程度的平衡、和谐和完善。他们能把需要、动机、态度、理想和行为统一起来，做到态度与行为相一致。心理健康的学生对自己的气质、性格、能力等都能作出较为客观的评价。对于自己的优点不沾沾自喜，妄自尊大；对于自己的缺点也能坦然接受，不妄自菲薄。能够把"理想的我"与"现实的我"有机统一起来，始终与环境保持平衡。

(5)社会适应良好,能保持积极的人际关系。马克思说:"人是社会关系的总和。"心理健康的学生能够客观地认识自己所处的社会环境,拥有和谐的人际关系。在环境条件不利时,不怨天尤人,自暴自弃,而是主动转变自己的观念,积极适应环境并改造环境。在与人相处时,心理健康的学生应掌握一定的社交技巧,在与人交往时做到诚实守信、宽容有爱、平等和善。

(6)心理活动特点符合心理发展的年龄特征。人的心理活动是一个不断发展的过程,心理发展的不同阶段会表现出不同的特征。心理健康的人的一般心理特点应该与其所属年龄阶段人的共同心理特征相一致。心理健康的学生应该表现出积极向上、勤学好问、反应敏捷等特点。消极厌世、依赖幼稚都是心理不健康的表现。

【观点交流】

1. 你是否认同以上评价标准?为什么?
2. 在你的国家,人们采用怎样的评价标准认定心理是否健康?

(二)心理健康水平的等级划分参考

一般而言,我们将心理健康水平大致划分为三个等级:一般常态心理、轻度失调心理和严重病态心理(见图 6-1)。

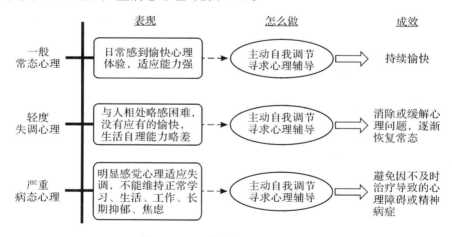

图 6-1 心理健康水平的三个等级

三、心理健康的人能够享受和谐的生活

（一）心理健康的表现是能够获得心理和谐

心理健康的主要表现是个体在拥有正确的人生观、世界观、价值观的基础上，能将需要、动机、理想和行为统一起来，形成一个和谐完整的统一体，能够获得和谐生活的心理体验。

【概念解析】

"和谐"，意为事物协调匀称的状态。"和"是中华文明的精髓之一，它是中华民族长期孜孜以求的理想状态。和谐，是中国传统哲学辩证法和马克思主义哲学辩证法的落脚点，是中国人追求的人与自然、与自我内心和睦协调的美好状态。

（二）心理健康的表现是能够享受和谐的生活

人们通常在日常生活中寻求着身体、社会、心理和精神各个层面的平衡，也会发现在现实生活中不可避免地存在不够协调的方面，这就需要人们通过扩大视野、提升能力来面对困难和挑战，同时积极调整心理状态，享受和谐的生活。

【知识拓展】

和谐生活

学者认为身体、成就、社交及未来愿景是构成和谐生活平衡的四个象限。每一人对自身的四个方面都有所估量，并总在追寻着各方面的平衡。那么，请大家试一试，根据自己当前现状，在下面坐标图中标记各象限的自我评估分值（每个象限值为 0～100），再将 4 个点用线连起来，看看画出的四边形是什么样吧！

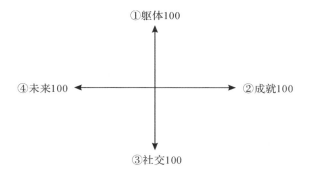

步骤1:首先,你需要先对自己提问:

(1)你对自己的身体、外表满意吗？你对自己的身体投入了多少关注？你能在躯体方面给自己打多少分？

(2)你在学业、事业上投入了多少能量？关注多少？你在成就方面给自己打多少分？

(3)你在与家人、社会交往上花了多少精力？你在社交方面给自己打多少分？

(4)你对未来想象如何？悲观还是乐观？在人生观、世界观上花了多少精力？你在未来愿景方面给自己打多少分？

步骤2:现在,把你给自己的平分连成一个四边形。请观察如果它们的每条边是均衡的,说明你的生活是均衡的,反之则不均衡。

步骤3:试着跟你的同学分享并讨论:自己的四边形如何？是否平衡健康？自己因为在哪方面经历放的特别多才成这样？有什么积极意义？需要做什么样的调整？

第二节　应对环境变化　增强适应能力

一、跨文化与跨文化环境

(一)高校国际生身处于跨文化环境之中

随着全球化进程的加深,社会流动性不断增强,不同文化、不同民族之间的接触往来推动着人与人之间的互动关系。跨文化,指的就是跨越不同国家与民族界线的文化及其状态。它要求对与本民族文化有差异或冲突的文化现象、风俗、习惯等有充分正确的认识,并在此基础上以包容的态度予以接受与适应。

对于高校国际生而言,离开自己的国家前往另一目的国家学习,也就离开了自己熟悉的生活环境,并开始经历跨越国家与民族界线的文化和生活体验。

(二)跨文化环境的定义与特征

跨文化环境,指的是人们处于两种或两种以上不同文化背景的群体之间,跨越不同国家、民族及群体文化体系的环境。

跨文化环境最显著的特征表现在以下方面。

(1)母语交际、社会习俗、文化背景、政治经济体制、法律法规等方面与自身熟知的成长经历环境之间存在诸多明显差异。

(2)要求处于该环境的群体或个体,不只依赖自己的语言代码、认知习惯、观念和行为方式,更要同时了解并掌握对方的语言代码、认知习惯、观念和行为方式,以适应文化环境差异。

(3)文化环境中的差异因素,容易导致经历者感到心理困惑,甚至遭遇事件冲突。

二、跨文化适应是高校国际生必须应对的挑战

国际留学生自离开母国到达留学目的国起,就不可避免地需要面对学习生活环境的变化,以及这种变化可能对心理健康状态带来的冲击和影响。因此,掌握跨文化知识、了解跨文化环境中自身所面临的冲突与挑战及其可采取的适应策略,是留学生群体维护自我心理健康的必要保障。

(一)跨文化适应的内涵

跨文化适应(intercultural adaptation),指的是人们处于跨文化环境中,对于与母国或本民族文化有差异、冲突的文化现象、风俗习惯等,在充分认识的基础上,采取包容的态度积极地接受、适应、融入当地生活,以达到自身文化认同与新文化认知接纳之间的平衡和谐的状态。

每一位来华高校国际生,从母国来到中国学习生活,面对汉语语言环境及中国社会的行为准则,甚至遇到与自身有别的文化价值取向时,都需要进行跨文化适应。

【知识拓展】

高校国际生来华留学跨文化适应情况测试

(二)跨文化适应的不同阶段与表现

跨文化适应不是一蹴而就的,而是一个对新的文化环境逐步认知与反应的动态过程。美国人类学家奥博格(Kalvero Oberg)将跨文化适应过程分为四个阶段。

刚进入陌生国度的阶段,个体在积极预期的作用下,在新的文化环境中情绪高涨,对新鲜的文化差异持一种积极态度,表现特征为着迷、兴奋、乐观。由于遭遇文化差异或冲突等现实问题,与先前的期望存在差距,导致心理倍感挫折,因此个体对目的国产生一定的敌意和偏见。

随着个体的目的语水平提升,对新文化环境的适应能力增强,对新文化环境适应能力提高,个体开始重新从积极方面看待目的国的人和事。

个体能够了解、接受并享受目的国的社会规范和习俗,适应程度增加,焦虑情绪基本消失,与跨文化环境产生和谐之感。

由于不同的跨文化个体,具备不同的个性与经历,有着不同的际遇或社会支持,因此,跨文化适应的四个阶段所需要的时间、所消耗的心力因人而异。

【观点交流】

1.你认为自己当前处于什么阶段?处于这一阶段的原因有哪些?

2.哪些因素可以帮助高校国际生更快到达跨文化适应期?

(三)跨文化适应不良易导致文化休克现象

就高校国际生跨文化适应的现实表现而言,有的能够及时进行自我心理调整,适应良好,顺利进入适应期,享受留学国家的学习生活;而有的则存在适应不良,甚至出现文化休克现象。这就需要我们对跨文化适应问题引起重视。

【概念解析】

"休克"，中文词义指的是一种细胞急性缺氧导致呼吸困难的病理状态。

Oberg首先提出了culture shock这一概念，中文释义为"文化休克"。它指的是处于跨文化环境中的个体失去了自己熟悉的社会交往符号，包括语言符号、文化习俗和社会规范等非语言符号，对于对方的社会符号不熟悉，而在心理上产生的深度焦虑症。中文的"文化休克"一词非常形象地说明了这种个体对于旅居国家的陌生文化环境不适应而导致"缺氧"的身心状态。

根据Oberg等人的描述，"文化休克"大多表现为心理不适，有的也有生理上的反应。一般来说，高校国际生群体到达留学目的国家的最初阶段都难免经历"文化休克"现象，而个体持续时间及其严重程度却有不同。有的人仅会感受到轻微的"文化休克"，且持续时间仅几周，而有的人的感受却会持续很久，甚至整个留学阶段都一直存在这种现象；有的人会在心理和情绪上感到不适，有的人却会因为心理焦虑而引发生理上的疾病，如头痛、失眠、胃痛、腹痛等。

快快对照自查小清单，了解自己有哪些文化休克的表现吧！

□感到孤独、无助，极度想念家人和朋友。

□感到心情烦躁、心理焦虑。

□害怕被欺骗、受欺负或受伤害等。

□强迫性地关注自我卫生与健康。

□过度认同自己原生文化，面对新的文化环境中的人采取敌视态度。

□回避与他人接触。

□感觉身体不适，如头痛、失眠、胃痛、腹痛等。

三、跨文化适应过程中存在的难点

高校国际生群体在对留学目的国家的文化适应过程中的难点，大致可概括为生存环境适应、人际适应、学业适应等三个方面。

（一）生存环境适应

对于高校国际生而言，留学期间需要适应的生存环境，即在留学目的国生存、成长的环境,包括所生活的地域、居住条件、气候条件等自然环境,以及当地的饮食、交通、生活习惯、治安法规等社会环境等。

【案例分析】

请阅读下面的案例,试分析讨论案例中的高校国际生遇到的问题。

案例1:一位来自埃塞俄比亚的 A 同学,到中国学习 2 个多月了,时常心情不好,常常抱怨,比如课程太难,学习汉语、认识汉字也太难;又如中国南方的冬天很湿冷,让人不舒服,教室里没有暖气,而宿舍的空调不太暖等等。他跟自己的同乡说,在中国的生活中,他开始时常抱怨,变成了一个易生气的人。

案例2:印尼学生 B 没来中国之前,一直对中国很向往。可刚来中国两个月后她抱怨当地的天气太冷,不敢走出宿舍。饮食上,中国的菜太油腻了,非常不喜欢,但自己也不太会下厨所以每天吃不好,还犯了胃病。此外,时常想家,很容易落入思乡情绪,学习时很难集中注意力。

(二)人际适应

不同的文化背景使得人们所习惯的社交礼仪、地方风俗、宗教行为方式等规约也不尽相同,高校国际生在新的文化环境中则还需要适应新的人际交往方式。

【案例分析】

请阅读下面的案例,试分析讨论案例中的留学生遇到的问题。

案例3:来到中国学习后,波兰学生 C 发现中国人很喜欢问一些私人问题,比如"你今年多大了?""你的衣服是什么牌子的? 多少钱?""你的丈夫是做什么工作的?"等等,这些都让她很不舒服,也不喜欢与当地人交流。外出时她也需要面对很多问题,比如打车软件没有英文,操作太复杂,而地铁、公交车都太过拥挤;很多公共场所人们不排队等,这都让她非常烦躁。她学会了很多粗话来发泄情绪。可是她的内心认为她原本不是这样的人,因此常常陷入自我怀疑与困惑之中。

(三)学业适应

学习是高校国际生群体进行跨文化交际活动的根本目的。若学习者个体能尽早适应留学国家的文化环境,积极调动自身的动机、情绪、态度与行为协调一致,对顺利完成学业有着重要的促进作用。然而,由于留学目的国家与高校国际生母国在教育、教学方式乃至校园管理文化上的种种差异,学业上的跨文化适应反而成为高校国际生无法绕开的严峻考验。

【案例分析】

请阅读下面的案例,试分析讨论案例中的留学生遇到的问题。

案例4:来自德国的同学D在中国某高校学习语言类课程。他与一位专业课老师的关系很好,经常与老师进行各种话题上的交谈。但在一次教师评教中,同学D给这位老师的评分很低。这位老师看到评分后感觉很不解,认为自己可能有让同学D不满的地方,所以在一次课后老师委婉地询问同学D原因。同学D表示他认为这是一个客观的评价,应向老师提出的教学建议,并没有考虑到与教师的个人关系,提出建议并不影响与老师之间的关系。但这位老师觉得学生给出较低评价很受挫。看到老师失落的表情,同学D也开始觉得很不理解,而后与老师的交谈也越来越少了。经过此事后,同学D开始对当地人产生了偏见,认为他们很虚荣,不太愿意与之交往了。

案例5:同学E是在浙江高校就读的2018级的国际研究生,来自非洲刚果。他是一个不善于表达、性格内向的学生。在准备论文开题报告的过程中,辅导员老师发现同学E的写作进度很慢,问其原因,他告诉辅导员老师自己跟导师的关系不太好,中国学生也不愿意帮助自己,不知道如何独自完成课题研究。他一直强调导师不喜欢自己,不尊重他自己选的研究方向,并且不能理解为什么导师要求他跟着其他中国学生一起做他们的研究项目,并认为他帮了中国学生,而中国学生又不肯帮自己,自己也不知道如何跟他们沟通。他甚至发觉,导师会给中国学生一些学习实践机会,而不会给留学生,认为老师有差别对待自己。因此同学E心里很痛苦,对学习也失去了兴趣,所以常常旷课,也不参与实验,更别提论文开题报告了。

案例6:同学F是来自非洲科特迪瓦的留学生,本科就读于中国某高校国际贸易专业,目前在浙江某高校土木工程管理专业读研。同学F的汉语水平不错,能与老师和同学用中文交流,但由于自己跨专业读研,学习压力很大。他表示自己需要花费比别的同学多三四倍的精力去完成课业,这让他十分疲惫。同学约他参加课余活动,他总是拒绝到公众场合,给人一种难以接近的感觉。而每当考试来临前,自己都会无比焦虑,因为他不知道自己是否能行。他清楚自己国家本专业的工作机会很少,而在中国本专业的研究生之间竞争压力也特别激烈,他时常怀疑自己未来能否找到工作,时常难以入眠,甚至在深夜哭泣。

四、跨文化适应策略

一般而言,高校国际生群体的跨文化适应过程,也是个体采取不同策略,逐渐认识、融入留学目的国家文化的过程。

(一)跨文化适应的策略类型

加拿大跨文化心理学家 John Berry 提出的跨文化适应模式理论认为,跨文化适应的本质是不同个体改变自我的过程,而个体采用何种自我调整策略主要由两个因素决定:一是个人对接触异族文化建立新的人际关系的态度,另一个则是个人对保持自我原有文化传统和身份的态度。在这两种因素相互作用并形成了整合、同化、分离和边缘等四种跨文化适应策略(见图 6-2)。

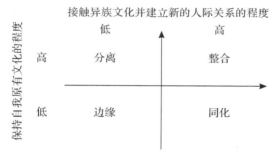

图 6-2　Berry 的跨文化适应策略

(1)整合(integration)。采取这种策略的高校国际生,既能保持自我的原有文化,又能同时接受中国文化中的价值观念和行为方式,既与本国或本民族群体保持着联系,又能融入中国群体进行良性的社交互动,从而达到相互融洽的适应模式。

(2)同化(assimilation)。采取这种策略的高校国际生,较少保持原来的文化传统和身份,努力寻求与当地中国人交往的机会,日常交流尽可能使用汉语,积极建立新的人际关系,尽量把自己视为当地人的适应模式。

（3）分离（separation）。采取这种策略的高校国际生，更愿意保持自我文化身份，即便在中国生活，也坚持自己原有的生活习惯和行为方式，交往群体仍限于本国或本民族的同胞群体，和中国人则保持距离，尽量避免接触与交流。

（4）边缘（marginalization）。采取这种策略的高校国际生，既对同胞保持自我原有文化传统兴趣不大，也不认同中国文化的价值观和行为方式，不愿与其他不同文化群体进行交流，只愿选择一个人独来独往的适应模式。

【观点交流】

1. 你倾向于使用什么跨文化适应策略？你认为自己的适应效果如何？
2. 你认为哪一种策略对于维护跨文化环境中的心理健康更有利？为什么？

研究表明，采用整合策略的人在接触新文化的同时也能保持比较稳定的自我认知，吸收、融合两种文化养分，对跨文化心理健康是最有利的，因此适应效果最佳。而边缘策略的效果是最差的，尤其是选择切断各种社交往来，十分不利于自我认知发展，严重者还容易陷入极端心理，造成抑郁等心理疾病。

（二）高校国际生跨文化适应策略的选择应该自由而灵活

事实上，对于高校国际生而言，有时候适应策略的选择也并不是个体能够主动进行的，无须有心理压力。

一方面是跨文化交际本身是一个双向互动、不断发展的过程，周围人对高校国际生的态度及其跨文化水平的高低，都相应地影响着其采取的策略。例如，遇到的当地人性情越亲切友好，性格越外向，或跨文化水平和对外接纳程度越高，越懂得相互尊重，高校国际生也越倾向于采取文化适应程度越高的策略；反之亦然。

另一方面，随着来华时间增长，高校国际生的汉语水平的提升，跟老师、同学、邻居等当地人接触程度越高，采取的策略就越容易转变为整合。因此，作为高校国际生，并不需要强迫自己马上采取整合策略，特别是初来乍到时，汉语水平较低、对陌生环境缺乏安全感，不得已选择分离，通过与本国同胞一起探索新环境，待逐渐熟悉适应中国的文化环境之后，再慢慢转变采取适应策略也无不可。

总之,在面对具体的跨文化适应问题时,大家可以根据自己的具体情况自由灵活地进行选择和调整。

第三节　掌握调适方法　提高心理素质

语言的障碍、习俗的差异、价值观的冲突等因素都可能导致身处异国他乡的高校国际生产生文化休克,即跨文化适应不良导致的焦虑、烦闷、怀疑、敌对情绪等心理健康问题。情况严重的学生,甚至可能出现如极度抑郁、精神分裂、自杀等极端表现。因此,身处跨文化环境中的高校国际生群体,应当掌握科学的心理调适方法,维持自身健康的心理状态是完成异国求学任务的基础。

一、克服文化休克的方法

要知道,每个身处跨文化环境的个体都在经历着各种各样文化冲突的挑战,以及这种经历给个体心理带来的冲击。因此,为了更好地适应跨文化环境,高校国际生群体必须了解一些常见的克服文化休克的方法。

(一)提升目的国语言运用水平

语言是交际的工具。要想融入留学目的国的社会生活和学习环境,目的国的语言熟练程度直接决定着个体在该环境中与他人进行交际的顺利程度。也就是说,高校国际生的汉语水平越高,越容易融入中国的生活和学习环境,越有助于减少跨文化适应的难度和过程。因此,提升汉语水平,不一定是来华留学的目的,但一定是在华学习生活中对于避免文化冲突最基础、最行之有效的工具。

(二)通过良好的人际交往建立社会支持系统

人们需要的社会支持系统,即个人在自己的人际关系网络中所能获得的来自他人的物质和精神上的帮助和支援。这个人际关系网络,往往包括自己的亲人、朋友、师长、同学、同乡、同事、邻里、合作伙伴等。当人们身处异国他乡,除了家乡亲人的情感支持外,我们需要积极地结交更多师友,争取在留学目的国建立良好的人际关系。较多良好的人际沟通,如进行交流与倾诉、获得他人理解和心理支持等,能减少孤独感;遇到困难时,还能获得及时而有力的帮助。这对跨文化交际者保持良好心态、避免走极端想法是十分有利的。

(三)熟悉目的国的文化常识

知己知彼,百战不殆。认知目的国的文化、习俗、规约等,了解交际对方的言行及其原因,无疑能够帮助自我在面对跨文化冲突时,保持正向的思维方式,及时化解自身不良情绪,甚至能够对一些矛盾和困难一笑了之。在跨文化交际过程中,对目的国文化常识越熟悉,越有助于在跨文化适应过程中保持理解和包容的心态。

(四)参加更多的文化活动或集体活动

人们在心理上往往对于陌生人、陌生环境有着天然的距离感,但是要避免封闭的自我环境,就应当鼓励自己走出一个人的"交际舒适圈",结交朋友、参与集体活动,积累丰富的跨文化交际的实践经验。通过参加各种各样的当地活动,跨文化交际者能够获取更多对自身感知当地社会文化有效的信息,更好地融入目的国文化。

二、自我心理调适的方法

当遭遇文化休克现象较为严重时,可以尝试通过自我调适的手段来渡过难关,这就需要我们掌握一些专业的心理调适方法。

在心理咨询过程中,心理咨询师常使用一些行之有效的方法来帮助来访者缓解心理问题,如放松技术、合理情绪想象等。对这些方法的合理使用可以帮助我们缓解生活中遇到的一些情绪或行为问题。

(一)放松技术

放松技术也称放松疗法,是一种通过有意识地控制自身的心理和生理活动、降低唤醒水平、改善机体功能紊乱的心理治疗方法。放松疗法认为,一个人的情绪发生有相应的躯体反应,如果改变个体的躯体反应,那么个体的情绪也可以得到改善。放松疗法就是通过意识控制使肌肉放松,进而舒缓紧张情绪,有利于个体身心健康。

近年来经过不断的发展,放松训练包括五大类型:(1)渐进性肌肉放松;(2)自然训练;(3)自我催眠;(4)冥想;(5)生物反馈辅助下的放松。在心理咨询过程中,放松技术主要是在咨询师的指导下使来访者完成放松。

在日常生活中我们也可以按照以下步骤进行放松。具体操作步骤如下：

——以尽量舒适的姿势靠在沙发或躺椅上。

——闭目。

——将注意力集中到头部，咬紧牙关，使面颊感到紧张，体会这种紧绷的感觉。然后再将牙关松开，体会松弛的感觉。依次逐一将头部各肌肉放松下来。

——将注意力转移到颈部，尽量使脖子的肌肉感到紧张，体会紧绷的感觉。然后把脖子的肌肉全部放松，体会松弛的感觉。

——将注意力集中到双手，用力紧握双手，体会紧绷的感觉。然后将双手逐渐松开，体会松弛的感觉。

——将注意力集中到胸部，开始深吸气憋气一分钟左右，缓缓吐气。再吸气吐气，反复几次，体会过程中紧张和松弛的感觉。

（二）合理情绪想象技术

合理情绪想象技术是理性—情绪疗法中最常用的方法之一。在心理咨询的过程中，咨询师通过对来访者进行合理的想象引导，帮助来访者运用合理想象替代或体验压力情境，以此缓解症状。

具体的实施步骤如下：

（1）通过咨询师的引导，使来访者在想象中进入他自感不适的情境之中，体验在这种情境下的强烈的情绪反应。

（2）帮助来访者使用合理想象，体验在合理信念下自身情绪的变化，体会合理情绪想象下的适度情绪。

（3）停止想象，让来访者讲述他是怎么想的，而使自己的情绪发生了变化。此时咨询师要强化来访者的新的合理的信念，纠正某些不合理的信念，补充其他有关的合理信念。

【观点交流】

1. 在日常生活中遇到压力事件时，是否可以进行自我引导，用合理情绪想象的方法使自己体会适度情绪，缓解情绪问题？请试举例说明。

2. 在你的国家，采用什么有趣的方式缓解情绪压力？你有可以分享的心得吗？

例如：有一位女大学生，对要在即将举行的一个会上发言感到恐惧，认为自己肯定不行，会出丑、"砸锅"，一切都会变得非常之糟。我们可以做下面的想象练习以缓解恐惧：

（1）闭上眼睛，使自己坐得很舒服。想象自己到了会场（要尽量想象得与真实情况一致）。现在该轮到自己发言了，有点紧张，讲得有点磕磕巴巴……（现在可能感到非常恐惧，可能有些坚持不下去）

（2）把这个场景保持在脑海中，同时把那种觉得非常恐惧的感觉变成只是有点紧张，想象自己仍在会场上发言，只是有点紧张。（需要坚持几次）

（3）检视自己的感觉或想法的变化，用合理信念代替不合理信念。（如果现在从会场逃走会更糟，反正我得在这坚持讲完。我已经站在这儿开始讲了，虽然讲得不好人家会笑话我，但我要是中间停下来不讲跑掉了，人家更会看不起我。不管别人说我什么，我也得讲完该讲的话。不管别人怎么想，现在要做的最关键的事，是要完成这次大会发言；不管别人会怎样看，可能发言不如某些人讲得好，但自己并不是个一无是处的人。）

（四）自我心理测量

一般地，我们可以采用的心理健康状况自评量表，如《症状自评量表SCL-90》。它将从感觉、情感、思维、意识、行为直到生活习惯、人际关系、饮食睡眠等多种角度，评定一个人是否有某种心理症状及其严重程度如何。它对有心理症状（即有可能处于心理障碍或心理障碍边缘）的人有良好的区分能力。适用于测查某人群中哪些人可能有心理障碍、某人可能有何种心理障碍及其严重程度如何。

三、寻求专业机构的帮助

如果长期处于孤独、失落、焦虑等令自己不安的心理状态，而自己已经无法调节某种不良情绪的时间长达 2 周，则应当主动寻求专业心理机构的帮助。

【知识拓展】

学校心理健康教育中心

【思考题】

1. 在你成长的社会环境中,人们感到心理不适时,是否习惯联系心理医生,或寻求专业机构的帮助? 你怎么看?

2. 你认为自己是否已经适应中国的生活学习? 有什么实用的跨文化适应策略和技巧可以分享给同伴?

Chapter Six　Maintaining Mental Health and Improving Adaptability

The 21st century is an age marked by highly advanced technology, but it is also filled with immense pressure. This makes it possible to achieve mental well-being for modern individuals while also demanding higher levels of psychological resilience from them. A healthy psyche is a necessary condition and foundation for the comprehensive development of human beings. This is especially true for international students who leave their familiar cultural environment to study abroad, as good mental qualities and strong adaptability are the key to their academic and career success.

【Mind Map】

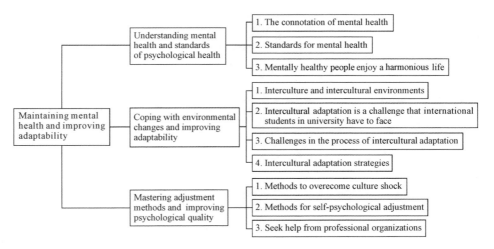

Section One   Understanding Mental Health and Standards of Mental Health

1. The Connotation of Mental Health

(1)The concept of Health is Constantly Evolving

The concept of health is constantly evolving over time under the influence of social and cultural factors.

In 1948, the World Health Organization (WHO) Constitution defined health as "a state of complete physical, mental and social well-being, and not merely the absence of disease or infirmity".

In 1989, the WHO further developed the concept of health, arguing that it should include four aspects: physical health, good social adaptation, moral health, and mental health.

(2) The Modern Concept of Health Emphasizes the Integration of Physical and Mental Well-being

Compared to the traditional notion of health, the modern concept of health refers to not only physical health from the biomedical perspective, but also a state of well-being in terms of mental and social adaptation. As human beings have both physiological and psychological activities, the body and mind integrate into a cohesive entity, jointly responding to the external environment.

When a person is in poor physical condition, his mental health may be affected, leading to decreased attention, low mood, irritability, and even various types of mental disorders. On the other hand, when a person's mental health is at risk, such as one who suffers from chronic depression or high levels of stress, he is more prone to displaying a range of physical symptoms. Thus, physical and mental health are inseparable.

(3)The Definition of Mental Health

The WHO constitution states: "Health is a state of complete

physical, mental and social well-being and not merely the absence of disease or infirmity".

More specifically, mental health refers to a state of good adaptation to life, in which an individual experiences positive psychological well-being and is able to use effective coping strategies to maintain this state. For example, seeking support from friends when feeling anxious.

Mental health can be divided into narrow and broad perspectives. The narrow perspective of mental health mainly focuses on preventing or treating mental disorders or behavioral problems. The broad perspective of mental health aims to help individuals reach their optimal state of well-being, enabling them to better adapt to the social environment.

【Knowledge Expansion】

May 25th, National College Student Mental Health Day

China's Youth Day is on May 4th. For a long time, May has been endowed by the Chinese with the same vitality and passion as those commonly associated with young people. In 1999, students from Sichuan University established National College Student Mental Health Day on May 25th, which sounds like "I love myself" (pronounced similarly to "525" in Chinese). The purpose was to promote the idea that college students should care for others by starting with caring for themselves first, as one can better love others only when they love themselves. In 2000, Beijing Normal University proposed to designate May 25th as Mental Health Day for students in universities in Beijing, and put forward the slogan "I love myself, and give a clear sky to my psychology!" In 2004, the All-China Youth Federation and the National Student Federation officially designated May 25th as National College Student Mental Health Day.

The aim of establishing Mental Health Day is to promote the idea of self-love, respect for life, seizing opportunities, and creating a better and more successful life among college students. At the same time, starting with taking care of oneself, it aims to develop a sense of caring for others and society among young people. A mentally healthy person is first and foremost someone who can recognize and accept themselves, affirm their self-worth, and maintain an optimistic and confident outlook. At the same time, they are able to interact with others with respect, trust, love, and tolerance. They can share, accept, and give love and friendship, and can work together with others to create a better life.

2. Standards for Mental Health

(1) The Criteria for Evaluating Mental Health are Influenced by Specific Factors

Mental health is not a static state, but rather being in a constantly changing process, and it is also influenced by factors such as social environment and cultural background. So developing a unified standard for assessing mental health is a complex issue. Experts and scholars in the field of psychology analyze this issue from different perspectives.

【Knowledge Expansion】

The famous American humanistic psychologist Abraham H. Maslow proposed 10 criteria for mental health:

1) Having sufficient self-security.

2) Fully understanding oneself and appropriately evaluating one's abilities.

3) Having realistic life goals.

4) Keeping in touch with the society.

5) Maintaining integrity and harmony of personality.

6) Being good at learning from experience.

7) Maintaining good interpersonal relationships.

8) Appropriately expressing and controlling emotions.

9) Showing one's personality within the limits of collective requirements.

10) Meeting one's basic needs without violating social norms.

Based on the research findings of psychologists and the current situation of university students in China, we generally evaluate the mental health status of students according to the following criteria:

1) One has normal intellectual development and performs well in the learning process. Intelligence refers to a comprehensive ability that mainly includes attention, memory, thinking, imagination, etc. Normal intelligence provides the basic psychological condition for students' learning, life, and work, and it is also the primary condition for international university students to adapt to the environment and seek personal development.

2) One has positive and stable emotions, and exhibits profound emotional harmony. Emotions refer to the positive or negative experiences that individuals have due to varying levels of environmental satisfaction of their personal needs. Positive emotions can increase a person's level of activity and therefore are beneficial to their mental health, while negative emotions can easily lower a person's level of activity, thus being detrimental to the mental health. Generally speaking, mentally healthy students often exhibit more positive emotions. Emotions belong to a higher level of social motional that are linked to individuals' social needs. So psychologically healthy students often have good interpersonal relationships and a strong sense of social responsibility.

3) One's willpower is sound, and his behaviors are coordinated and consistent. Psychologically healthy students typically demonstrate well-developed qualities of consciousness, decisiveness, tenacity, and self-control. They can consciously adjust their behavior according to their needs; make decisions and execute them; persistently strive under the guidance of goals until the goals are achieved; consciously resist unreasonable desires and effectively restrain their behaviors.

4) One's personality is harmonious and unified, and his character is complete and independent. Personality encompasses a range of important and enduring psychological traits of a person. Psychologically healthy individuals maintain a certain degree of balance, harmony, and perfection

in all aspects of their personality structure. They are able to unify their needs, motivations, attitudes, ideals, and behaviors, achieving consistency between their attitudes and actions. And psychologically healthy students can provide a relatively objective evaluation of their own temperament, character, and abilities. They do not become complacent or arrogant about their strengths, nor do they become overly self-deprecating about their weaknesses. They are able to integrate their "ideal self" with their "real self", and maintain balance with their environment.

5) One can be well adapted to the society and maintains positive interpersonal relationships. Marx said: "Human nature is the sum of all social relations." Psychologically healthy students can objectively understand their social environment and have harmonious interpersonal relationships. When faced with unfavorable environmental conditions, they do not blame the others or themselves, but take the initiative to change their mindset, adapt to the environment positively, and transform it. When interacting with others, they should master certain social skills, be honest and trustworthy, tolerant and loving, equal and kind.

6) The characteristics of one's psychological activities correspond to the age features of their psychological development. The psychological activities of individuals are a continuous process of development, and different stages of psychological development demonstrate different characteristics. A psychologically healthy person should generally demonstrate psychological characteristics that are consistent with the common psychological characteristics of individuals in their age group. Psychologically healthy students have positive attitudes, a strong desire to learn, and quick responsiveness. And negativity, cynicism, dependence, and immaturity are signs of poor mental health.

【Opinion Exchange】

1. Do you agree with the above evaluation criteria? Why or why not?

2. What evaluation criteria are used in your country to determine someone's mental health is sound or not?

(2) Reference for Levels of Mental Health

Generally, we roughly divide the levels of mental health into three categories: normal psychological state, mild psychological disorders, and severe pathological psychology (see Fig. 6-1).

3. Mentally Healthy People Enjoying a Harmonious Life

(1) Mental health enables to attain psychological harmony

A psychologically healthy person is able to integrate his needs, motivations, ideals, and behaviors into a harmonious entity based on the correct outlooks of life and the world, as well as of values. They can obtain a psychological experience of a harmonious life.

【Conceptual Analysis】

"Harmony" refers to a state of coordination and balance among things. "Harmony" is one of the essences of Chinese civilization and is an ideal state that the Chinese nation has been pursuing for a long time. Harmony is the foothold of traditional Chinese philosophical dialectic and Marxist dialectic. It is an ideal state that the Chinese people pursue, where there is harmony between human beings and nature, as well as within one's inner self.

(2) Mental health enables to enjoy a harmonious life

People usually seek balance in various aspects of their daily lives such as physical, social, psychological, and spiritual dimensions. However, they may also encounter aspects that are not well-coordinated. This requires them to broaden horizons, to enhance abilities to face difficulties and challenges, and to proactively adjust their psychological states to enjoy a harmonious life.

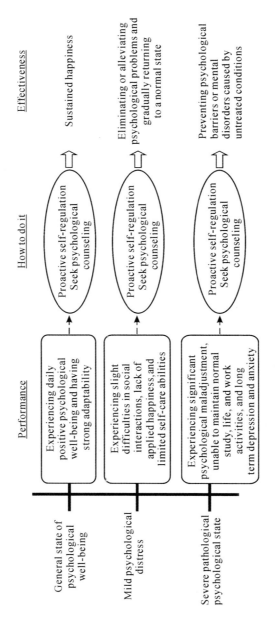

Fig. 6-1   The three levels of psychological health

【Knowledge Expansion】

Harmonious Life

Scholars believe that body, achievement, social communication, and future vision are the four components of a balanced and harmonious life. Each individual has their own estimation of these four aspects and is always striving for balance in all areas. Please evaluate yourself on each aspect and mark your score (0~100) on the coordinate graph below, and connect the four points with lines to see what kind of quadrilateral is formed.

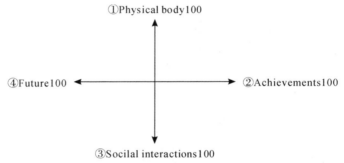

①Physical body100

④Future100 ←——————→ ②Achievements100

③Socilal interactions100

Step 1: First, you need to ask yourself these questions:

1) Do you feel satisfied with your body and appearance? How much importance do you place on maintaining your physical health? How would you rate yourself on this aspect?

2) How much effort have you put into your academic or career pursuits? How much attention have you given to your achievements? How would you rate yourself on this aspect?

3) How much effort have you put into your family and social relationships? How would you rate yourself on this aspect?

4) How do you imagine your future? Are you optimistic or pessimistic about it? How much effort have you invested in your outlook on life and the world? How would you rate yourself on this aspect?

Step 2: Now, connect the scores you gave yourself and form a quadrilateral. If each side is balanced, then your life is well-balanced, otherwise it is not.

Step 3: Discuss with your classmates about your quadrilateral: whether it is balanced, which part you have exerted more effort and why, what positive aspects you have gained, and what kind of adjustments are needed.

Section Two   Coping with Environmental Changes and Improving Adaptability

1. Interculture and Intercultural Environments

(1)   International   University   Students   Situated   in   an Intercultural Environment

With the deepening of the globalization and the continuous increase in social mobility, the interactions between different cultures and ethnic groups have promoted the development of interpersonal relationships. Interculture refers to culture and its characteristics that transcend national and ethnic boundaries. It requires a full understanding of cultural phenomena, customs, habits, etc. that differ from or conflict with one's own culture, and on this basis, acceptance and adaptation should be made with an inclusive attitude.

For international students in university, leaving their own country to study abroad also means leaving their familiar living environment and beginning to experience cross-border culture and life.

(2)Definition and Characteristics of Intercultural Environment

Intercultural environment refers to a setting where individuals are situated in two or more groups with different cultural backgrounds, spanning across different countries, ethnicities, and cultural systems.

The most significant features of intercultural environment are as follows.

1) There are significant differences in aspects such as mother tongue

communication, social customs, cultural background, political and economic systems, and laws and regulations between the foreign cultural environment and one's own familiar growth environment.

2) Individuals or groups are required not only to rely on their own language codes, cognitive habits, concepts, and behaviors, but also to understand and master those of the other groups to adapt to such cultural differences.

3) The differences in culture can easily lead individuals to experience psychological confusion and even encounter conflicts.

2. Intercultural Adaptation Is a Challenge International Students in University Have to Face

International students face a number of changes when leaving their home country to study abroad. These changes can have a significant impact on their mental well-being. Therefore, it is important for them to have a good understanding of intercultural knowledge, as well as of the conflicts and challenges they may encounter in a new cultural environment, and of the adaptation strategies they can adopt. This knowledge serves as a necessary safeguard for international students to maintain their mental health.

(1) The Connotation of Intercultural Adaptation

Intercultural adaptation refers to the process where individuals in an intercultural environment, actively accept, adapt to and integrate into the local lifestyle by having a tolerant attitude towards cultural phenomena, customs, and habits that differ or conflict with their own culture, in order to achieve a balance between their cultural identity and acceptance of new cultural knowledge.

For international students who come to study in China, they need to undergo intercultural adaptation when being in the Chinese language environment, facing Chinese social norms and even cultural values that differ from their own.

【Knowledge Expansion】

Cross-Cultural   Adaptation   Assessment   for International Students Studying in China

(2)Different Stages and Manifestations of Intercultural Adaptation

Intercultural adaptation is not something that happens overnight, but rather a dynamic process of gradually recognizing and responding to a new cultural environment. American anthropologist Kalvero Oberg divided the process of intercultural adaptation into four stages.

In the initial stage, individuals who just come to an unfamiliar country keep their mood high at the very beginning due to their positive attitude towards the fresh culture. They feel fascinated, excited, and optimistic about the differences.

When individuals encounter cultural differences or conflicts that do not align with their previous expectations, it can result in psychological setbacks. This may lead to hostility and prejudice towards the foreign country.

As individuals enhance their proficiency in the target language, they tend to become more adaptable to the new cultural environment, and begin to view the people and things of the foreign country from a positive perspective again.

Individuals are able to understand, accept, and enjoy the social norms and customs of the foreign country. Therefore, their adaptability improves, and their anxiety disappears, and they get along well with the intercultural environment.

As individuals in different interculture have different personalities and experiences, as well as different opportunities or social support, the time and effort required for the four stages of intercultural adaptation varies from person to person.

【Opinion Exchange】

Which stage do you think you are currently in? What are the reasons for being in this stage?

Which factors can help international university students reach the intercultural adaptation period more quickly?

(3) Poor Intercultural Adaptation Can Easily Lead to Cultural Shock

In terms of the performance of intercultural adaptation among international university students, some are able to make timely self-psychological adjustments, adapt well, smoothly enter the adaptation period, and enjoy the learning life in a foreign country; while others experience poor adaptation and even cultural shock. This requires us to pay attention to the issue of intercultural adaptation.

【Conceptual Analysis】

"Shock" in Chinese refers to a pathological state in which acute cell hypoxia leads to respiratory distress.

Oberg (1958) first proposed the concept of culture shock, which refers to the deep psychological anxiety that individuals experience in an intercultural environment when they lose their familiar social symbols, including language, cultural customs, and social norms, and are not familiar with those of the other groups. The Chinese term "文化休克" (culture shock) vividly illustrates this state of physical and mental "hypoxia" that individuals experience when they do not adapt to the unfamiliar cultural environment of a foreign country.

According to Oberg et al., "culture shock" is mainly manifested as psychological discomfort, and sometimes accompanied with physiological reactions. Generally speaking, international university students inevitably suffer from "culture shock" during the initial stage of their arrival in a foreign country, but the duration and severity of this experience varies among individuals. Some may only experience mild "culture shock" for a few weeks, while others may experience it for a long time, even throughout their study period; some may feel uncomfortable psychologically and emotionally, while others may suffer from physical illnesses such as headaches, insomnia, stomach pain, and abdominal pain.

Refer to the checklist and see what your culture shock symptoms are!

☐Feeling lonely, helpless, and longing for family and friends intensely.

☐Feeling restless and experiencing psychological anxiety.

☐Feeling afraid of being deceived, bullied, or harmed.

☐Compulsively focusing on self-hygiene and health.

☐Excessively identifying with one's native culture and adopting a hostile attitude towards people in a new cultural environment.

☐Avoiding contact with others.

☐Feeling physically uncomfortable, such as experiencing headaches, insomnia, stomachaches, or abdominal pain.

3. Challenges in the Process of Intercultural Adaptation

The difficulties that international university students face during the process of cultural adaptation to a foreign country can be broadly summarized into three aspects: adaptation to living environment, interpersonal adaptation, and academic adaptation.

(1)Adapting to Living Environment

For international university students, the environment they need to adapt to during their study abroad, namely, the environment they live and grow in the destination country, includes aspects such as the region, living conditions, and climate conditions, as well as local diet, transportation, living habits, and safety regulations.

【Case Analysis】

Please read the following cases and discuss the problems encountered by international students in universities in the cases.

Case 1: Student A from Ethiopia has been studying in China for more than 2 months. He often feels unhappy and complains about the difficulties of the courses, of learning Chinese and of recognizing Chinese characters. He also finds winter in southern China very damp and uncomfortable, as there is no heating in the classroom and the air conditioning in the dormitory is not very warm. He tells his fellow countrymen that he complains frequently in China, and becomes a person who is easily irritated.

Case 2: Before coming to China, Student B from Indonesia had always been fascinated by the country. However, two months after arriving in China, she complains that the weather is too cold, so she is afraid to go out of the dormitory. And she also finds the Chinese foods are too greasy to eat. Besides, Student B does not know how to cook herself, so she eats poorly every day and even gets a stomach problem. In addition, she often feels homesick, making it difficult for her to concentrate on her studies.

(2) Interpersonal adaptation

Different cultural backgrounds breed different social etiquettes, local customs, religious practices, and other norms. So international university students need to adapt to new ways of interpersonal communication in a new cultural environment.

【Case Analysis】

Please read the following case and analyze the problems encountered by the international university students.

Case 3: Student C from Polish, who came to China to study, finds that Chinese people like to ask personal questions, such as "How old are you?", "What brand is your dress? How much is it?", "What does your husband do for a living?" etc. These questions make her feel uncomfortable, so she doesn't like to communicate with them. When going out, she also has to face many problems, such as the taxi app not being in English, the operation being too complicated, the subway and buses being too crowded, people not being in queue in the public places. Such situations make Student C feel very irritable, and she learns a lot of swear words to vent her emotions. However, she feels that this is not who she really is, and she often falls into self-doubt.

(3)Academic Adaptation

The fundamental purpose of intercultural communication activities for international university students is to facilitate study. If the individual learners can adapt to the cultural environment of the destination country as soon as possible, they can actively integrate their motivation, emotions, attitudes, and behaviors into a unity, which promotes the success in completing their studies. However, due to the stark differences in education, training methods, and campus management between the foreign country and the international students' motherland, intercultural adaptation has become a severe test that international students cannot avoid.

【Case Analysis】

Please read the following cases and analyze the problems encountered by the international university students.

Case 4: Student D from Germany is studying language courses at a university in China. He gets along well with one of his teachers and often communicates with him. However, Student D gave the teacher a low score for the evaluation of his performance. The teacher was puzzled and asked Student D for the reason after class. Student D believed that the evaluation was fair and objective, and that the teacher should receive constructive feedback regardless of any personal relationships. However, the teacher was very disappointed, while Student D also felt misunderstood and their conversations became increasingly infrequent. After that, Student D develops prejudices against the local people, thinking that they are very vain and becomes less willing to socialize with them.

Case 5: Student E is an international graduate student from Congo who enrolled in a university in Zhejiang, China in 2018. He is introverted and not good at expressing himself. His counselor notices that he is proceeding slowly with the preparation of his research proposal and asks for the reason. Student E explains that he does not have a good relationship with his supervisor, and the Chinese students are not willing to help him. He consistently emphasizes that his supervisor dislikes him and does not respect his research direction. He is also unable to understand why his supervisor requires him to work on research projects with other Chinese students and feels that he has assisted them without receiving any help in return. He even perceives that his supervisor provides Chinese students with more opportunities for hands-on learning experiences compared to international students, leading him to believe that he is being treated unfairly. As a result, Student E is in great psychological distress and losses interest in his studies, which makes him frequently skip class and not participate in any experiments or research.

Case 6: Student F is an international student from Cote d'Ivoire. He completed his undergraduate studies in International Trade and is currently pursuing a graduate degree in Civil Engineering Management at a university in Zhejiang. Although he has a good command of Chinese, he is under a lot of pressure due to the inconsistency between his undergraduate and graduate majors. He usually needs to devote three or four times more effort to complete his coursework than his classmates, which makes him very tired. And he always refuses the invitation to participate in extracurricular activities, giving others a sense of being unapproachable. When exams are approaching, Student F feels extremely anxious because he is unsure whether he can perform well. He knows that job opportunities in his motherland are scarce and that the competition is fierce in China, which leads him to frequently doubt whether he is able to find a job in the future. As a result, he often struggles to fall asleep and even cries late at night.

4. Intercultural Adaptation Strategies

In general, intercultural adaptation for international university students is a process of adopting various strategies to gradually understand and integrate into the culture of their destination countries.

(1) Types of Intercultural Adaptation Strategies

Canadian intercultural psychologist John Berry (1990) proposed the Intercultural Adaptation Model theory, which suggests that the essence of intercultural adaptation is the process of individual change, and the choice of self-adjustment strategies mainly depends on two factors: first, an individual's attitude towards building new interpersonal relationships with a different culture, and second, an individual's attitude towards maintaining his own cultural traditions and identity. These two factors interact and form four types of intercultural adaptation strategies: Integration, Assimilation, Separation, and Marginalization (see Fig. 6-2).

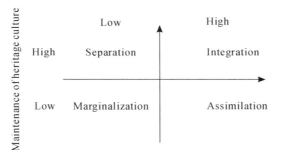

Fig. 6-2   Berry's model of cross-cultural adaptation illustrated

1) Integration. By adopting this strategy, international students are able to maintain their original cultural identity while also accept the values and behaviors of Chinese culture. They maintain connections with their own ethnic group while integrating into the Chinese society to create positive social interactions, thus achieving mutual adaptation.

2) Assimilation. International students who adopt this strategy tend to maintain less of their original cultural traditions and identity. Instead, they actively seek opportunities to interact with Chinese people, to communicate in Chinese as much as possible, to establish new interpersonal relationships, and to adapt themselves as locals.

3) Separation. International students who adopt this strategy prefer to maintain their cultural identity. Even when living in China, they insist on their original lifestyle and behavioral norms. They tend to limit their social circle to their own ethnic group, while keeping a distance from Chinese people and trying to avoid contact and communication as much as possible.

4) Marginalization. International students who adopt this strategy are not interested in maintaining their original cultural traditions or identifying with Chinese cultural values and behaviors. They are unwilling to interact with different cultural groups and prefer to be solitary and independent.

【Opinion Exchange】

1. Which intercultural adaptation strategy do you prefer? How do you think about your adaptation effect?

2. Which strategy do you think is more advantageous for maintaining mental health in an intercultural environment? Why?

Previous studies have shown that individuals who adopt an Integration strategy can maintain a relatively stable self-awareness while also being exposed to a new culture. This approach allows for the absorption and integration of nutrients from both cultures, which is the most favorable for intercultural mental health, thus having the best adaptation effect. The Marginalization strategy, on the other hand, has the worst effect. Especially for those who choose to sever social interactions, it is extremely detrimental to the development of self-awareness and can even lead to extreme psychological problems such as depression.

(2)The Choice of Intercultural Adaptation Strategy for International University Students Should be Free and Flexible

In fact, for international university students, the choice of adaptation strategies is not always something that individuals can control, so there is no need to feel pressure.

On the one hand, intercultural communication is a two-way and constantly evolving process. The attitudes of those around international students and their levels of intercultural competence also influence the strategies they adopt. For example, if local people are more friendly and open-minded, and have higher levels of intercultural competence and acceptance, international students are more likely to adopt strategies that are more culturally adapted. Otherwise, the opposite is true.

On the other hand, as their time in China increases, their Chinese language proficiency improves, and their contact with local teachers, classmates, neighbors, and others increases, they are more likely to adopt an Integration strategy. Therefore, as international students, they do not need to force themselves to adopt Integration strategies immediately, especially when they first arrive and may have lower Chinese language proficiency and lack a sense of security in an unfamiliar environment. In such cases, they may choose Separation strategy and explore the new environment with their compatriots, and gradually shift to other adaptation strategy as they become more familiar with the cultural environment in China.

In summary, when facing intercultural adaptation problems, everyone can choose and adjust their strategies according to their own situation.

Section Three   Mastering Adjustment Methods and Improving Psychological Quality

Factors such as language barriers, differences in customs, and conflicts in values may cause cultural shock for international students, making them encounter mental health problems such as anxiety, frustration, suspicion, and hostility. In severe cases, students may even have extreme performances such as severe depression, schizophrenia, or suicide. Therefore, international students should master scientific psychological adjustment methods to maintain their mental health, which is the foundation for completing their studies abroad.

1. Methods to Overcome Culture Shock

It's important to understand that individuals in an intercultural environment face various challenges of cultural conflicts and bear the psychological impact of such experiences. Therefore, in order to better adapt to an intercultural environment, international university students need to know some common methods to overcome culture shock.

(1) Improving Proficiency in the Language of the Destination Country

Language is a tool for communication. In order to integrate into the social and learning environment of a foreign country, the proficiency of target language directly determines the smoothness of individual communication with others. In other words, the higher the Chinese proficiency of international students, the easier it is for them to adapt to the life and learning in China, and the more helpful it is to reduce the difficulties during the process of intercultural adaptation. Therefore, while improving Chinese language proficiency may not be the primary goal for international students studying in China, it is undoubtedly the most fundamental and effective tool for them to avoid cultural conflicts in academic and daily life.

(2) Building a Social Support System through Good Interpersonal Relationships

Social support systems are essential for individuals, providing them with both material and emotional assistance and support from others within their personal social network. This network typically includes family members, friends, teachers, classmates, compatriots, colleagues, neighbors, and partners. When individuals find themselves in a foreign country, it is important to seek out more friends in order to establish positive interpersonal relationships in the destination country. Individuals with good interpersonal communication skills, such as exchanging ideas and expressing oneself, gaining understanding and emotional support from others, can reduce feelings of loneliness. When faced with difficulties, they can also receive timely and effective help. This is very beneficial for intercultural communicators to maintain a positive mindset and avoid extreme ideas.

(3) Be Familiar with the Cultural Norms of the Destination Country

Know the enemy and know yourself; in a hundred battles you will never be in peril. Understanding the culture, customs, and conventions of the destination country is crucial for individuals to navigate intercultural interactions successfully. By understanding the behaviors and beliefs of the people one is communicating with, individuals can avoid misunderstandings and resolve conflicts in a positive manner. The more familiar individuals are with the cultural knowledge of the country, the better they will be able to maintain an attitude of understanding and openness during the process of intercultural adaptation.

(4) Participate in More Cultural or Group Activities

People often have a natural sense of distance from strangers and unfamiliar environment. However, in order to avoid a closed self-environment, they should encourage themselves to step out of their "social communication comfort zone," make friends, participate in group activities, and accumulate rich intercultural communication practical experience. By participating in various local activities, intercultural communicators can obtain more effective information about the social culture, and better integrate into the culture of the destination country.

2. Methods for Self-psychological Adjustment

When encountering severe culture shock, one can try to overcome the difficulties through self-psychological adjustment, which require us to master some professional psychological adjustment methods.

In the process of psychological counseling, psychologists often help clients relieve psychological problems by using some effective methods, such as Relaxation techniques and Rational Emotive Imagery. The appropriate use of these methods can help us alleviate some emotional or behavioral problems encountered in our lives.

(1)Relaxation Techniques

Relaxation techniques, also known as Relaxation therapy, are a form of psychological therapy that involves consciously controlling one's own mental and physical activity, reducing arousal levels, and improving the functioning of the body. Relaxation therapy believes that a person's emotions have corresponding bodily reactions, and if the individual's bodily reactions are changed, their emotions can also be improved. The therapy works by consciously controlling the relaxation of muscles to alleviate tense emotions, which is beneficial for an individual's physical and mental health.

In recent years, relaxation training has developed into five major types: 1) Progressive Muscle Relaxation; 2) Natural Training; 3) Self-hypnosis; 4) Meditation; 5) Biofeedback-Assisted Relaxation. Relaxation techniques are mainly used to help clients relax under the guidance of psychologists.

We can follow the following steps to relax:

—Sit or lie down in a comfortable position on a couch or reclining chair.

—Close your eyes.

—Focus your attention on your head; clench your teeth, and feel the tension in your cheeks. Then, release the tension in your jaw and feel the sensation of relaxation. Proceed to relax each muscle in your head one by one.

—Shift your focus to your neck, and try to tense the muscles to feel the sensation of tension. Then, release the tension and feel the relaxation.

—Focus your attention on your hands, clench your fists tightly, and feel the tension. Then, gradually release your hands and feel the relaxation.

—Focus your attention on your chest, take a deep breath and hold it for about a minute, then slowly exhale. Repeat the process of inhaling and exhaling a few times and feel the tension and relaxation throughout the process.

(2)Rational-Emotive Imagery

Rational-emotive imagery is one of the most commonly used techniques in rational-emotive therapy. Therapist guides clients to use Rational-Emotive Imagery to relieve their symptoms.

The steps are as follows:

1) Through therapist's guidance, clients imagine entering a situation in which they feel uncomfortable and experience strong emotional reactions within the context.

2) Help clients use rational-emotive imagery to let them have rational beliefs and experience their emotional changes.

3) Stop imagining and ask clients to describe how their thoughts have changed and how their emotions have changed. At this point, therapist should reinforce clients' new rational beliefs, correct any irrational beliefs, and supplement other relevant rational beliefs.

【Opinion Exchange】

1. Can self-guidance and rational-emotive imagery be used to alleviate emotional problems when encountering stressful events in daily life? Can you give an example?

2. How do people in your country alleviate emotional stress? Do you have any related personal experiences to share?

For example, a female college student is experiencing fear and self-doubt about giving a speech at an upcoming event, believing that she will embarrass herself and everything will turn out badly. If we were in her position, we can do the following exercise to alleviate such fear:

1) Close your eyes and get comfortable in your seat. Imagine yourself at the meeting (try to imagine it as realistically as possible). Now it's your turn to speak, and you're a little nervous, and you stutter a bit... (you may feel very afraid at this point and may not be able to continue).

2) Keep this scene in your mind, and at the same time, transform the feeling of extreme fear into just a bit of nervousness. Imagine yourself still speaking at the meeting, but just feeling a bit nervous. (This exercise needs to be practiced several times to be effective.)

3) Reflect on the changes in your feelings or thoughts, and replace irrational beliefs with rational ones. For example: "If I run away from the meeting now, things will only get worse. I have to stay here and finish my speech. I'm standing here to speak, and even if I don't speak well, people might laugh at me. I would be even more ashamed if I stopped speaking in the middle and ran away. The most important thing now is to complete this speech. Although others may speak better than me, I am not worthless".

(4) Self-psychological Assessment

Generally, we can use a self-assessment scale to assess mental health status, such as the "Symptom Checklist-90 (SCL-90)". It evaluates whether a person has any psychological symptoms and the severity of those symptoms from various perspectives, such as sensation, emotion, thought, consciousness, behavior, lifestyle habits, interpersonal relationships, sleep and eating habits. The scale can effectively distinguish individuals with psychological symptoms, including those who may be experiencing or at risk of developing psychological disorders. It is useful for identifying which individuals in a given population may be affected by psychological disorders, the specific type of disorders they may experience, as well as the severity of their symptoms.

3. Ways to Seek Help from Professional Organizations

If one finds himself in a prolonged state of psychological distress such as loneliness, depression, anxiety, etc. , and has been unable to regulate such negative emotions for more than 2 weeks, then he should seek help from a professional psychological institution.

【Knowledge Expansion】

School Mental Health Education Center

【Questions for Discussion】

1. Do people in your social circle have the habit of contacting a psychologist or seeking help from a professional institution when they experience psychological discomfort? What is your opinion?

2. Do you feel that you have successfully adapted to life and study in China? Can you share any practical strategies or techniques for intercultural adaptation that you have found helpful in adapting to life and study in China?

后 记

    高校国际生有其各自的本国意识形态和文化背景,他们的成长环境和受教育环境与中国存在着较大的差异,而且他们都已经成人,已经有了自己的思想行为标准,他们的世界观、人生观、价值观已基本形成。特别是来华初期,他们在语言、沟通、生活、跨文化交际等方面存在的困难,使他们不能高效地融入中国高校的教育和生活,部分学生甚至在思想上出现抵触的消极心理和偏颇狭隘的言论。针对这些问题,绍兴文理学院通过管理育人、课程育人、文化育人、实践育人,多维度统筹推进高校国际生德育工作。绍兴文理学院从2019年开始设置德育课程"高校国际生成才导论",作为本科学历留学生通识公共必修课,按照学校课程设计的要求,筛选专业相关的授课师资,开展专题备课研讨会,研究确定课程体系和课程内容,完善课程专业化建设。绍兴文理学院在课程建设中得到了浙江大学、北京理工大学、中央民族大学、浙江师范大学、井冈山大学等学校的相关领导和专家的大力支持与帮助。通过几年的实践探索,我们编写了这本《高校国际生成才导论》新形态教材。本教材针对教学的重点、难点内容采用二维码方式,在纸质教材中融入数字化教学资源,使教材兼具生活化、情景化、动态化等特点,不仅体现了实用性和丰富性,而且适应国际生的汉语语言水平和阅读习惯。

    本书写作分工如下:导论由白文杰编写;第一章由奚梦澜、许大平编写;第二章由洪波编写;第三章由杨奎编写;第四章由葛天博编写;第五章由钱佳莹、金程程编写;第六章由杨伊凡、吴晶编写。张宏对全书的章节结构谋篇布局,并负责全书的修改、统稿和审定工作。寿永明、章越松、方小利、宋浩成、杜坤林、令狐文生、胡琦蓉、张颖、李文、王臣、钱能、邵咪咪等参与了提纲论证和书稿审定。胡朋志牵头负责本书翻译工作。胡琦蓉负责本书编写过程的联络工作。由于作者团队水平有限,难免存在风格不统一和纰漏之处,敬请诸君批评指正。我们将总结经验,寻找差距,砥砺前行,争取不断进步。

Postscript

International students in universities have their own national ideologies and cultural backgrounds, and their upbringing and educational environments are also significantly different from that in China. Moreover, as adults, they have largely formed their own worldviews, outlooks on life, values as well as their own standards of thought and behavior. When they come to China, especially in the initial stage, they would encounter problems in language use, daily life and intercultural communication, which make it difficult for them to effectively integrate into the education and life of Chinese universities. Some students even have negative resentful mindsets and produce biased narrow-minded remarks. In response to these problems, Shaoxing University has taken a multi-dimensional approach to promote the moral education of international students through management, curriculum, culture and practice. Since 2019, Shaoxing University has adopted the moral education course "An Introduction to Development of International Students in Universities" as a compulsory course for undergraduate international students. The University has designed the course based on a specific curriculum, selected professional teaching faculty, organized lecture preparation seminars, determined the curriculum system and content through detailed research, and gradually improved the quality of the course. During the process of course development, we have received strong support and assistance from leaders and experts from Zhejiang University, Beijing Institute of Technology, Central University for Nationalities, Zhejiang Normal University, Jinggangshan University, etc. With several years' teaching practice, we have finally compiled this new-form textbook—*An Introduction to Development of International Students in Universities*. The textbook adopts QR code integration for key and difficult teaching content, incorporating digital teaching resources into the physical textbook and making the textbook practical, situational, and dynamic. It not only embodies practicality and richness in teaching, but also adapts to the Chinese language proficiency and reading habits of international students.

Authors of the textbook include Bai Wenjie (Introduction), Xi Menglan & Xu Daping (Chapter 1), Hong Bo (Chapter 2), Yang Kui (Chapter 3), Ge Tianbo (Chapter 4), Qian Jiaying & Jin Chengcheng (Chapter 5), and Yang Yifan & Wu Jing (Chapter 6). Zhang Hong is responsible for the overall structure and layout of the book, as well as the editing, compilation and finalizing of the entire book. Shou Yongming, Zhang Yuesong, Fang Xiaoli, Song Haocheng, Du Kunlin, Linghu Wensheng, Hu Qirong, Zhang Ying, Li Wen, Wang Chen, Qian Neng and Shao Mimi have participated in discussions determining the outline or approving the manuscript writing. Hu Pengzhi is responsible for the translation of it into English. Hu Qirong also served as the liaison during the writing process of this book. Due to the limitations in both the team members' professionality and their cooperation, there must be some inconsistency or inadequacies. Thereby, criticism and correction to the textbook are welcomed. We will learn from the experience, identify gaps, forge ahead and strive for further improvement.